Growing Barn Owls in my Garden

Growing Barn Owls in my Garden

Paul Hackney

Whittles Publishing

For my parents, Grace and Ron

Published by
Whittles Publishing Ltd.,
Dunbeath,
Caithness, KW6 6EG,
Scotland, UK

www.whittlespublishing.com

For information on the Barn Owl Trust see page 152

ISBN 978-184995-027-5

Printed by
Charlesworth Press, Wakefield

Contents

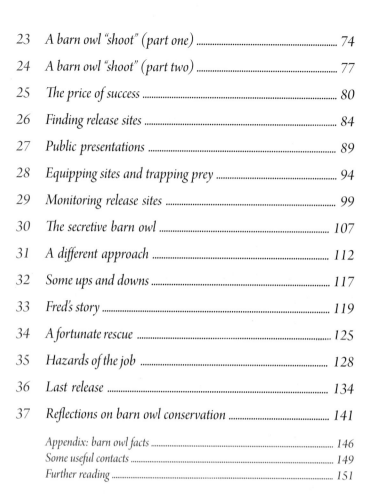

Growing Barn Owls in my Garden

Acknowledgements

I should like to thank all those who have helped me with the barn owl conservation work I describe in this book. They are far too numerous to mention individually, but include both professional and amateur conservation workers, landowners, organisations and statutory bodies. With very few exceptions, I have disguised people's identities. Should anyone recognise themselves, however (or think that they do), I hope they will forgive me if I have gently poked fun at them or their actions. An ability occasionally to see the funny side of things is, I believe, essential to maintaining a balanced approach to such a serious activity as species conservation. In summary, my fundamental feelings are of intense gratitude to, and admiration for, all those who gave their time, effort, financial and physical resources so readily.

I should also like to thank Janni Howker for her helpful comments on an early version of my manuscript, and Dr Carole M. Hackney, Jeff Cohen, Smith Davies Press, Paul Adams and Sam Connolly who have all kindly given me permission to reproduce their photographs in my book.

Paul Hackney's book, *Growing Barn Owls in my Garden* is a wonderful insight into the life of a long-term conservationist. His obvious passion for the natural world and its creatures is reflected in his delightful descriptions of his encounters with the wildlife and the human characters of the British countryside. His story leads the reader from the years of his childhood to his passion for Barn Owls and their conservation.

As Paul explains in the book, in the 1980s the breeding and release of captive Barn Owls was a fairly controversial thing to do. There were thought to be far more Barn Owls in captivity in Britain than in the wild. Rumours abounded of well-meaning individuals who thought they were helping to restore the balance by giving birds bred in captivity their 'freedom'. Unfortunately for these birds most of them died, often a slow lingering death from starvation. This story is from a man who really thought about his conservation work. He carefully selected his birds, his release sites and his methods of release.

At the end of the book Paul reflects on whether his work was worthwhile. Having many years of personal experience of both breeding and release and wild Barn Owl conservation, I would say yes. There are almost certainly young Barn Owls flying around in the countryside today that are descended from his released birds but, more than that, there are the people and their friends and families whose lives his project touched; people who discovered this amazing bird because his work gave them a glimpse of its incredible beauty. Farmers that put up nestboxes or landowners who changed their farming practices to encourage Barn Owls on their land, thereby benefiting many other kinds of flora and fauna.

By giving so much of his time and his energy to his Barn Owl project, Paul Hackney has raised awareness of this wonderful bird that has shared our countryside for thousands of years. This book tells the story of how one man can make a difference.

Frances Ramsden
Co-founder & Trustee
Barn Owl Trust

1   *Escape to the Lakes*

It must be possible to be raised in the Lake District without taking an interest in nature, but only with a lot of determined effort. To me and my brothers – one older, one younger than me – the place was little short of paradise. We found ourselves living on the edge of the Lakes because of our parents' decision, taken well before any of us was born, to flee at the first opportunity from the suffocating pea-soupers and stultifying landscapes of 1950s inner-city Manchester. The lure of lakes and mountains prompted a move that six years' effort by the Luftwaffe during World War II had failed to achieve – an exodus from the familiar grimy terraces and factories of the conurbation to the clear, fresh open air of the lakes, valleys and fells of Cumberland and Westmorland. Yet it would be wrong to suggest that this was some spur of the moment decision, involving reckless abandonment of family and friends in favour of exploration and adventure in some unknown, far-off place. On the contrary, Mum and Dad knew the area intimately, having spent every atom of their spare time there as young adults, cycling, walking and youth hostelling with a group of like-minded friends.

Their mentor at that time had been one M.J.B. Baddeley, B.A. - a forerunner of Alfred Wainwright - who declared grandiloquently in his famous guidebook:

> 'In the effect which it produces on the eye and mind of the spectator, mountain scenery is much more dependent on the proportion of its component parts than on the foot-and-line measurement of any of them, and in this attribute of proportion there is probably no beauty-spot in the world which can equal English Lakeland.'

This was pretentious stuff indeed for youngsters from the backstreets of Manchester who, during their disrupted wartime education, had encountered similarly grandiose claims in the flowery poetry of William Wordsworth and his fellow Lakeland scribblers. Possibly they were seduced by such literary hype, but it is more likely that my parents were convinced by the evidence of their own eyes; they upped stakes and moved north as soon as the opportunity arose, in the shape of an engineering draftsman's job for Dad.

At first, they rented a stone-built farm cottage just outside Kendal, an idyll that could not have been in starker contrast with the austere nineteenth-century redbrick terraced house that they had been sharing with Mum's parents. As soon as possible, though, they moved into Kendal itself. Here, things took an unexpected turn one day when a shotgun-toting distant relative, Uncle Jim, arrived on the doorstep to invite Dad out for a day's 'shuttin'. Despite his young wife's protestations, Dad was soon hooked, and became a keen wildfowler. In later years he would recount his adventures to a wide-eyed audience of his three young sons: tales of how he and his friends crouched completely still at night on the salt marshes of the Solway Firth, straining all the while to hear the honking of the geese as they flew in at daybreak, and praying that they would arrive before the tide turned and icy salt water began to race through the channels and ditches to flush the hunters from their only cover or, even worse, cut them off from the safety of the shore.

'But didn't Mum mind?'

The naïve enquiry would prompt an embarrassed silence from Dad, an enigmatic frown from Mum. The truth was that, even though she did object, Dad loved the sport too much for her to be able to persuade him to give it up.

One particular story from Dad's repertoire has always stuck in my mind: the tale of how, one night, he'd been lying in complete stillness out on the estuary, safe from the retreating tide, when he had looked up to see a pale, wraith-like form floating just a few inches above his head. Bathed in the crisp light of a full moon, the eerie presence turned out to be a barn owl, hovering low over an unfamiliar intrusion into its hunting grounds, and staring hard in an effort to understand its meaning.

'It gave me quite a fright, lads, I can tell you', Dad explained, 'appearing from nowhere like that'.

Just like a ghost, it had disappeared again as mysteriously as it had arrived, but not before emitting an ear-piercing scream of alarm.

At other times, the evidence of Dad's hunting trips was more tangible: a brace of mallard hanging by their necks in our tiny larder, or the kitchen knee-deep in the feathers of a freshly-plucked goose. His tales could shock as well as fascinate us. Once, he explained, with more than a hint of admiration in his voice, how he'd watched a gamekeeper on a foxhunt (they do it on foot in Lakeland) shoot dead one fox directly ahead of him, then turn immediately through 180 degrees to dispatch, with equal efficiency, another animal that had attempted to slink away behind the hunters' backs. It was with obvious distaste, though, that he would tell us that a wounded hare would 'scream like a human baby'.

Then suddenly, one day, everything changed. Dad took up his gun. He walked determinedly into town to Atkinson's Sports Shop (or 'Tommy Ack's', as it was better known), banged the fowling piece down on the counter and enquired brusquely,

'How much will you give me for this?'

In response to the shopkeeper's look of puzzlement, he offered a terse explanation:

'Guns and children don't mix!' As he told his sons many years later, it wasn't pressure from Mum that had finally prompted his decision, or embarrassment that he had once seized his shotgun in the dead of night to confront a garden prowler which turned out to be a harmless hedgehog, but the steady stream of fatal accidents that he'd heard of over the years (a particularly deadly, and not uncommon, combination seemed to be the carrying of a loaded shotgun whilst climbing over a stile or fence). There was however rather more to his Damascene conversion than a fear of accidents. There was undoubtedly a bit of 'doing a Peter Scott' involved too. The one-time wildfowler had himself unexpectedly hung up his shotguns and devoted his energies to conserving instead of killing. His founding of the Wildlife Trust at Slimbridge in Gloucestershire, coupled with his many natural history broadcasts on television and radio, had helped to spread the word about the virtues of habitat and species conservation.

'At one time, you'd have been called a crank, saying things like that!'

In a short, pithy phrase, Dad summed up the popular view of conservationists from a few years before. Little did he realise, though, that by moving to the Lakes and later handing in his gun, he might, literally and metaphorically, be sowing the seeds of a new generation of committed conservationists.

2   A budding naturalist

It was indeed a glorious childhood: dreamy Swallows and Amazons days frittered away in the stony shallows of the Rivers Mint, Sprint and Kent where, ever so gingerly, as if prising the lids off bottles of fizzy pop, we would ease up the larger rocks to reveal treasures that lay beneath. Maybe we'd find a caddis fly larva in its protective tubular case, like a miniature concrete drainpipe, or some ugly bullheads, common little brown fish with flat heads and thick, protuberant lips, that would dart amongst the stones and around our feet. Known by some as 'millers' 'thumbs', we always referred to them as 'snotty bullies'. Perhaps it was as well that we didn't know the fish's Latin tag, *Cottus gobio*, as we would undoubtedly have dreamed up even more imaginative nicknames. Best of all, on our excursions to the rivers, would be the discovery of a crayfish, a miniature freshwater lobster, a prize with a hint of danger attached, the danger being that the creature itself might become attached – to us. Its formidable pincers were capable of delivering a nasty nip to an unprotected finger or toe.

They seemed truly to be days of innocence, when small bands of children, still of primary school age – brothers, sisters, cousins, friends – could take themselves off to the lanes, fields and rivers lying a short walk from home. The nearest we came to inappropriate behaviour was when the girls tucked their skirts (there were no jeans for young ladies in those days) into the legs of their knickers so they wouldn't get wet when we were splashing about in the river; or when we were playing on the fields, and they performed handstands without taking the same precautions, so that their skirts fell forward over their faces, to sly sniggers from us boys.

There was occasionally a savage side to our activities too. One day, an older boy, whose presence we tolerated rather than welcomed, caught a 'snotty bully'.

'Hey, watch this!' he yelled, and before anyone had a chance to protest, he held the squirming fish down firmly on a flat rock, grabbed a sharp-edged shard of slate in his other hand and decapitated the poor creature with a single cut. The reaction with which we all greeted his cruel display seemed genuinely to puzzle him, and he never associated with us again.

We were not beyond acts of thoughtless cruelty ourselves, however. On fishing trips to Grasmere or Windermere, we would think nothing of skewering earthworms on barbed hooks for use as bait, or catching minnows in traps made from jam jars and using them for the same purpose, hooking them through the mouth and casting them out on a line in the hope of tempting a resident perch, or even a razor-toothed pike, to take a mouthful. More often, the damage was unintentionally inflicted. My older brother, Mike, was a keen birder, forever roaming the hedgerow-lined lanes in search of nests. He would take us to see his finds, excitedly persuading us to peer closely into a dense thicket or a hollow in a tree trunk to catch sight of the brooding hen bird, or the brightly-coloured gapes of a band of scrawny nestlings, straining to be fed. Although we never touched the nests or their occupants, our mere presence was enough to cause distress and possible abandonment, or act as an unintended signal to predators to investigate the site as a potential food source once we had departed. Our dangerous curiosity was fuelled by others. A neighbour, whom we called Mrs D., whose husband kept a fan-tailed pigeon called Prunella, one day presented Mike with an old chocolate box full of blown birds' eggs, each individually wrapped in its own thick wad of cotton wool. Clearly the work of an informed and determined collector, the labelled specimens included the eggs of common and rare species, as well as raptors such as buzzards and kestrels. Long since smashed to pieces and thrown away, this treasure could well have prompted one or all of us to take up egg-collecting to accumulate an even bigger and more varied selection. Fortunately, Dad's new-found aversion to shooting, and his respect for wildlife, combined with our own experiences to produce greater sensitivity towards the world around us, though sometimes there were regrettable lapses.

On one memorable summer's evening we all took off for a ride in the car. If there was a luxury our parents insisted on having, it was a means of independent transport. Constantly strapped for cash, the best they could manage was a series of old bangers. But, as Dad proclaimed, 'I don't care what it looks like, just so long as it gets us from A to B'.

We weren't too bothered about the vehicle's appearance either, treating it during most journeys as a mobile hide from which we could look out for nature during our frequent safaris into deepest Lakeland.

'Keep your eyes peeled'. Dad would borrow a popular phrase from Hollywood cowboy films, pointing out that this was a good place to see such-and-such a creature in a desperate attempt to distract us from fidgeting, rioting or even fighting each other on the back seat. More often than not, however, the predicted such-and-such – buzzard, kestrel, red squirrel, hare – would put in an appearance bang on cue. As kids, we thought it distinctly uncanny, but simply put the phenomenon down to Dad being perfect.

That evening, Dad's sixth sense (or whatever it was) didn't let him, or us, down. As we tootled along the road that runs round the western side of Thirlmere ('a good spot for deer', we were told), we peered to our left towards the steep, wooded slopes tumbling down from the rocky heights of Fisher Crag. We knew that deer could be spied in such terrain, half-hidden amongst the upright, serried trunks and gloomy shadows of the fir trees. Unexpectedly, the car came to a stop. Slowly and with great deliberation, Dad leaned into the back where we were sitting and whispered:

'Have a look down towards the lake, boys – just back there.'

He nodded to the right, while we'd all been looking left. Regrettably, our father's example of calm and quietness was not emulated by his sons, as we pushed and shoved, scrambling over each other in a tangle of arms, legs and rock-hard heads to get the best view.

'Ow, gerroff, will yer!'

'Shh!' both parents hissed.

But we finally quietened down only when we at last spotted our quarry.

'Oh, look at that', someone muttered, and pointed to a magnificent red stag, stooping low on the stony shore to take a drink from the clear, fresh waters of the reservoir. Like

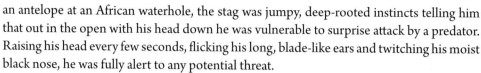

an antelope at an African waterhole, the stag was jumpy, deep-rooted instincts telling him that out in the open with his head down he was vulnerable to surprise attack by a predator. Raising his head every few seconds, flicking his long, blade-like ears and twitching his moist black nose, he was fully alert to any potential threat.

We wanted a closer look. Whispered pleas to avoid making a noise went unheeded as my younger brother, Alan, and I tumbled from the car, raced across the road and crouched behind the neat stone wall that separated us from the lake shore. Now my atavistic urges really took hold. Grabbing a fallen branch, I popped up from behind the wall, like a gunfighter at the OK Corral, took aim and fired.

'Bang! Bang!' I cried.

The stag's reaction was instant. Spinning round, wide-eyed and with his head held high, as if bearing a pile of books to aid deportment, he trotted across the shingle beach and, gathering speed, raced up the gentle slope towards the road. With a single, graceful leap, he cleared the wall, clattered across the narrow road and melted into the fir plantation, like a cartoon ghost gliding effortlessly through a solid structure.

The inevitable recriminations followed as soon as we'd all absorbed what we had just seen. The accusation that Alan and I had broken the golden rule, not to disturb wildlife, seemed to me to be somewhat wide of the mark. If the stag hadn't been startled, I thought, we would have all missed an apparently effortless display of grace and power by an animal that was breathtakingly in tune with its environment. On more mature reflection, I would have realised that, from the stag's point of view, our thoughtlessness had resulted in an interrupted drink, a sudden rush of fear and the unnecessary expenditure of precious energy.

Like any curious child, I wasn't always willing to leave the natural world where I found it, especially if it was easily portable. Reasonably enough, given that we lived in a small, three-bedroom semi, Mum made it plain that, whilst a nature table – an eclectic mix of pine cones, acorn cups, sheep bones, teeth and horns, and bird feathers (the most prized of all being the electric blue- and black-striped feathers from the wing patches of a jay) – was just about tolerable, the real, living, breathing thing was not.

'I can't be doing with (this, that or the other)' or 'I know exactly who'd end up looking after (it/them)' were the sort of reasons she gave for banning live specimens. So, for a time, the best I could do was to assemble, lay out and label my collection of inanimate bits and pieces to gather dust on a bedroom shelf. As time went on and our requests became more specific and persistent, so Mum's responses were honed and practised until she had them off pat, ready to be deployed at a moment's notice:

'Can't we have a mouse?'

'Too smelly!'

'A rabbit?'

'We haven't got a lawn.'

'What about a budgie?'

'You killed the last one by pulling out its tail feathers, poor thing.'

So apart from an ancient and gun-shy springer spaniel (a singularly unsuccessful relic of Dad's wildfowling days) and occasional sickly goldfish won at the local fair, we had to do without pets. There was, however, always the possibility of making illicit acquisitions:

buckets of frog spawn or jam jars full of tiddlers smuggled into the house when no-one was looking. Soon discovered, they were ordered to be promptly returned ('because they won't survive in captivity'). In fact it was to be Mike who managed to break through our mother's sophisticated defences, if only for a short time.

'It says here', he announced one day, brandishing a well-thumbed library book, 'that grass snakes can make good pets' and without waiting for a response, continued: 'I know, I'll make a vivarium – it shows you in here how to do it.'

Now mice, rabbits, budgies and the like were clearly within Mum's experience, but at the mention of a reptilian house guest, she was completely nonplussed. Before she could recover her composure and utter a word against his proposal, Mike had run from the room, clutching his book and planning the challenging construction job that lay ahead. Over the next few days, not much was seen of him as he worked hard with plywood, saw and nails to produce a rectangular box, roughly the size of a small fish tank, with a sliding lid. Immensely proud of his handiwork, he declared that the next step was to catch himself a snake.

'There's plenty around. I'll soon get one.'

Several warm, sunny days passed – ideal snake-catching weather –with no further mention made of either grass snake or vivarium. Supposing that he must be having more difficulty finding a pet than he'd anticipated, I couldn't resist the opportunity for a bit of teasing. Feigning an innocent interest, I asked him how his project was going.

'Oh, yes'. He looked distinctly sheepish. 'I showed Mum the library book and she pointed out that captive snakes have to be fed on baby mice, preferably live ones. It also says they can squeeze through incredibly small spaces, just by flattening their bodies....' His voice trailed off, whilst I sniggered at his reluctant revelations. Seasoned campaigner that she was, Mum had clearly bided her time and seized on the first opportunity that presented itself to subvert this latest threat of a wild incursion into the family home. Sadly, I later discovered, the lovingly-constructed vivarium had been cast into the inner reaches of the coal shed, there to remain for many months, unused and gathering a coating of bright green mould.

3   Bannisdale days

Within a short drive of home lay our secret valley, a place we would have been entitled to own if depth of emotional attachment had counted for anything. Unspectacular and virtually unknown, unlike the adjacent valley Longsleddale, Bannisdale (or 'Banniz' to us), could be reached only by a winding single-track road, which the authorities had thoughtfully barricaded at regular intervals with sturdy five-bar gates. Part of the ritual of getting to Banniz involved a member of the party hopping out of the car just ahead of every such obstruction, opening the gate to allow the car through, then closing it again once the car had passed by (thus complying with another rule of the countryside – to close all gates behind you). Needless to say, we three boys fought furiously to secure the middle position on the back seat, entitling the winner to argue, reasonably enough, that he couldn't possibly be expected to get in and out of the car easily to perform the necessary gate-keeping duties.

Bannisdale is a glacial valley, wide and long, with a small meandering river, and a rough track running its whole length and ending at an isolated farm. Comfortably low ridges and hills, marked occasionally by rocky outcrops or small stands of windswept trees, hold the valley floor in a gentle embrace. Unfit for much else, the land is grazed by hardy Herdwick sheep. Though apparently unremarkable – certainly no Buttermere or Langdale – the place held some irresistible attractions for us. The best of these lay at the valley's entrance. Descending into the valley from the 'pass of many gates', the road crossed a small limestone bridge spanning the river, Bannisdale Beck. Negotiating one last gate just past the bridge, we could park the car on the grass at the point where the tarmac road changed into a rough track. Here there was a wide greensward, close-cropped by the resident sheep, that formed the lower slope of the first little peak encountered when entering the valley, Lamb Pasture, all of 1205 feet high. Ideal for picnicking on, this area also lay within a few yards of the beck and its bridge.

On our early visits, we'd soon discovered that, as the water approached the confining arch of the bridge, its rate of flow slowed to even less than its customary sluggishness, resulting in a modest pool no more than a couple of feet deep. Once beyond the bridge, the beck passed through a small, neglected fir plantation. Deploying a cunning combination of dead and rotten tree trunks (which we soon learned to manoeuvre in the water with the skills of a Canadian logging gang), large rocks and stones, and clods of earth (often leading to perfectly legitimate requests to 'bring that little sod over here'), we found we could dam the stream just inside the wood to create a magnificent outdoor swimming pool. As well as providing this private facility, fortuitously hidden from view beneath the bridge, our construction activities provided excellent opportunities to indulge our long-standing passion for dabbling amongst the fish and invertebrates that inhabited the stream. As time went on, we became as keen and proficient at damming the watercourse as any band of beavers.

Once we were past the initial shock of plunging into the icy water, drained not long before from the surrounding fells, the pool became a refreshing alternative to lying out in the sun, or partaking of yet more scrumptious picnic food. It was not only the aquatic environment that fascinated us: we also had a private swimming pool where we could lie back in the water, our heads cradled in our hands, and watch buzzard, raven or kestrel as they drifted, high above, across the vast emptiness of a cloudless bright blue sky, or engaged in aerial dogfights if they happened to encounter each other. We could relax to the soporific call of the cuckoo proclaiming the boundaries of his territory – apart from the gentle tinkling of the water, often the only sound in the valley. Looking further afield, we might spot a small herd of deer grazing on a hillside, or in later years, once the effects of DDT and persecution had subsided and the population recovered, a peregrine falcon twisting and wheeling against the remoter crag faces.

Ever mindful that the land was privately owned, by a very indulgent farmer who would occasionally wave in greeting as he sped by in his Land Rover, we nonetheless adopted a somewhat proprietorial attitude towards 'our' valley. We rescued sheep from tangles of barbed wire or steep-sided rocky gullies, and Mum became even more of a heroine to us when she once plucked a small lamb from the swirling waters after it had foolishly launched itself into the beck. The hardiness of Lakeland sheep can only be admired, but their ability to find ways of killing themselves is simply uncanny: there must be at least 101 different methods that I've come across. We carefully dismantled our dams before we left, heaving the materials out onto the grassy banks, and took home all litter and other alien detritus that we had brought with us, or found already there. In a sense, I think, we felt we were repaying our valley's hospitality. Like the cuckoo, though, we became fiercely territorial, greeting the occasional arrival at our picnic spot of even one other vehicle with a disgruntled cry:

'Blimey, it's getting like Blackpool here!'

If the interlopers persisted, we would, as likely as not, peremptorily pack up and leave for home, hoping that we had made our point.

Even in all its picturesque tranquillity, the valley could occasionally reveal a darker side to its nature. It wasn't uncommon, for instance, following a swim, to discover a little further upstream the decomposing remains of a sheep (method number 65: death by drowning). Worse still was evidence of human activity, beyond intruding picnickers. One day we found, nailed to a fence post, an official notice. In the cold, detached phraseology of bureaucracy (in this case, the Water Board) it announced that equipment had been installed to gauge the quantity and rate of flow of the beck, because Banniz was being surveyed as the possible site of a new reservoir. We were beside ourselves with panic.

'They can't do that, can they, Dad?'

'Well, they flooded a whole village, called Mardale, in the 1930s to create Haweswater reservoir. People in Manchester do need fresh water, you know'.

It was the engineer talking: Dad's working life was devoted to the design and installation of turbines of the water-powered variety often used at reservoirs. Clearly his sympathies were not wholly with us on this one. Six months later, to our great relief, we learned from

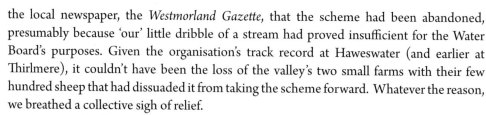

the local newspaper, the *Westmorland Gazette*, that the scheme had been abandoned, presumably because 'our' little dribble of a stream had proved insufficient for the Water Board's purposes. Given the organisation's track record at Haweswater (and earlier at Thirlmere), it couldn't have been the loss of the valley's two small farms with their few hundred sheep that had dissuaded it from taking the scheme forward. Whatever the reason, we breathed a collective sigh of relief.

As an avid collector of natural objects, especially skulls and other bones, I was thrilled one day by the discovery of something more unusual than a mouldy sheep's cranium. Behind the stone wall that encircled the plantation, I came across a jumble of bones, picked clean of flesh and fur, scoured by the Lake District's driving rain, and bleached to a shining white by the summer sun. The best preserved pieces of this treasure trove were lower jaws, which I confidently identified, after consulting my *Dumpy Book of Nature*, as those of a fox. I was closely acquainted with fox physiology thanks to the pastime of one of my school classmates. Tony was an inveterate foxhunter, so dedicated to his sport that – to the obvious disgust of most of Class 4 at Stramongate County Primary School – he insisted on bringing his various trophies into school. Where most children of his age would try to impress with football cup winners' medals or Wolf Cub badges, Tony's proudest possessions were foxes' masks, paws and brushes, crudely mounted on blocks of wood. Whenever he produced them, these gruesome objects simply refuelled the ongoing debate around cruelty v. pest control that raged through classroom and playground. To my mind, however, the Bannisdale hoard (as thrilling, I thought, as discovering a cache of old coins) fell into a completely different category. They were the remains of an animal that had lived and breathed in our valley, not the mangled off-cuts of some poor creature that had been chased and killed by a gang of cruel huntsmen. Treating them like rare pieces of delicate porcelain, I transported the luminescent white finds home with utmost reverence and accorded them pride of place on the bedroom cupboard that served as my nature table. Transfixed by my find, I never gave a thought to why, or how, the remains had come to be where I had discovered them. A few weeks later, though, the likely provenance of the bones was to become all too clear.

About halfway up the gentle slope of Lamb Pasture, well away from our picnic area, the sandy soil had been excavated to form a series of burrows. Realising that they were too large to be the work of rabbits, we were convinced that they were home to badgers or foxes, or even both. Occasional finds of bits of bone, tidy piles of dried bracken and an odd strand or two of black or red hair around these excavations provided additional clues. But for all our detective work (which included sticking our heads as far down the holes as we could and yelling 'Is there anybody home?'), we never had conclusive proof, such as a sighting of one of the animals entering or emerging from its burrow. Perhaps, we reasoned, they waited for noisy visitors like us to disappear and for peace to descend on the valley like a comforting blanket, before emerging for their night's foraging.

Our theories about the burrows' inhabitants were eventually proved right in an unexpectedly terrible way. Playing by the stream one hot and sunny day, we were intrigued to see a battered white van drawing up at the gate. There was the sound of an unfamiliar voice, and then Dad calling,

'Come and have a look, boys! They've got something to show us'.

We all gathered excitedly at the rear of the van, expecting to see a litter of cute sheepdog puppies, or perhaps a newborn lamb. With a wide grin, the scruffy-looking driver and his mates flung open the van doors. The scene that greeted us was not the wondrous revelation of new life we were anticipating; on the contrary. At first we started as half-a-dozen pairs of hostile eyes, black and malevolent, stared back at us from the gloomy interior of the van. A group of small, wiry terriers, their muzzles bloody and encrusted with soil, stood guard amongst a tangle of rusty old picks, spades and iron bars. As we stood gaping, wary of the growling dogs, our gaze was drawn to the objects that they were so fiercely defending: on a piece of heavily-soiled sacking, like meat on a butcher's slab, lay a heap of little corpses – badger and fox cubs piled roughly on top of one another, their eyes dull and lifeless, rivulets of blood weeping from their nostrils.

'Ugh!' someone gasped.

As my brothers recoiled from the grisly scene, I suddenly felt an urge to reach out and pat the piggy plump bellies of the badgers and run my fingers through the sleek fox fur, murmuring words of comfort. But my time for sorrowing was short-lived. Without a word, we were shoved rudely out of the way, the doors were slammed shut, and the van sped off up the road

'Bloody idiots!'

Dad's tone was venomous as he shouted after the men.

'They did that on purpose; they probably thought it was funny'.

He was furious, partly at his own gullibility and its unintended effect on his children. It was pretty clear that he'd either said something to the men, or the expression on his face had made clear his feelings about their trick, and this accounted for their sudden departure.

'Did they say where they got them from, Dad?' I asked, strongly suspecting his likely answer.

There was no reply, just a curt nod of Dad's head, as I'd feared, in the direction of Lamb Pasture. It dawned on me then that the fox remains I'd been so excited to find a few weeks earlier had probably come from a previous victim of this roving country death squad. In a few awful moments, there had been revealed to us a dark side of our serene and beautiful valley.

Where people work the land to provide themselves with a living, there are bound to be clashes between its owners and other inhabitants. A line of mouldering 'mowdiewart' corpses impaled on a barbed wire fence following a visit by the mole catcher was a common enough sight during my childhood in rural Westmorland; it somehow seemed acceptable, as did the occasional carcass of a carrion crow, strung up in a similar way to act as a literal scarecrow. But some practices, like the brutal digging out and slaughter of animals, as so vividly portrayed to us in Bannisdale, stand out in my mind as symptoms of a system that had become seriously unbalanced.

'Dad, I need a wee… now!' My younger brother Alan's urgent needs finally prompted a sudden left turn down a narrow country lane, the first available exit from the straight, fast road along which we were travelling, somewhere in the badlands of northern Cumberland, reiver country close to the Scottish border. Taking the opportunity to relieve myself too, I wandered a little way from the parked car in search of some privacy. Spotting a gap in the roadside hedgerow, I stepped smartly into the overgrown grass verge and began fumbling with my fly buttons. Only when I looked up did I realise that someone before me had found a very different use for the space between the bushes. Stretched between two rough posts was a single strand of wire, from which hung, like a grisly row of fairy lights, a line of bodies, each one attached to the wire by its individual string. Instantly forgetting the purpose of my visit, I simply stood, mouth and flies agape, staring at the grim spectacle. As well as commoner species – members of the crow family such as jays and magpies – the display included rarer predators: raptors such as kestrels and buzzards, and mammals such as weasels and stoats, all dangling by their necks, lifeless shapes at the end of slender nooses. What I had stumbled across, of course, was a gamekeeper's gibbet, a proud advertisement of the countryman's proficiency in eliminating potential predators from his employer's land. In those days, any wild creature sporting tooth, claw or curved beak, or combining a sharp intelligence with determined opportunism in the search for food, qualities vividly displayed by all corvids, would be viewed as a threat to the game being reared or conserved on the land. The chicks of game birds such as pheasants and partridges were regarded as particularly vulnerable and the extermination of predatory species was both determined and thorough. During my childhood, the gibbet was fortunately becoming a rare sight in the countryside, more a testament to the successful eradication of so-called pests than an indication of the landowners' conversion to the cause of nature conservation. However, the few that I did see had a profound effect on my interest in wildlife and its conservation.

Despite my suspicions, based on considerable evidence, that the owners of the countryside were largely a bunch of murderous villains, at least as far as wildlife was concerned, I never wavered throughout my primary school years in the answer I gave to the teacher's question: 'What would you like to be when you grow up?'

'A farmer, Miss,' I would reply, without a moment's hesitation.

It wasn't that my vision of farming was some glamorised ideal of golden corn ripening in the summer sun and cute fluffy lambs gambolling in lush green pastures. On the contrary, it was completely realistic, based on a detailed knowledge and close-up experience of the whole messy business.

4 *Down on the farm*

Just outside Kendal, in the hamlet of Selside, stands Yewdale Farm, known to us simply as 'the farm', as if it were the only one in the country. It was a jumbled collection of buildings, ranging from a centuries-old stone farmhouse with thick, irregular walls, through to modern, utilitarian steel and corrugated-iron barns, all nestling in a shallow depression in the undulating countryside. Whether old or new, the buildings and their layout were functional, rather than picturesque, and the whole atmosphere of the place – the cobbled yard with its foraging hens, the huge midden silently steaming away in a corner, the rickety gates secured with wire or straggly orange binder twine – suggested bustling, breathless activity, far too busy to concern itself with keeping up appearances. Bill and Pat Hague, the farmers, had been firm friends of Mum and Dad ever since my older brother Mike, during a summer fête held in one of their fields, had stumbled backwards into a water trough, soaking his pants, and been supplied temporarily with a pair of Bill's trousers, big enough to cover him from head to foot. We all enjoyed a good laugh at Mike's expense – a rare treat, as he was older and bigger than us and so usually the one making fun of others.

Pat was every inch the archetypal farmer's wife – large, round, red-faced, jolly and always swathed in a great, grease-stained apron. She was perfectly happy, on receiving a request for a fresh chicken, to grab a passing hen from the farmyard and wring its neck for you there and then: instant customer satisfaction guaranteed. Her husband, Bill, a more reserved character, was a strong individual, hardened by long hours of physical toil in the fields, but capable nevertheless of amazing delicacy and patience in pursuit of his hobby, photographing garden birds. Taking a rare break in the day's routine, he would disappear without a word into the crooked old farmhouse and emerge with a photographic print clutched in his large, rough hands, the fingers the size and shape of Cumberland sausages holding a sharp, well-composed study of a bluetit feeding from a bag of peanuts, or a robin holding a wriggling worm firmly in its beak. He would hand these round in proud silence before explaining how they had required hours of patience, waiting in the small, neatly-tended garden at the back of the farmhouse which clearly served for him as an oasis of order and calm amidst the hustle and bustle of his daily life on the farm.

Yewdale Farm, though, was far from providing our only experience of agriculture. Within a couple of hundred yards of home stood the county auction mart, where we could help the farmers – always glad of some labour, provided it was free – to load and unload their trucks of cattle, sheep and pigs. We learned various tricks of the trade, such as never to hit a pig, even lightly, with a stick because its skin is extremely delicate; nor to sit directly

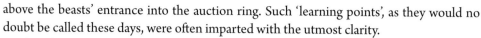

above the beasts' entrance into the auction ring. Such 'learning points', as they would no doubt be called these days, were often imparted with the utmost clarity.

'Git fookin' away from up theer!' I remember the stockman bellowing at us as he struggled to control a bull that we'd inadvertently spooked, and which was dancing around the ring like a bucking bronco at a rodeo.

Once a year, we would be given a day off school for the Westmorland County Show and would gleefully spend the morning helping the owners to clean and polish their beasts of various shapes and sizes in preparation for the afternoon's competitions. We would each be rewarded with a free pass to the formal event and would look out for animals we had helped to prepare, such as a Jersey cow we'd rubbed down with handfuls of powdered chalk to make her hide look sleeker and more shiny.

For me, though, an interest in livestock was only part of the attraction of places such as the auction mart and the agricultural showground. Just as fascinating were the people you could see there: big, beefy men (and women) came down to these events 'from t'fells', either still dressed in their working clothes, spattered with cow muck and a variety of other unpleasant substances, or else squeezed awkwardly into their Sunday best, reeking of mothballs and damp wardrobes. Both gatherings provided a mixture of business and social opportunities, sometimes necessitating financial outlay, – an uncomfortable prospect for any Westmerian farmer. At the merest mention of a proposed price, he would instantly blanch and ask with shocked incredulity: "*Ow* much?'

Even when the sum was settled, he would complete the transaction resentfully, extracting a fat roll of bank notes from the recesses of a deep trouser pocket and counting out, almost ceremonially, the agreed amount. As often as not the buyer's evident distress at parting with his beloved cash would be met with a gruff riposte from the seller: "Tha's gittin' a baargin fer a gert thing like that!' – a cow, a tractor, anything – 'A's damn'd near *givvin* it yer!'

I was clearly an agricultural groupie from an early age. But lacking a family background in farming, and certainly having no landholding to speak of – a small, three-bedroom semi-detached house with pocket handkerchief-sized garden, mainly concreted over, hardly qualified – a certain amount of realism in career planning had begun to intrude by the time I moved to secondary school. Seeking an intellectually- challenging and reasonably lucrative occupation, I plumped for a training in the law. After all, as my careers teacher helpfully commented when I broached the subject:

'Never mind, if it doesn't work out, you can always become a second-hand car salesman.'

Unable to break completely free from my bucolic tendencies, however, I soon opted to specialise in town and country planning law. It was therefore ironic that my first job, with a local planning authority in rural Cheshire, saw me resisting many farmers' attempts to create substantial nest eggs by gaining planning permissions for lucrative executive housing to be built on their holdings.

Fortunately, my parents continued to live in Kendal and it was through them, and Mum in particular, that I met someone who was to help me combine my two lifelong passions: farming and conservation. To describe Jane Ratcliffe as feisty would be a gross understatement. Her husband Teddy was, by contrast, a gentle man in every sense. With his unswerving support, Jane had devoted much of her life to wildlife conservation, not only rescuing and rehabilitating individual animals and birds at her Lakeland home, but also promoting improvements in attitudes to animal welfare through writing, lecturing and broadcasting. One of her greatest triumphs was to help bring about changes in the law to give protection to badgers and their setts, outlawing the kind of cruel activity I'd witnessed as a child in Bannisdale.

Once I had come to know her quite well, I could imagine even the most battle-hardened MP buckling under a barrage of scientific facts and cogent arguments unleashed by Jane in her assertive and uncompromising style. Intelligence provided by my mother, who had attended a couple of Jane's lectures, illustrated as always with Teddy's beautiful photographic slides, only confirmed Jane's reputation as a difficult person.

'She doesn't stand any messing'. Mum spoke admiringly.

'You know, she doesn't tame the birds she's trying to rehabilitate; she says she shouts at them and bangs on the netting of their aviaries to make sure they stay wild'.

I could imagine her using pretty much the same sort of technique on hapless MPs who failed to get the message.

Once I had come to know the Ratcliffes, through a combination of demonstrating an intense interest in their work and an obvious commitment to natural history – like them, I'd done a good deal of practical wildlife rehabilitation over the previous few years – I discovered that one of their greatest conservation interests was the barn owl. Not only did these birds make ideal subjects for Teddy's stunning photography – one amazing shot showed a bird in what Teddy described as the heraldic attitude, wings and tail outspread, legs outstretched and head tilted skyward – the species was also an excellent subject for a variety of conservation measures. Jane and Teddy explained that the wild population of the 'white owl' had noticeably declined throughout the country, although they readily bred in captivity; that as a relatively sedentary species, controlled introductions into the wild could be carried out over a long period of time; and that, although the precise reasons, or combination of reasons, for population loss were hotly disputed amongst naturalists, practical measures such as habitat creation and nest box provision could be taken to help reverse the decline. These might have been the ostensible reasons for action, but the attraction for me was, in truth, an emotional one: memories from childhood of catching occasional glimpses of an ethereal form, fluttering like a spirit across lush meadows on a long, moonlit summer's evening, or dancing over sparkling snow on a freezing winter's day; a bird whose presence was closely interwoven with the folklore of the Lake District, where it was known by the locals as 'Jenny Howlet'.

There were more deep-seated reasons too. My wife and I had been trying for some time to start a family, without success. We'd consulted the medical profession and been variously poked, prodded, tested and counselled by our GP and hospital specialists alike, but to no avail. We both came from strong, conventional family backgrounds, where a married couple producing two or three children was explicitly treated as the norm. To our great distress, it was beginning to dawn on us that following the family way might not be quite as easy as we'd unthinkingly assumed. The prospect of a life of childlessness had begun to loom before us, alongside the dread anticipation of expensive fertility treatment or complicated adoption processes. Subconsciously, perhaps, we imagined that the nagging, dull ache of our reproductive failure might be lessened by the acquisition of a surrogate family which we could nurture and cherish as if they were our own offspring.

5   Getting to know Jane and Teddy

'You get great satisfaction from releasing birds into the wild after you've nursed them back to health', Jane explained, referring to her rehabilitation work, 'but you can have much more effect on population levels with a captive breeding and release scheme'.

In her book, *Fly High, Run Free*, she talked of establishing breeding barn owls in the wild and of her delight at watching, as she sat writing, a third-generation owl from one of these pairs. Although she was determined to convince me of the value of release schemes, I was already pretty much a convert: John Love's book on the return of the sea eagle to western Scotland, describing the introduction of young birds taken from established nests in Scandinavia, had seen to that.

Jane and Teddy, speaking in turn like partners in a professional double act, with Teddy only occasionally contradicting his wife's more extreme claims, explained the techniques they used. There were two main ones. The method they favoured – the adult pair release – involved a sort of blind date approach, allowing two adult owls to form a compatible pair, confining them in a barn or other suitable building from January onwards, providing them with daily food, a safe and secure home in the form of a nest box and everything they needed for breeding, including privacy and freedom from disturbance. Pretty much the same as humans, in fact, though sadly it hadn't done the trick in our case. And then it would come down to waiting patiently. Four weeks after first hearing the patter of tiny talons, the building would be opened up to allow the parents to fly freely in and out. Because their offspring would as yet be unfledged and unable to leave the nest box, the adults would – so the theory went – go out to hunt in the surrounding countryside and instinctively return to feed their dependents until they became able to fly and fend for themselves.

The second method – juvenile release – involved breeding from adult stock kept in captivity, removing the resultant offspring when they reached five – six weeks of age, while they were still unfledged but less dependent on their parents – the equivalent of human teenagers – and relocating them in a nest box on a suitable site. Here they would be provided with food by a human foster parent until they fledged and learned how to hunt in the surrounding countryside. This technique, explained Jane and Teddy, was sometimes called 'hacking back', although this is a term usually used to refer to a method of releasing tame or former falconry birds into the wild.

My enthusiastic mentors went on to emphasise that the aim of both methods was to habituate the birds to the release site so that, in future years, they might return to breed or at least to roost there. Feeling bombarded with information about methods, including several variations on the main ones, laced with Jane's strong views on their respective merits and demerits, all imparted in her rapid-fire style of talking, I decided to try to steer the conversation towards some practical concerns.

'Er, you mentioned food,' I muttered tentatively during a nanosecond's pause in the proceedings.

At least I knew – or thought I knew – something of this subject, thanks to my occasional experience of nursing back to health injured raptors such as kestrels and sparrowhawks. Knowing that birds like this need roughage from whole food to stimulate their digestive systems, I'd followed the example of falconers, who take advantage of surplus chicks from poultry hatchers to feed to their hawks and falcons. There is no way to sex a hen's egg, or rather its contents, before hatching. Once the chicks emerge, though, they can be sexed by an experienced poultry sexer (a step above pheasant plucker on the poultry dealer's career ladder). As the overwhelming commercial demand is for hens, the vast majority of those identified as male sadly do not live to see the dawn of another day. Large quantities of these dead day-old chicks can therefore be bought cheaply and fed to captive birds of prey.

Thinking that I was ahead of the game on this topic, I was sure that Jane and Teddy wouldn't be able to tell me anything that I didn't already know, and I could therefore bring the conversation to an end, or at least slow it down. My confidence, though, was severely misplaced. Jane simply launched into another lengthy discourse.

'Yes', she declared, 'you can't just give them dog meat, or anything like that!' I had known worse, I thought, recalling a lady who'd tried, without success, to interest an injured sparrowhawk in strips of best-quality boiled ham floating in a bowl of milk.

'No, they need feather, bone and fur to stay healthy. Chicks – dead ones –', she emphasised, 'are alright, but I prefer mice'.

A picture flashed briefly across my mind of Jane about to tuck into a plate of small rodents, and I managed, only with great difficulty, to suppress a guffaw.

'Brown ones, too,' Jane thundered on, 'it's no good feeding them white mice – they won't find any of those when they go out hunting in the wild, will they?'

It was a rhetorical question. Still expounding the virtues of the brown mouse diet, she shepherded me out of the house and down to an ordinary-looking shed at the bottom of the garden.

The pungent stench alone, as we drew near, left no doubt as to the building's purpose, and belatedly confirmed Mum's determined stand against our keeping pet mice at home. Inside, the shed looked like a ramshackle pet shop, with cages of various shapes and sizes full of brown mice at all stages of development, from newborn 'pinkies' to full-grown adults. Though breeding them as food for her owls, Jane was clearly fascinated by her mice and keen to care for them properly. Like the geneticist Gregor Mendel, with his garden peas, she took a keen interest in the animals' genetic mix. Assuming equal enthusiasm on my part, she attempted to describe the complex web of relationships, waving her arms excitedly from one cage to the next as she explained.

'This is the mother of those ones – and these are the offspring of him – but they aren't related to those over there'.

Feeling the onset of dizziness, brought on by a combination of information overload and the reek of a shed full of mice, I seized on a pause in Jane's monologue in the hope of diverting her back to the subject of owls.

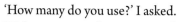

'How many do you use?' I asked.

Without apparently pausing to draw breath, Jane responded with the exact details:

'Each owl needs three mice per day. If you're feeding an adult pair and, say, four owlets, you'll need to give them at least 18 every day. Of course, that's full-grown mice – they'll take more if you're giving them young animals. It's all about food value, you see'.

I knew that I shouldn't, but I just had to ask about the use of day-old chicks. I couldn't picture myself in the intensive mouse-rearing business. Again, the answer was fired back, straight to the point. Jane dismissed the use of chicks as an inferior practice but insisted that, if they were to be used, they should be disguised by having their heads and legs cut off, so that the parent owls wouldn't mistakenly assume that their newly-hatched offspring were also on the menu.

'You also need to add a powdered vitamin supplement'.

I knew this already and recognised instantly the tub of SA37 that she was now waving under my nose. I would sprinkle a few grains over the birds' food, anticipating that a small amount would be ingested during feeding. Jane, of course, had her own technique.

'What I do', she continued, 'is slit open the chest of each chick and sprinkle a pinch of the powder beneath the skin'. By now, the full menu had been explained. The unappetising choice seemed to be mutilated, doctored day-old chick or home-reared, 'wholemeal' brown mouse.

6   My first barn owls

Eventually I was permitted to retreat from the mouse production unit, following Jane and Teddy indoors to receive further instruction on many bizarre activities involved in wildlife conservation, some of which I already practised. These included regular disinfecting of perches to prevent 'bumblefoot' (a septic condition of birds' feet leading to abscesses) and the provision of heated feeding platforms in outdoor aviaries during winter to prevent food from freezing. Teddy's ingenious device to prevent the inadvertent production of chick or mouse lollipops was to install a 40W light bulb in a tin box directly beneath the feeding platform, creating sufficient warmth to counteract the effects of sub-zero temperatures.

Having finally extricated myself with assurances that I was keen to try captive breeding and release of barn owls, and with my head buzzing with information and ideas, it wasn't long before I was summoned to return. Although Jane and Teddy were by then living in the Lake District, in a wonderful house overlooking Windermere that they'd designed and built themselves, they had also spent many years living and working in Cheshire. They were busy releasing barn owls in Cumbria but had seemed particularly interested, on my previous visit, to hear that my wife and I were based in Cheshire. However, when I arrived in answer to the summons, I had little idea what I was in for. I was soon to find out.

'They're a breeding pair,' Jane insisted as we stood peering into one of her aviaries, in which two barn owls were flapping wildly about. The formalities of my arrival had been quickly disposed of.

'Quite clearly male and female'.

You could've fooled me, I thought, not daring to say that both birds looked exactly the same. There was no obvious size difference, as there is in many other raptor species – the male sparrowhawk, for instance, is around one third smaller than his partner. Nor did their plumage seem to differ, both being predominantly white with grey-gold backs and upper wings. I must have been looking particularly gormless.

'It's obvious – look!' Jane pointed out (quite patiently, for her) that the male bird's colouration was generally paler than the female's; that she bore a subtle band of golden-brown shading, like a broad necklace draped around her breast, and a spattering of small black spots in the same area, extending beneath the wings, as if a naughty schoolchild had flicked ink from a fountain pen all over a sheet of pristine white paper. Again, the female showed bronze feathering that framed her facial disc –the set of modified feathers that gives an owl its characteristic round 'face' and acts as a sound-gathering device, like a TV satellite dish. The male owl showed no such markings, Jane emphasised, his breast, underwings and face being pure, unsullied white.

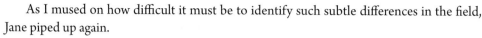

As I mused on how difficult it must be to identify such subtle differences in the field, Jane piped up again.

'Of course, this is an exemplary pair – some males have spots and golden colouration, and you do get very pale hen birds.'

Even more confused, I decided it was time to move the conversation swiftly on.

'About transporting them...' I began.

Once again, Jane and Teddy had all the answers. It turned out that a good old cardboard box was ideal, even better if it was specifically designed for carrying pets. The bird could be kept confined in the dark, so that the jumpiest of captives couldn't injure itself or damage its delicate feathering.

Given the speed with which Jane and Teddy responded to my expression of interest, it was fortunate that I'd spent the intervening weeks planning suitable accommodation in our back garden. With years of rescuing, rehabilitating and sometimes permanently accommodating all manner of wild birds, I was well versed in the art and practice of aviary construction. Largely self-taught, I'd also picked up a few tips on various visits to zoos and wildlife sanctuaries, where I would always take as much interest in the details of the enclosures as in their inhabitants. I did, however, aspire more to the Snowdon aviary style than the Casson and Conder approach, both of which I'd encountered as a young boy on a rare family trip to London zoo. To me, the latter seemed more interested in creating clever works of art than in simply providing appropriate environments for animals and birds.

I had carefully chosen the site for the construction of an aviary. First, I identified the most secluded spot in my back garden, close to the house but screened from it by a large garden shed. Then I built the framework of my aviary from 'rustic poles' bought from the local garden centre, covered the sides and top with wire netting, and laid a generous covering of limestone chippings on the ground, having first removed all the turf. Following my mentors' meticulous instructions, I roofed over part of the aviary with corrugated plastic sheets, more conventionally used for carports and lean-tos, and fastened a nest box, converted from an old tea chest, high up in the most sheltered area, the corner bordered by the garden shed on one side and my neighbours' domestic oil storage tank on the other. Finally, the interior was fitted out with all the necessary mod cons, including perches made from tree branches, alternative sheltering or roosting places, also roofed over with corrugated plastic, a drinking and bathing facility (consisting of a cat litter tray, minus cat and litter, of course), and a small wooden shelf for use as a feeding platform. I'd also installed a sturdy hinged door, which I would keep padlocked to deter intruders; and, to exclude potential raiders of a different kind – foxes, squirrels and the like – the side netting of the aviary was sunk well into the earth and held in place by hefty poles laid on the ground around the entire perimeter. After several days' hard work, I finally stepped back to admire my handiwork.

'There vill be no escape from Colditz!' I muttered to myself.

My elaborate constructions had become a bit of a family joke, prompting facetious re-marks about their being strong enough to contain a rhinoceros. I prided myself, though, on the fact that none of my charges, even the smaller, nippier varieties such as bluetits, had ever escaped. Given the provenance of the barn owls, I thought that now was not the time to get careless.

When my owls arrived, I began the process of introducing them with the utmost care to their new home. Taking them into the aviary in the separate pet carriers in which I'd transported them down from the Lake District, I closed the door behind me and pulled on a pair of gloves as if I was a surgeon preparing for a delicate operation. I was keen to examine the birds before releasing them into the aviary, both to check their condition and to get one last close-up look at their subtle markings. Having witnessed at close quarters the birds' ferocious talons, I was convinced that I needed to protect my hands. An old pair of bee-keeper's gauntlets seemed the ideal solution, as they were made of soft leather that was thin enough to ensure sensitivity when handling the owls, but also sufficiently thick to withstand the talons' piercing grip. The canvas sleeves attached to the gloves offered extra protection to my arms as far up as the elbows.

To my great surprise – and relief – both birds appeared docile and cooperative as I gently lifted each in turn from its cardboard box. I put this down to the rigours of their journey in a dark, confined space and the sudden move into the bright, sunny environment to which they were now being introduced. I was well-practised in the proper handling of small birds, where the general rule is to use your hand to form a cage behind the creature's back without putting undue pressure on its body, whilst gently extending your first and second fingers around the captive's neck to prevent it from escaping forwards. This leaves the legs relatively free and the rest of the bird safely restrained. I was far less confident about handling bigger species, particularly well-armed raptors, where it was the legs and feet that specifically concerned me. Fortunately, I had paid close attention to Jane's and Teddy's technique, which involved grabbing these parts first. Once the legs were firmly gripped in one hand, the bird could be held gently against my body with the other, thus preventing either wing from being extended. The only disadvantage of this approach seemed to be that it left the bird's head free and, given the well-known flexibility of an owl's neck, both birds had the opportunity not only to stare directly – and, I thought, menacingly – at my face, but also to make use of their sharp, curved beaks to emphasise their displeasure. To my great relief, my bee-keeping gloves proved to be more than capable of withstanding their vicious pecks.

Not wanting to stress the owls any more than necessary, I was nevertheless keen to make full use of this rare chance to study them at close quarters, as I was still unsure about my ability to detect plumage differences between the sexes. I therefore decided to examine their wings more closely. This involved gently extending a wing with the fingers of one hand whilst continuing to grip the bird's legs and feet firmly with the other, keeping the second wing folded by continuing to press the bird's body gently against my own. Once extended and viewed in close-up, I could see clearly what a remarkable structure the barn owl's wing is. First of all, its overall shape is broad and rounded, rather like a lady's fan, although an asymmetrical one. The feathering, particularly on the underside, appears almost in soft focus because of its velvety texture, and the leading edges of the wing feathers are clearly barbed, like a miniature comb. These and other characteristics are, of course, vital components of the owl's ability to fly silently. Most impressive of all, perhaps, is the decoration on the fan: a subtle background of gold, grey-blue and white, barred with darker markings that create several irregular horizontal lines, studded at random with small, tear drop-shaped flecks of black on white. Two other features struck me from these careful examinations:

the stubbiness of the bird's tail compared with its total body length, and the large size of its head, although I soon found, from gentle probing with my fingers, that this was mostly made up, along with the facial disc, of very dense feathering rather than bone.

Having tried the owls' patience for long enough, and reassured myself that they remained in good condition after their journey, I was convinced that now was the right moment to release them into their new home. Although I appreciated that the barn owl is a predominantly nocturnal species, I had chosen to carry out the procedure in daylight, rather than after dark, for two reasons: firstly, to enable me to intervene more easily if anything untoward should occur, and secondly, because I imagined that there would be a greater chance of the birds heading for the reassurance of the nearest dark hole, the nest box in which I wanted them to become established. Sure enough, my guess proved right. After a few feeble and directionless flaps around the new and unaccustomed home, both birds dived into the nest box and scrambled noisily, like two dogs scratching at a kennel floor, into its comforting innermost depths.

So far, so good, I thought, as I breathed a huge sigh of relief. It was only then that the enormity of the task I'd undertaken struck me. It was one thing to rescue distressed animals and birds, look after them and return them to the wild, if and when they were fit, as I had been doing for a number of years; but it was a hugely different challenge to breed deliberately from captive stock and release large numbers of offspring into the unknown. Though immensely thrilled to have such beautiful creatures in my back garden, I suddenly felt an enormous weight of responsibility resting on my shoulders. It was self-inflicted, of course, but that wasn't going to make the job any easier, or guarantee its success.

7 Other owl encounters

Over the next few days, I restricted my interactions with the owls to observing them from what I thought was a safe distance, venturing into their aviary briefly, only once a day, to pop a handful of food onto the feeding platform located high up, just inside the door. At the first sound of my approach, there would be a flash or two of white, sometimes preceded by a high-pitched screech of alarm, followed by the now familiar, but still puzzling, scratching noises. When I finally plucked up courage to peer into the box itself, I soon discovered the cause. Both birds were fighting to get as far away from me as possible at the back of the box's dark interior. Straining to brace themselves against the furthermost wall, they leaned backwards, holding out their legs rigidly, then scrabbling frantically to gain purchase by sinking their talons into the box's smooth floor, like a pair of mountain climbers trying to anchor their crampons in solid ice. Frequently, a foot would slip, making its owner, in panic, grab onto the nearest object, such as its companion's leg or wing. Not once threatening to fly past me – I was fully prepared to duck, if necessary – the birds seemed more inclined to climb the walls as if terrified by the sudden appearance of some great monster. I didn't think I was that ugly, until a friend pointed out one day that the human face – circular in shape, pale-coloured and with large eyes separated by a prominent 'beak' – represents a super stimulus: an enormous and threatening barn owl. In other words, what I was doing to them was the equivalent of a human giant staring in at me through my front door. No doubt that would have had me climbing the walls too.

Although I've never felt in the least bit intimidated by barn owls, whether in the aviary or in the wild, the same cannot be said for a friend of mine. Watching my captive owls one dark night from an upstairs bedroom window, she quickly realised that the loud and tremulous screeching that suddenly arose had been prompted by some unexpected visitors. Seeing that my birds were careering manically round their aviary in a highly agitated state, she spotted two other barn owls sitting on the roof of a neighbour's bungalow, one of them screeching for all it was worth. The aviary birds were hissing and screaming in response – there was obviously a heavy territorial dispute in progress – and in a moment of thoughtlessness my friend opened the bedroom window and emitted a passable imitation of an aggressive barn owl's call. Without hesitation, one of the wild owls, presumably the male, launched itself from the bungalow roof and shot at speed towards the source of this latest intrusion. Fortunately, my friend managed to close the window a split second before the angry bird arrived, with wings outspread and talons raised to strike at her face. It was certainly a magnificent sight, but one that could have resulted in nasty injuries had the bedroom window not intervened.

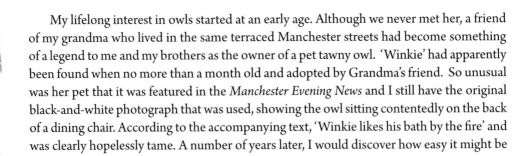

My lifelong interest in owls started at an early age. Although we never met her, a friend of my grandma who lived in the same terraced Manchester streets had become something of a legend to me and my brothers as the owner of a pet tawny owl. 'Winkie' had apparently been found when no more than a month old and adopted by Grandma's friend. So unusual was her pet that it was featured in the *Manchester Evening News* and I still have the original black-and-white photograph that was used, showing the owl sitting contentedly on the back of a dining chair. According to the accompanying text, 'Winkie likes his bath by the fire' and was clearly hopelessly tame. A number of years later, I would discover how easy it might be to obtain a 'Winkie' of my own.

By now an undergraduate at Manchester University, I had soon discovered how much free time law students were allowed each week, theoretically to devote to private study. One day, having turned up for and endured the required one-hour lecture, I decided to enjoy the rest of that sunny afternoon by walking back to my room in a hall of residence, rather than catching a bus. Bowling along in a reasonably contented state of mind through the leafy suburbs of Didsbury, I suddenly became aware of a high-pitched, regular squeaking noise, as if an overweight child were using a rusty swing, or someone were rhythmically opening and closing a gate whose hinges were in serious of oiling. My curiosity aroused, I continued in the direction of the strange sound, which grew louder and more grating to the ear with every step I took. Eventually I reached the stretch of pavement outside a solid, red-brick suburban villa set in a pleasant, well-groomed garden from which the harsh squeaking seemed to emanate. It didn't take long for me to spot the cause: sitting in the lower branches of a small tree, no more than 20 yards from where I stood, was the unmistakable plump brown form of a young tawny owl. My presence failed to prompt even the slightest pause in the owlet's monotonous call which, close to, sounded rather like a distress signal, as it rose and fell – 'I'm here! I'm here! I'm here!' To my astonishment, the bird did not attempt to move away. Although there were no other people around, I could see how vulnerable the youngster might be to cats and other ne'er-do-wells, whom it seemed, perversely, to be doing its best to attract. On the point of hopping over the garden wall to rescue the owlet, I suddenly recalled some advice given in one of my childhood natural history books that tawny owlets found out of their nests are best left alone. With some reluctance, but also relief – how would I have looked after a little 'Winkie' of my own in a student bed sit? – I turned and continued on my journey, the grating squeak echoing, almost mockingly, in my ears, until I turned a corner into the next street.

Incidents like these, involving possible wildlife casualties, tend to prey on my mind for years afterwards. Did I do the right thing? I ask myself, in anxious self-doubt. At other times, I will kick myself for missing an opportunity: wouldn't it have been great to have had a pet owl? Confirmation that my masterly inactivity had been the right approach in this instance did, however, eventually come along.

'Never even think of picking up a young tawny owl!' It was Jane Ratcliffe declaiming in her inimitable way at one of her public lectures. 'It's perfectly natural for them to leave the nest before they can fly. Their parents know exactly where they are and they can climb up a tree if danger threatens.'

Jane went on to advise her audience – which included me – that the most they should consider doing if concerned about a grounded owlet was to pick it up and pop it into the lower branches of a nearby tree.

'If you bring it to me,' she narrowed her eyes menacingly as she surveyed her audience, 'I'll tell you to take it straight back to where you found it!'

I smiled to myself. I had done the right thing all those years ago after all, and I was greatly relieved to be hearing it from a renowned expert in the care and rehabilitation of wild animals and birds.

Whilst tawnies are most commonly taken from the wild, usually by well-intentioned members of the public, barn owls are widely bred in captivity and the offspring bought and sold. Given my interest in the bird, I am sometimes asked, usually by someone who's spotted an advert – 'Barn owls for sale' – in their local newspaper, whether this is illegal. To their obvious surprise, I tell them that it isn't, provided that the breeder follows certain rules. Key amongst these, and the clearest sign that a bird has been bred in captivity for sale, is the presence of a close ring fitted round one of its legs. These light metal bands are fitted when an owlet is no more than a few days old and its hind toe is still supple enough to be bent back against the leg, allowing the ring to be slipped over the foot. As the owlet grows and the toe joint stiffens, the ring can no longer be passed back over the foot and removed.

In contrast with close rings, British Trust for Ornithology (BTO) rings are made from stainless steel, or an alloy, and are split. They are fitted to a bird's leg by a licensed ringer, using a special pair of pliers. These rings, too, are impossible to remove over the bird's foot. Although both types of ring serve the same general purpose – the identification and tracing of individual birds – the underlying motives for their use could not be more different: close rings form part of a commercial approach while BTO rings are fitted purely to further scientific research. While I have enjoyed years of BTO ringing, I have never needed to use close rings, because I have never been involved in the buying and selling of birds.

8 The arrival of Barney

And yet it was through a commercial transaction, rather than scientific endeavour, that I eventually came to acquire a pet owl, Barney. Her story was commonplace, even comical in parts, and would have ended tragically had not common sense intervened, at a critical moment, in the shape of Mildred, a middle-aged lady who helped to run a local bird sanctuary.

Paving the way with great diplomacy during a visit to my house one day, Mildred told me of a barn owl that had been bred in captivity the previous spring and subsequently bought, as a pet, by Seamus, a friend of hers. As a veterinary surgeon, Seamus should have known better, Mildred agreed, but seemed reassured when I told her that, provided the bird was close-ringed, he didn't appear to have done anything illegal.

'He had the bird from a very young age – from a dealer in Blackpool – and raised it by hand', she continued, 'and when it had fledged, he let it fly free around his flat'.

'He's a bachelor', she added quickly, shrewdly interpreting my disapproving reaction, an involuntary grimace at the thought of the health risks of bird droppings, salmonella and other noxious by-products of the average bird.

'Well, he acquired a girlfriend'. Mildred paused, savouring the moment. 'Apparently, she took one look at the domestic arrangements and delivered an ultimatum: 'Either that bird goes, or I go!'

'I can't say I blame her', I muttered. My limited experience to date of the barn owl's lifestyle had demonstrated how thoroughly obnoxious they were in many of their personal habits. Feeding, I'd found, could be a particularly unpleasant business, as the owls tend to pull apart food items such as day-old chicks, devouring the tastiest cuts and abandoning less desirable parts to rot wherever they fall. The natural results of the digestive process are no pleasanter, consisting either of pellets of compacted bone and feather regurgitated at one end, or foul-smelling white liquid droppings ejected at high velocity from the other.

'He chose to keep the girlfriend', Mildred remarked drily. 'But then he had a problem about what to do with his *other* bird. He said he was going to take it into the countryside and just let it go'.

'But a tame owl wouldn't last five minutes!' I was horrified at the thought of such irresponsibility. 'It would have no idea how to hunt, or look after itself'.

'That's exactly why I stepped in', Mildred explained.

Although quiet and conventional on the outside, I was beginning to appreciate this lady's steely determination to do the right thing when it came to bird rescue and rehabilitation. She explained that she had heard about my breeding and release scheme, and had worked on Seamus until he had finally given up his hare-brained plan and agreed instead to donate his pet to me, if I would take it.

Mildred now nodded towards the cardboard box that she'd quietly deposited on the kitchen floor when she first arrived. Only too aware that my own claimed expertise would now be under close scrutiny, I gingerly opened the lid. The last thing I wanted was for the occupant to escape and fly around the room – something it was obviously used to doing – but even worse, I thought, would be a cack-handed demonstration at this stage of how not to handle an owl. Pulling on my bee-keeper's gloves, I tensed in preparation for the combination of fear and aggression that many birds display when they encounter unfamiliar circumstances for the first time. But to my enormous relief, as I eased back the lid, I was met not by the warning hisses and aggressive talon strikes I'd expected from an upset owl, but by the quiet chirruping noises and placid, friendly gaze of a thoroughly unflustered bird, like a baby gurgling with contentment in its pram. Two jet-black eyes set in a heart-shaped white face stared coyly up at me, whilst the bird swayed its body rhythmically from side to side, as if waggling its hips and deliberately flirting. I moved back, the owl seemingly content to stay where it was.

'It's oddly named – for a female'. I turned towards Mildred, confident of my new-found expertise.

'Oh, I'm sure the breeder told Seamus it was a male'. Mildred was nonplussed.

'Well, I could be wrong, of course, but we'll obviously know for sure if she manages to produce eggs and young'.

Clearly impressed by my great knowledge, Mildred agreed to leave Barney with me, on the proviso that she could bring the erstwhile owner, Seamus, to see her some time.

Only after Mildred had left did I begin to appreciate the extent of Barney's problems. Firstly, she had no idea that she was a barn owl. Just like the young goslings that trailed behind the naturalist Konrad Lorenz because he was the first living creature they saw after hatching, Barney had no fear of humans, viewing them only as a source of food or comfort. Like a pet parrot, she would amble quite amiably along my outstretched arm, and even perch on my head, sinking the needle-sharp points of her talons painfully into my scalp whenever she felt slightly insecure. I imagined the shock she would have given someone if she'd been released and tried such tricks in the wild. There was no doubt that she would soon have been hurt, or even killed.

In effect, the bird was an emotional cripple, and although I was fascinated to have such close contact with a gorgeous creature, I was also intensely saddened by her deeply unnatural behaviour. It was as depressing as watching an elephant perform in a circus ring.

Though thoroughly habituated to man, my new charge was certainly not acclimatised to the weather. When I placed her in an outdoor aviary on her first night, she puffed out her feathers and proceeded to shiver violently. It was January, after all, and she had been kept indoors all her life. Although the last thing I wanted was to prolong the owl's unsuitable lifestyle, she did look so cold and miserable that I felt obliged to introduce her more gradually to the joys of outdoor living. She therefore spent the first night in a cage, next to a warm radiator in my spare bedroom. Over the ensuing weeks, I gradually changed her location – from heated bedroom to unheated bedroom; from unheated bedroom with window open to draughty garage – until, like a tender plant, she had been sufficiently hardened off to

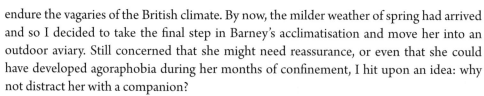

endure the vagaries of the British climate. By now, the milder weather of spring had arrived and so I decided to take the final step in Barney's acclimatisation and move her into an outdoor aviary. Still concerned that she might need reassurance, or even that she could have developed agoraphobia during her months of confinement, I hit upon an idea: why not distract her with a companion?

Feeling that she was probably still suffering from an identity crisis, I rejected the idea of finding another barn owl. Instead, I thought a miniature version might be more acceptable, like a dwarfish familiar in a medieval royal court whose job it was to cheer up the depressed monarch. As it happened, I was temporarily accommodating a disabled little owl, called Ollie, who was usually in the care of Jane and Teddy. After a collision with a car, the bird's wing had healed in a crooked fashion, limiting its ability to fly. The recent history of this species contrasted markedly with the barn owl's remorseless decline. Deliberately introduced into England from the Continent over a hundred years ago, it had become well established in much of Britain by the middle of the last century. While the barn owl's habitat was fast disappearing, the little owl found and occupied a profitable niche – quite literally – by nesting in a wide variety of holes and crevices, often at ground level, and showing a catholic taste in food, from beetles and earthworms to larger items such as small mammals, reptiles and amphibians. Though a seriously anthropomorphic notion, I can't help thinking that the little owl's colonisation of this country owed much to its apparently fierce and tenacious character, indicated by its bright yellow eyes set under permanently glowering brows. The barn owl seems a much more sensitive creature, with a kinder expression and gentler disposition, accounting perhaps in part for its downfall. Whatever the reason, the success of the little owl and other species, such as the red kite and the white-tailed sea eagle, in gaining a foothold in the British countryside, demonstrates at least that carefully controlled releases can have positive outcomes, provided that they are closely tailored to the needs of the particular species.

Making sure that both birds had their own nest boxes to retreat into – the little owl's being a cosy nine inches square with a circular hole at one end, about four inches in diameter – I placed them both in a small aviary near the house. Normally, the barn owl is nocturnal, whereas little owls are commonly seen throughout the day, sitting in prominent positions like fence posts or on the roofs of buildings. As a result of her unusual upbringing and desperate craving for human attention, however, Barney was also diurnal in her habits. This at least had the advantage of allowing me to monitor the birds' interactions, or so I thought.

Far from making any moves, friendly or otherwise, towards her diminutive cohabitee, Barney treated Ollie with lofty disdain, preferring to peer across at the house, bobbing her head and chirruping with pleasure whenever I came into view. The little owl, by contrast, reacted to the perceived intrusion on its privacy rather badly, taking to its box for much of the night and day and staring out malevolently from the entrance hole like an ill-tempered gnome. At least they never came to blows, even if they did act rather like the figures in a weather house, alternating their appearances in the open and never emerging at the same time. It was with some relief that I was eventually able to return Ollie to the Ratcliffes' care, leaving Barney on her own in the small aviary near the house from where she was most able to see and continue to dote on her new owner – me.

9   *Home-bred success*

With the arrival of spring, I knew I had to shift my attention from Barney – at best a potentially productive breeding bird – and concentrate instead on the pair of owls provided by Jane and Teddy. Following their strong advice, I had been using a non-interventionist approach, which was just as well, given the distractions offered by my new acquisition. I was keeping an eye on the pair as much as possible, to see whether I could detect any changes in their behaviour – not that I actually knew what I was looking for. I did, though, begin to notice that the female owl was leaving the nest only infrequently, and then just for short periods, whilst the male was consistently taking food from the feeding platform to present to his partner. Scouring my bird books for clues, I became convinced that I was seeing patterns of behaviour consistent with the early stages of breeding. I was desperate to confirm my theory, but equally keen not to do anything that might upset the owls. Above all, I appreciated that a repeat of the 'giant owl' trick – suddenly peering into the nest box - was too risky in terms of potential disturbance. I then remembered an observation technique, recommended by the Ratcliffes, that required a small mirror, some strong sticky tape, a bamboo cane, a powerful electric torch and a certain suppleness on my part.

Choosing a fine, quiet evening, I crept with my equipment into the aviary and crouched beneath the nest box. Slowly, I raised the bamboo cane until the mirror, which I'd taped to one end, came level with the entrance hole of the box. I froze for several seconds as, above my head, I could hear dull 'thump, thump' noises made by the birds as they shuffled about. Probably, I imagined, they were unsettled by the sudden appearance of a strange object outside their box. Deciding, after an interval, that I should risk the next stage, I switched on my torch, accurately directing its beam onto the mirror. Sure enough, as Jane and Teddy had predicted, I was rewarded with a clear image of the box's interior. The first and most obvious sight was of two nonplussed owls, both standing upright and staring into the mirror, their eyes gleaming like polished black stone in the powerful torchlight. But I could justify the disturbance to myself simply on the basis of what I could now see on the floor of the box just in front of the nervous owls: there, to my delight, sat a small cluster of shiny white eggs – five or six in number, each about half the size of a domestic hen's egg – neatly arranged in a shallow saucer formed from regurgitated pellets. Having had such clear visual confirmation of my suspicions and now even more anxious to minimise any disturbance, I quickly switched off the torch, withdrew the mirror and scrambled out on all fours through the aviary door.

For the next few weeks I resisted the almost overwhelming temptation to take further indirect peeks into the nest box. Instead, I placed the aviary under the closest possible

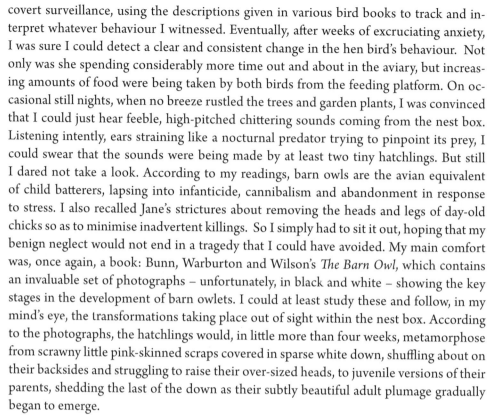

covert surveillance, using the descriptions given in various bird books to track and interpret whatever behaviour I witnessed. Eventually, after weeks of excruciating anxiety, I was sure I could detect a clear and consistent change in the hen bird's behaviour. Not only was she spending considerably more time out and about in the aviary, but increasing amounts of food were being taken by both birds from the feeding platform. On occasional still nights, when no breeze rustled the trees and garden plants, I was convinced that I could just hear feeble, high-pitched chittering sounds coming from the nest box. Listening intently, ears straining like a nocturnal predator trying to pinpoint its prey, I could swear that the sounds were being made by at least two tiny hatchlings. But still I dared not take a look. According to my readings, barn owls are the avian equivalent of child batterers, lapsing into infanticide, cannibalism and abandonment in response to stress. I also recalled Jane's strictures about removing the heads and legs of day-old chicks so as to minimise inadvertent killings. So I simply had to sit it out, hoping that my benign neglect would not end in a tragedy that I could have avoided. My main comfort was, once again, a book: Bunn, Warburton and Wilson's *The Barn Owl*, which contains an invaluable set of photographs – unfortunately, in black and white – showing the key stages in the development of barn owlets. I could at least study these and follow, in my mind's eye, the transformations taking place out of sight within the nest box. According to the photographs, the hatchlings would, in little more than four weeks, metamorphose from scrawny little pink-skinned scraps covered in sparse white down, shuffling about on their backsides and struggling to raise their over-sized heads, to juvenile versions of their parents, shedding the last of the down as their subtly beautiful adult plumage gradually began to emerge.

Eventually, unable to contain my curiosity any longer, I chose a warm, balmy evening to creep as stealthily as I could to the bottom of the garden. There, I secreted myself in a flower border, sitting stock-still amongst the foliage like a piece of garden statuary. As the sun went down, swarms of midges descended on every inch of skin I had foolishly left exposed and proceeded to take their fill of my blood. Hardly daring to breathe, let alone move position, I did eventually resort to a few feeble sweeps of the hand when the savagery of the midges' attacks became truly unbearable.

'I only hope it's worth it!' I muttered darkly to myself, resentful of my unintended function as a feeding station for hungry insects.

After a seemingly endless wait, something other than the midges eventually stirred. From the nest box came a series of odd, muffled bumps and bangs, an occasional short hiss, like a brief blast from a spray can, and a high-pitched squeak or two. Straining my eyes to see clearly in the rapidly fading light, I all but gave myself away by gasping in surprise as the two adult owls shot from the nest box in rapid succession and zoomed around the aviary at top speed. Clearly wide awake, they behaved like a pair of dedicated fitness fanatics, leaping out of bed and promptly setting off on a fortifying jog. After completing several circuits of the aviary, the birds came down to rest on separate perches.

My gaze, however, was still fixed on the small wooden platform immediately in front of the nest box. I'd watched the parent birds' manoeuvres through the corners of my eyes, not daring to move my head, and I could swear that I'd seen some strange protuberance momentarily projecting from the entrance hole.

'Surely not, it must have been some trick of the light'. I dismissed the apparition from my mind.

By now, the sun had disappeared completely from the sky and the whole scene was bathed in a ghostly half-light. Praying that there would be no disturbances, such as the sudden emergence of my neighbours and their boisterous dog into their garden, I decided to watch for only a little longer. Just as I was about to give up in total frustration, I spotted two strange forms moving out from the shadows and into view on the platform, like a pair of actors arriving on stage from the wings. But this was no confident, dramatic entrance – far from it. The shapes made jerky, shuffling movements as they moved uncertainly forward, more like extras overcome by stage fright. So shambling was their performance that I was convinced that one or both would shortly wobble off the platform and crash to the ground. As I peered more intently through the gloom, the two figures began to look even more bizarre than they'd appeared at first sight. Both hunched, ugly creatures were covered in off-white down, apparently so loosely attached that the slightest breeze would send clouds of the stuff sailing through the air, like the seeds from a dandelion clock. Their heads were as unattractive as the rest of their bodies – bald, elongated faces dominated by sharply curving beaks, with none of the soft roundness so characteristic of all owls. For a moment, I feared there must have been some terrible mistake - my back garden had somehow become home to a pair of baby vultures, or even weird mutants. Only then did I remember the set of photographs from my book illustrating the barn owl's developmental stages: at around a month old, owlets would still be shuffling about on their haunches and only just beginning to acquire their facial discs. It was an enormous relief.

After several more minutes' wobbling around and shedding copious quantities of down, the ungainly twosome retreated into their box, from which once again there came a variety of muffled bumps and bangs. Keen to end the experience of being eaten alive, now that I'd seen all I wanted to, I seized the opportunity to stir from my hideout and head indoors. But anxious not to blow my cover completely, I resisted the urge to dash straight for the kitchen door, and instead strolled as nonchalantly as I could around the lawn, giving the impression, I hoped, of a gardener conscientiously tending his herbaceous borders. I knew that the adult owls were watching me, and it was them I was trying to fool into assuming that my nocturnal excursion was nothing they hadn't witnessed many times before. Eventually satisfied that my subterfuge had worked and that the owls were not feeling unduly agitated, I withdrew into the house, where I promptly rifled through the first-aid box and applied as much soothing balm as I could find to my well-chewed skin.

Over the next few weeks, I continued to monitor my charges from the impromptu foxhole in the flower bed. I watched in silent wonder as, little by little, the scruffy hunched forms that I had first seen shambling around their platform, like baby penguins on an ice floe, transformed themselves into creatures of beauty. Like butterflies emerging from their chrysalises, the youngsters wriggled and stretched, shedding clouds of wispy down to reveal, beneath, the velvety plumage of fully-fledged barn owls: gold and grey, flecked with black and white tear drops above, and pure radiant white below. Their heads, too, changed shape, becoming more rounded with the development of heart-shaped facial discs made up of specially-modified feathers. Regular consultations with Bunn *et al.* were essential throughout the owlets' transmogrification to reassure me that all was progressing absolutely normally.

Like an anxious parent monitoring his child's progress – or so I imagined, in the absence of any personal experience – I tracked the birds through all their key stages in turn, feeling particular pride whenever the smaller of the two seemed to be catching up with its older sibling. It was no more than an illusion, however: since barn owl eggs are laid, and hatch, at intervals of two to three days, the older owlet would always outstrip the younger. (The most extreme demonstration of such age differences I witnessed was when one of my pairs unexpectedly produced nine young in one go, meaning that the oldest bird in the brood was at least two weeks, and possibly three weeks, older than its youngest sibling). But once they approached maturity, the youngsters became virtually indistinguishable from each other, though not from their parents, as vividly demonstrated during one of my nightly vigils. In the fading light of evening, there was a sudden explosion of owls as all four of the inhabitants burst simultaneously from their nest box. Judging by their plumage, they were all pretty much alike, except perhaps for the adult female, whose feathering was showing distinct signs of wear and tear from the effort of raising her brood, but it was the birds' behaviour that was the real giveaway. While two of them – the adults – flew strongly and confidently around the aviary, the other two flapped clumsily about, trying, often unsuccessfully, to coordinate their wing and leg movements, particularly when effecting landing and take-off. They were clearly at that gawky, teenage stage, provided with all the necessary equipment, but still naïve and unskilled in its use.

No longer concerned about disturbing a family with vulnerable youngsters, and while their flying abilities were obviously so poorly developed, I decided to catch both juveniles so that I could have a go at sexing them. There's all the difference, I reminded myself, between studying them from the sidelines and holding them in the hand for a close-up view. Anticipating trouble, I pulled on my beekeeper's gloves and stepped smartly into the aviary, taking great care to fasten the door securely behind me. Secretly, I was hoping for trouble – I feared that an upbringing in a suburban back garden might somehow have had a taming effect, which might hinder their eventual release. But I needn't have worried on that score. As I caught each of the youngsters in turn, they hissed and struggled, striking out with their needle-like talons just as fiercely as any wild-bred barn owl would have done.

Now for the interesting bit, I thought. I'd discounted an attempt at what the reference books called 'direct visual inspection of the cloacal anatomy', as used for poultry. I wouldn't have known what I was looking at. Nor did I want to submit the birds to surgical sexing by the vet, a complex-sounding procedure involving anaesthesia and laparoscopy to facilitate a 'quick inspection of the gonads'. For a variety of reasons – squeamishness being the main one – I opted instead for the gentler, non-invasive technique shown to me by Jane and Teddy. This involved careful visual inspection of a bird's plumage, looking particularly for the darker markings that might signify the female sex: black spotting on the underwings and breast, a bronze 'necklace' effect and a dark edge to the outer rim of the facial disc. Manipulating each struggling bird in turn as best I could, I finally concluded that both were probably female.

10   Hunting skills

There was one life skill in particular that I wanted to be sure all the owls could master. It was particularly important because, as fascinating as I found them, I had no intention of keeping a garden full of barn owls forever and a day. Besides, they were not, and never had been intended to be, pets. On the contrary, the whole justification for what I was doing was the release of captive-bred barn owls as a conservation measure aimed at supplementing existing populations and restocking areas from which wild-bred birds had disappeared. Although back-up food supplies would be provided, it was vital that released owls should first of all recognise prey, and then know what to do when they found it.

Although greatly concerned about the ethics of my plan, I was convinced that there could be no substitute for the real thing – live prey. Contrary to Jane's uncompromising advice, all four of my owls had been fed predominantly on day-old chicks. I knew therefore that I ought, at least, to test their food recognition abilities before letting them loose in the wild.

Having scrounged several live brown mice from Jane, I set about making elaborate preparations for my experiment. First, I constructed an arena from a sheet of plywood about 1 metre square, to each corner of which I fastened a short (30 cm) wooden post. The walls of the arena were then formed from strips of heavy duty plastic sheeting, which I stretched tightly around the posts and fastened securely in place. Inside, the arena floor was covered with turf cut from my lawn, designed to provide a reasonably natural environment. Next I had to acclimatise the owls to this strange construction, so I manoeuvred it into the aviary, where I left it for several days. At first, the object prompted a degree of panic, especially when the slightest of breezes made the plastic sides flap about noisily. Gradually, though, the owls calmed down and appeared to accept the new object, much as garden birds become accustomed, after a few days, to a new bird table or feeder.

When at last I decided that the time had come, I made sure the birds were sharp-set (a falconry term meaning hungry) and therefore keen. A mouse was placed in the arena at dusk and provided with a small pile of tempting food, such as muesli. I then retreated to observe proceedings, not into the flower bed foxhole, which was too distant, but into the adjoining shed, from where I could peer through the windows to get a grandstand view. To my great relief – I could almost feel my conscience being salved – the mouse showed not the slightest concern, but continued calmly exploring its generous supply of tasty food. I had already decided that if the animal did show any signs of distress, I would intervene, either to recapture it or allow it to make an escape and take its chances in the great outdoors. Amazingly, though, the rodent's nonchalance persisted even when the two young owls,

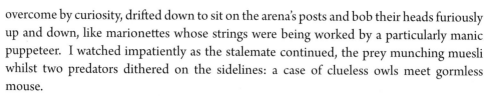

overcome by curiosity, drifted down to sit on the arena's posts and bob their heads furiously up and down, like marionettes whose strings were being worked by a particularly manic puppeteer. I watched impatiently as the stalemate continued, the prey munching muesli whilst two predators dithered on the sidelines: a case of clueless owls meet gormless mouse.

Uncertain about how long to let this strange situation continue, I began to speculate on what I might have to do to teach the owlets how to hunt, such as dragging dead food items on a string across the aviary floor, as if I were teasing a cat. What I hadn't reckoned with was that others were also getting impatient with the stand-off. In a flash the adult male owl, who, unnoticed by me, must also have been observing the scene, swooped down to grab the mouse from under the beaks of his feeble offspring, killing it instantly and repairing to a perch to enjoy his meal.

'Poor little bugger!' I muttered, thinking of the mouse, but then realising that I had just witnessed a master class in prey recognition and hunting skills. So had the owlets, and I could only hope that they were as impressed by their father's display as I was. There was one way to find out. I introduced a second brown mouse into the arena a few minutes later. Although much less hesitant than before, the youngsters once again allowed themselves to be robbed of a meal as the adult male quickly repeated his stylish but deadly manoeuvre.

These convincing displays clearly called for a change of plan. Abandoning the experiment for good, I decided to concentrate my efforts on releasing the adult pair of owls, rather than their apparently laggardly offspring, as I had originally intended. This would involve confining the pair in a suitable place from about mid-January until the following spring when, having bred, they would be released into the wild along with their brood. That, at least, was the theory.

11   Preparations for release

The Cheshire village where I was by then living had long before become something of a dormitory suburb of the nearby conurbation of Greater Manchester. I was a commuter myself, driving daily to and from work in north Manchester, weaving along the twisting, hedge-lined lanes separating the village from the motorway. The village is a classic of ribbon development, a narrow band of old-fashioned cottages mixed in with more modern houses bordering both sides of the main road as it winds its way through. Behind this residential veneer stretch the fertile Cheshire fields, grazed by great herds of Friesian cows, conspicuous in their magpie colours against the unnaturally bright, shiny green of their well-fertilised pasture land.

At the very end of my road, a mile or so from the village, lay a rather less intensive enterprise. Greenwood Farm was a family business run by a father and son, Jeff and Philip. There was certainly a small herd of cows, and also sheep and poultry, cereal and root crops, and even a part-time car repair business – what in town and country planning terms is called 'mixed use'. Infinitely more interesting to me, though, was the abundance of wildlife to be found in and around the farm. On the approach, where the lane passed through a steep-sided cutting, chestnut-brown bank voles could be seen scurrying through tangled undergrowth and twisted tree roots; just before you reached the farm, a frequently flooded, low-lying area might be playing host to a heron, or on one occasion to a moorhen trying, against the odds, to construct a viable nest there; and, most attractive of all, in the unkempt woodland that bordered the farm and provided its name, a tribe of badgers, occupying an ancient and enormous sett originally excavated many decades before from the sandy Cheshire earth. This secure and tranquil environment contrasted starkly with the roads on which I travelled to work, which were invariably littered with the mangled remains of any creature – fox, pheasant, hare – unwary enough to stray from the relative safety of the adjoining fields onto the deadly, tarmac killing zone.

Not only did the environs seem ideal barn owl territory, but the farm buildings and farmyard too were just what I was looking for. Though built in the local red brick, rather than the coarse grey limestone of the Lakeland buildings I'd been shown by Jane and Teddy Ratcliffe, the barns and other outbuildings were largely unused. With only limited storage now required at ground floor level, the upper floors were completely redundant, no longer needed to hold bales of hay because fodder to see the beasts through winter was supplied in cylinders of silage, like huge black puddings in their tight, shiny, plastic skins. Ironically, whilst this intensive silage production has resulted in empty farm buildings, producing potential homes for barn owls, the self- same process, involving the frequent, mechanical

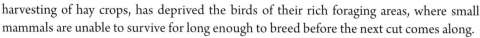

harvesting of hay crops, has deprived the birds of their rich foraging areas, where small mammals are unable to survive for long enough to breed before the next cut comes along.

It was in one of these disused haylofts, on the first floor, that the farmers, Jeff and Philip, agreed that I could carry out my first release. The room was situated in one end of a long, two-storey brick-built barn, with a neatly-fashioned circular opening, about four feet in diameter, in the gable end ('for chucking bales through', as Philip explained). At the opposite end of the loft was an internal dividing wall stretching the full height of the building, with a heavy wooden door at first floor level. There were therefore only two ways in and out – the circular opening and the door – both of them requiring the use of ladders. Using the hole involved setting ladders on a concrete yard adjoining the shippen. This yard, covered as it frequently was in a thin, treacherous coating of liquid cowshit, would be unlikely, I reckoned, to hold the ladder in place for long. If the cowshit didn't do the trick, the cattle surely would when they used the ladder as an impromptu scratching post or accidentally barged into it as they milled about the yard. Whatever the cause, the effect would be to maroon me in the loft with no means of escape. The safer bet therefore seemed to be to retreat inside the building and position a ladder against the whitewashed dividing wall so that I could access the loft via the elevated wooden door. Although this would involve a rather awkward stooping manoeuvre to step from the ladder and through the entrance, not least because the door opened outwards, I consoled myself with the thought that the sacks of cattle nuts piled at the foot of the wall would be more likely to cushion my fall than the unforgiving, slippery concrete of the yard outside.

Like most farmers, Philip was perfectly at ease climbing up and down ladders, and must have been amused as he watched my first, tentative steps up to the loft.

'You can do whatever you like!' he shouted up once he'd seen me safely over the threshold.

'I think I'll go home, then' I muttered in response, as an icy blast of winter wind swept in through the circular window to catch me full in the face.

In fact, I'd only ever intended this first ascent to be a reconnoitring exercise. Having had detailed orders from Jane, I was determined to follow them to the letter, as she would doubtless demand a full report back, and I wanted to work out what materials and tools I would need. With Jane's uncompromising words ringing in my ears – 'You'll have to block every possible exit – remember, barn owls can get through a two-inch gap!' – I worked my way painstakingly round the loft. Most obvious both in terms of owl-proofing and personal safety, parts of the floor had completely disappeared, providing a clear and disconcerting view into a row of cattle stalls below. Taking great care from then onwards to tread only on the joists, and as lightly as I could in case the remaining floorboards were in a similarly precarious state, I noted numerous small gaps in the brickwork, particularly where the roof met the walls. The more closely I looked, the more full of holes I imagined the loft to be and realised that, instead of importing quantities of DIY materials, I might have to improvise by plugging the gaps with anything that came to hand. The round opening was clearly a different matter. I would need to use netting there, I thought, partly because of the size of the gap, but also to provide the captives with a window onto the world, a place from which they could look out and familiarise themselves with the immediate locality during their forthcoming months of involuntary confinement. Fortunately, in contrast with the floor, the roof appeared to be well-maintained and completely sound. Eventually, I finished my survey by sizing up the central roof beam as a suitable place to attach the all-important nest box. That, at least, looked as if it would be a straightforward task.

Knowing how essential it was to rehouse the birds as soon as possible, I returned to the farm within a couple of days, equipped with every item that could conceivably be needed, and set to work. Unfortunately, the weather was still bitterly cold, encouraging me to work considerably faster than my normal, thoughtful pace. Working my way from the innermost point – the internal wall – I neurotically checked for any gaps of two inches or more. I took no chances, stuffing bits of brick, scrunched-up newspaper, sacking and handfuls of straw as tightly as possible into any space bigger than the merest crack. Edging painstakingly forward, towards the circular opening, I laid planks of wood to replace the vanished floorboards as I went. By the time I eventually reached the outer wall, I had already been at work for several hours.

Covering the circular opening presented me with my greatest challenge so far. It involved the construction of a lightweight wooden frame, square in shape and covered with netting, which could be easily fastened to the surrounding brickwork, and just as easily removed when the time came to do so.

As I banged and crashed about, a small gathering of young cattle assembled in the yard below, eyeing nervously this strange apparition, the warm air they anxiously snorted from their nostrils hanging like miniature cloud formations in the chilly air. Like a shoal of fish, they reacted as one, skittering noisily across the yard whenever they were startled by a particularly loud crash from my hammer or an occasional sharp cry of pain as I misjudged the blow and brought the hammer down on a semi-frozen finger instead of the intended nail.

'Oh, bloody hell!' I bawled, dancing around the loft like a madman, shaking my hand violently in a vain attempt to lessen the agony.

At times like these I was glad that the farmyard was so often deserted, my profanities heard only by an uncomprehending, yet spellbound, bovine audience. At least, I hoped so.

But my foul language wasn't the only thing that I might have wanted to keep to myself. Alone in my garret, cold, tired and hungry, I suddenly found myself talking to the cattle as if they were human, explaining what I was doing ('You'll have some new friends in here soon – that'll be interesting, won't it?) or trying to coax them back into the yard after they'd been spooked by a particularly noisy burst of hammering ('It's alright, steady now, that's good girls'). In reality, the last thing I wanted was to be regarded as sentimental or just plain mad, which probably would have worried me rather less. Throughout my dealings with site owners I've always been at great pains to stress the serious, practical conservation purposes of my project and minimise any fancy talk about 'the ethereal beauty of the barn owl, floating like an angel against a moonlit sky'. I certainly did not want my behaviour to undermine this approach and get me simply written off as a harmless eccentric. So, determined to stop talking to the animals, I decided to put all my energies into completing the loft conversion instead.

But there were other challenges to be overcome. The weather, bitterly cold and unpredictable throughout, tried one last time to drive me, finally frozen to the marrow, from the loft. Timing to perfection its most fierce onslaught, an undoubted skill of the British climate, the weather conjured up a particularly vicious blast of icy wind, accompanied by a

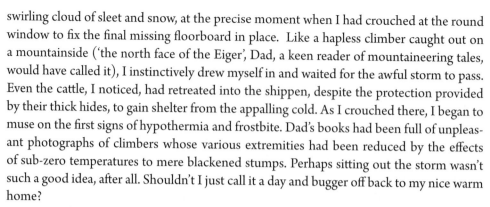

swirling cloud of sleet and snow, at the precise moment when I had crouched at the round window to fix the final missing floorboard in place. Like a hapless climber caught out on a mountainside ('the north face of the Eiger', Dad, a keen reader of mountaineering tales, would have called it), I instinctively drew myself in and waited for the awful storm to pass. Even the cattle, I noticed, had retreated into the shippen, despite the protection provided by their thick hides, to gain shelter from the appalling cold. As I crouched there, I began to muse on the first signs of hypothermia and frostbite. Dad's books had been full of unpleasant photographs of climbers whose various extremities had been reduced by the effects of sub-zero temperatures to mere blackened stumps. Perhaps sitting out the storm wasn't such a good idea, after all. Shouldn't I just call it a day and bugger off back to my nice warm home?

But just as I'd convinced myself that sticking it out any longer was not only unnecessary but also unwise, the weather suddenly changed once again. As unexpectedly as it had arrived, the storm passed, the howling wind dropped and, behold, the sun broke through the clouds, bringing a feeble but welcome warmth to my aching body. Even the cows were back.

'May as well carry on then, girls,' I muttered to them, as I felt a renewed enthusiasm to complete my task seep slowly back with the sun's rays. So, soldiering on, I finally managed to fit in place the square wooden frame that I had made and covered with wire netting. At last I could retreat into the relative comfort of the loft's interior and set about the final job: erecting a nest box.

I had thought that this would be the most straightforward task, as I'd brought with me a tea chest already adapted by the removal of its silvered lining paper, surplus tea leaves, protruding sharp nails and jagged strips of metal edging. I also had a cover, complete with entrance hole cut to the prescribed dimensions. The box, I naïvely thought, could simply be nailed in place on the central beam. It was while trying to implement my plan that I discovered several snags. Perched on a pair of stepladders, balancing the tea chest hard up against the beam with one hand and attempting to drive a large nail through the frame and into the beam with the other was, I soon discovered, a feat of gymnastics that I was incapable of sustaining for long. Even when I did achieve a brief equilibrium, I found it impossible to drive the nails home because of both the unyielding density of the oak beam and the sheer difficulty of taking a good back-swing with my hammer within the confines of an 18-inch square wooden box. As I toppled down from the ladder, releasing the box, hammer and nails to crash noisily to the floor, I once again howled curses of frustration.

Recovering my composure after a few minutes and deciding to make one last attempt, I convinced myself that the elegantly simple approach was not necessarily the only solution. So I opted to suspend the box beneath the solid beam, using a combination of heavy gauge wire, to form a cradle, binder twine and thin wooden laths, positioned vertically and nailed to the outside of the box and the less dense rafters that ran above the beam. Although this Heath Robinson construction was hardly pretty to look at, it was stable and secure as a roosting and nesting place. I had therefore achieved my main objective. Motivated now by thoughts of returning to a warm house and a decent meal, I quickly fitted out the loft with additional perching places, made from tree branches fastened across corners of the room. One of these I fastened close to the circular hole to encourage the owls to look out over the surroundings of their temporary quarters. And with that, and bidding farewell to my bovine friends, I jumped into my car and sped home, in desperate need of something that would defrost my severely chilled extremities.

No sooner had I completed my unconventional loft conversion than it was time to introduce its new occupants. January had all but passed and I was anxious to avoid carrying out the transfer when it might interfere with the birds' pairing and mating behaviour. I'd read that in the wild, established pairs maintain only a loose alliance, like being 'just good friends' during the winter months, meeting up again, if they both survive, early in the following year. One night I had a vivid demonstration of how such a rendezvous might be arranged. Hearing a racket going on outside my house, I first poked my head through the curtains to check whether all was well in the aviaries. Although it was a pitch-black winter night, I could make out my captive pair of barn owls by the light cast from an upstairs room. Both birds were in a highly agitated state, flying around wildly and coming to rest only to stare intently at the apparently featureless sky. As I strained to follow their gaze, the window by now propped wide open, I was surprised by a tremendous howling noise, as if a strong breeze had suddenly got up. Yet the night air was perfectly still. Then another sound, more akin to a screech, seemed to come from a different part of the sky. Still in my carpet slippers and indoor clothes, I grabbed a torch and shot out of the house into the nearby fields from where I was sure the strange noises were coming. As I stared up into the sky, waving my torch wildly in all directions as a feeble searchlight, more eerie sounds penetrated the night air, but, maddeningly, there was nothing to be seen. Like invisible rockets on bonfire night, the screams sped rapidly – sometimes erratically - across the sky, seeming to die away as they became more distant. Then, without warning, they would sound directly overhead, moving rapidly to left or right, never staying still. By now, I knew what I was witnessing, although a sighting or two would have provided conclusive evidence. I'd read about the courtship flights of barn owl pairs and was convinced that this was what I was now hearing: tremulous screeches uttered by both birds as they danced wildly together in the chill night air all around me. Oh, what I would have given at that moment for a pair of night-sighted binoculars, so that I could pick out these whirling spirits in their nocturnal courtship ritual. Instead, I could only imagine their twisting and turning pursuits as they uttered their mysterious calls.

Eventually, cold and exhausted from stumbling about the frozen fields, I had no option but to retreat indoors.

12 Bird ringing

I have always thought that an essential preliminary to any release – whether involving captive-bred creatures or wild ones that have been rescued, or treated in some way, and are ready for rehabilitation – is that they should be marked or tagged so that the success or failure of the activity can be gauged. Although such techniques are widely used by scientific researchers, they do not seem to be standard practice amongst the many well-motivated and dedicated individuals and organisations carrying out rescue and rehabilitation, or breeding and release, schemes. How then can any meaningful judgement be made about the effectiveness of their work?

On a trip to Australia, I once read – chalked up on an A-board – a story that vividly underlines the point. According to the author, the cost of treating each seal caught up in the Exxon Valdez oil disaster in Alaska was $80,000. When the time came for the release of two such patients, the whole of the local community came out to watch. Amid much cheering and self-congratulation, the seals were duly released into open water, but within a few minutes the jubilation turned to misery when both animals were promptly killed and eaten, in full view of the crowds, by a predatory killer whale. The tale had a moral, which the scribe highlighted at the end of his narrative: 'Have a nice day, because you never know what could be just around the corner!' For me, though, the vital lesson was a somewhat different one. Suppose that, rather than being seen to be butchered by a passing or lurking orca, the seals had swum into the next bay and met the same grisly end out of sight of their admiring spectators. No-one would have been any the wiser; the crowds would have departed thinking that they had witnessed a success story; and, worst of all from my point of view, there would have been no possibility of learning about the outcome of the release, unless the animals had been tagged. In this particular case, it was unclear whether the seals had been tagged or marked in some way. What is clear, however, is that, although tagging or marking cannot guarantee that information will be obtained about every individual, there is at least the possibility of gaining useful feedback on those that are subsequently found, whether dead or alive, in good health or poor. An objective judgement can then be made about the value of a particular activity, such as whether rehabilitated seals are likely to survive or will simply turn into incredibly expensive orca snacks.

The British Trust for Ornithology (BTO) has for many years run its tagging, or ringing, scheme for birds. The ring fastened round a bird's lower leg, or tarsus, bears a unique series of letters and numbers. A detailed record is kept of the ringing – the date, place and species – and anyone who later finds or catches the bird is encouraged to report it, with the following words impressed on every ring: 'Inform BTO British Museum Nat. Hist. London

SW7'. Since the Trust began the ringing scheme in earnest in 1937, invaluable data has been produced on such matters as the survival, migration and population size of many species of birds. My first encounter with the BTO, as a young boy, demonstrated both the value of ringing and the importance of good public relations. Finding a dead bird whilst beach-combing on holiday, I recovered the ring and carefully followed the instructions. A few days later, I was thrilled to receive back through the post an official notice, or recovery form, setting out details of the bird, including its species – it was a shag, or green cormorant – the date it was ringed, its age and the distance it had travelled. From that moment, I was totally sold on the merits of bird ringing. Twenty five years later, however, my enthusiasm had still not been translated into action. I wanted to ring my birds before placing them in the barn, but I knew that it was illegal for anyone without a BTO licence to ring a bird, even one bred in captivity for release – and I was not licensed. Desperate to practise what I passionately believed to be right, I was able, through a friend, to make contact with a couple of local ring-ers, Martin and Chris. When they arrived at my house I was apologetic, but soon found I had misjudged the situation.

'Don't worry, it's a pleasure,' came the reassuring reply. 'Wild barn owls are so rare, we're only too happy to ring captive-bred birds'. Not only were Martin and Chris keen to ring my owls, they also expressed their support for my project to supplement the meagre wild population with released individuals.

It was my job to catch and hold each bird in turn while Martin, the senior of the two ringers, carried out the ringing. I was reasonably well-versed in the procedure, having accompanied an expert, called Malcolm one summer at a site in Gloucestershire. The object there – part of a long-term study of the bird population of a particular wood - was to catch speculatively, using mist nets made from fine mesh. The lengthy nets, virtually invisible to birds, were stretched between vertical poles in a position designed to catch the maximum number of passers-by. Having flown, unseeing, into the net, a bird would quickly become entangled and be forced to wait helplessly until extracted, unharmed, by the ringer. In the course of a day, Malcolm and I patrolled his nets and disentangled, measured, weighed, ringed and recorded a wide variety of woodland species, ranging from an ill-tempered jay, which chiselled a lump out of his hand with its powerful beak, to a delicate but feisty little bluetit. Throughout a long, and at times trying, day I saw Malcolm lose his patience only once. It had nothing to do with the laborious and intricate task of extracting fragile catches from the nets' fine filaments, but was prompted by the discovery of a length of net that had been trampled down by a marauding bunch of heifers. Although no permanent damage had been done to either the net or any trapped birds, Malcolm charged at the miscreants waving a stick and screaming obscenities. He seemed to have so lost his self-control that I feared he would inflict some physical harm on the uncomprehending beasts. Only by risking a slightly lame quip – something about needing heavier-duty nets if he wanted to capture cattle – did I distract this usually mild-mannered ringer from his apparently murderous intent.

Bearing in mind all I had learned on my Gloucestershire field trip, I found handling the owls within the confines of the aviary surprisingly easy. Holding out each bird in turn, I watched as Martin skilfully fastened a stainless-steel split ring around the leg, using a special pair of pliers. He meticulously satisfied himself that that the two ends of the rings butted up closely against each other, and that the completed ring moved freely round the leg. Wearing

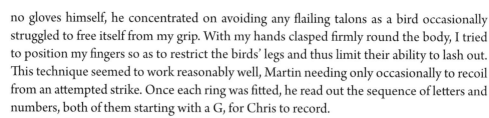

no gloves himself, he concentrated on avoiding any flailing talons as a bird occasionally struggled to free itself from my grip. With my hands clasped firmly round the body, I tried to position my fingers so as to restrict the birds' legs and thus limit their ability to lash out. This technique seemed to work reasonably well, Martin needing only occasionally to recoil from an attempted strike. Once each ring was fitted, he read out the sequence of letters and numbers, both of them starting with a G, for Chris to record.

With the ringing process complete, the owls were at long last ready to be removed to their new home down on the farm. I had already put the finishing touches to their quarters, covering the floor of the nest box with a thin layer of dry peat and sawdust, providing a shallow tray of fresh water and fixing a small feeding platform to the wall, just inside the door. It was much the same arrangement as I'd used in the aviary. I took Martin and Chris to the site to show them the set-up and let them watch the introduction of the owls, by now safely stowed in cardboard boxes for transportation. Once in the loft, I gently opened the boxes, allowing the owls to leave in their own time. As I retreated through the door and down the ladder, I could see them flapping around like a pair of huge moths, trying to find a spot to settle. Confident that they would calm down once we had all left, though much less confident that I'd plugged all possible escape routes, I took the additional precaution of padlocking the door to the loft. An accidental escape at this point would be little short of catastrophic.

I spent an anxious few hours back at home, before returning to the farm at dusk, a mishmash of worries and self doubt racing through my mind. Had I really managed to block up every gap of two inches or more? Would the birds find the place to their liking? Would they breed? Was I capable of managing their long-term care and eventual release? As I mounted the ladder, a bag of day-old chicks in hand, I willed everything to be in order – it would have been devastating to find out that it was not. Then, as I stepped from the top rung of the ladder over the threshold and into the loft, I had the immediate feeling that, contrary to my imaginings, all was well. Although at first the owls were nowhere to be seen, I could sense their presence, just as you can tell that there is someone there when you enter an apparently empty room. A quick peep into the nest box confirmed my supposition: both birds had assumed their customary positions, the hen trying to melt into the background by standing tall and thin, her eyes narrowed to oriental slits, whilst the cock stood defiantly on guard in front of her. Thrilled with the apparent success of my enterprise and needing to see no more, I quickly deposited the food on the ready-made platform, climbed back down the ladder, having padlocked the door, and sped home on a high of joy and relief.

13   *Increasing my breeding stock*

Meanwhile, my barn owl stock was expanding relentlessly. First, a cock bird had arrived, a wild specimen from the border country of Dumfries and Galloway. Apparently, he had been rescued by a farmer after being found shot – regrettably, not an uncommon event. Although his rescuer had cared for him for three years, she did not seem to have sought immediate veterinary attention and his injured left wing had healed in a crooked position, the forewing drooping unnaturally from a point just below the alula, or 'bastard wing'. Although able to fly short distances, it was clear that this bird would never be fit to return to the wild. A career at stud would therefore be his enviable fate.

The owl had been sent down from the Borders by train to Jane and Teddy. 'When we opened the box he arrived in, we were horrified by his condition,' Jane told me. 'His feathers were red with what we took to be blood. It was only when we examined him more closely that we realised it was dye for marking sheep – the farmer must have had it all over her hands when she caught him and put him in the box!'

Jane was holding the owl firmly in both hands as she spoke, and I was pleased to see that there was no longer any trace of red dye on his plumage. His behaviour, though, reminded me of an old joke – this bird wasn't just wild, he was furious. Like an enraged or terrified cat, the owl held both legs straight out and rigid, his toes splayed with their long, curved talons like miniature sabres, drawn back ready to slash at anything that might come within range. He was also hissing like a cat, moving his head menacingly from side to side and occasionally jerking it forward to stick his slender pink tongue out from the side of his beak and utter a single sharp click. I instantly recognised the sound as a display of aggression made by wild tawny owls I'd previously cared for, but I'd never seen them stick their tongues out at me first. I'd assumed that they were simply snapping together their upper and lower mandibles but, according to Bunn *et al.*, this is the subject of some controversy. After many years' observation, my strong suspicion is that the sound comes from the tongue, not the beak, and is like the sharp 'tock' noise human beings can make by pushing their tongue up against the roof of the mouth then quickly withdrawing it – a technique used by naughty school children, preferably when the teacher's back is turned, to enliven a silent interlude during lessons.

However fierce and unpredictable this bird might be, Jane and Teddy were determined to pass him on to me for use in my project. 'Remember, it's all about getting a good genetic mix!' Jane declared. And that was that.

The next addition to the gene pool was equally unexpected. One night, my telephone rang and the caller, Peter, identified himself as the warden of a nature reserve in north

Manchester. Elements of the tale he proceeded to tell me were to become all too familiar over the ensuing years.

'I've bought a barn owl…' he began.

'Oh yes?' My non-committal response must have contained more than a hint of disapproval, because he quickly added that he'd paid the money over only to be certain of acquiring the bird from its unsuitable owner.

'He'd kept it as a pet for a couple of years, but got tired of it', Peter explained.

Another one, I thought, recalling Barney's story.

Quickly making my decision, I told Peter that I would take the owl off his hands, but that I wasn't prepared to pay him for it. To his credit, he readily agreed.

'I don't mind about the money, just so long as you can use it in your breeding and release scheme – I think it's a female, by the way'.

When Peter arrived later that evening and produced his owl, the contrast with the Ratcliffes' bird could not have been greater. Here was no extravagant display of bravado, but a painfully shy creature, cowering in a cardboard box, rigid with fear rather than aggression. Its feet were tightly clenched and its facial disc drawn back, turning the eyes into narrow slits that emphasised the bird's unhappy appearance. Even a cursory inspection proved that it had been poorly cared for – its plumage was generally grubby and unkempt, and the wing and tail feathers broken and frayed. New feathers were beginning to poke through a bald patch on the owl's head. Like Barney, this bird had obviously been bred for the pet trade, as I noticed that an alloy close ring encircled one of its legs.

Saddened though I was by the owl's physical state and demeanour, I was heartened to realise that Peter's instinct had been correct in thinking it was a female. Unlike in Barney's case, the bird's original owner had made the right assumption and given her an appropriate, if unusual, name: Carrie. My first problem was where to accommodate her.

The two offspring of the previous year, whom I called The Sisters, were now living in an aviary with Barney, who had waited until they adopted one of the two nest boxes and then promptly evicted them, taking it over and fiercely defending her new home. With no experience of keeping several owls of the same sex in one aviary, I simply assumed that, now they had established some sort of pecking order, they were unlikely to fight or seriously harm each other, at least outside the breeding season. However, I was determined to keep a close eye on them all, so that I could intervene if necessary, and, besides, I was far from convinced about the accuracy of my sexing abilities – it was certainly possible that some of my hens were, in fact, cocks. I had much less doubt about the Ratcliffes' owl, which, Jane had insisted, was a male. I didn't want to try him out with any of the resident females because I thought that Barney was too tame and that The Sisters, only a few months old, were possibly too young to breed. But I now had an opportunity. With Carrie, a fully-grown female – or so I hoped – the cock bird could demonstrate his virility. First, though, I felt she needed to build up her strength with some rest and recuperation.

Providing her with a nest box, I began by housing Carrie in an aviary with two orphaned kestrels which I was also caring for. I reasoned that they would operate the day shift and the owl the night shift. Sure enough, I detected no signs of aggravation amongst the residents and Carrie's general state noticeably improved with the benefit of fresh air, exercise and good food, liberally dusted with the vitamin supplement SA37. So remarkable was the transformation within a few days that I could only imagine the poor conditions in which she must have been kept by her original owner.

After several weeks, when I was absolutely sure that the newcomer had settled in, I decided to take another major step towards introducing my two recent acquisitions to each other. By now, through a combination of observation, reading and discussions with experts, I thought I knew a thing or two about breeding barn owls. So I decided to make use of a set of three aviaries that I had acquired from Jane and Teddy, dismantled, transported from their Lake District home and re-erected in my back garden. The great advantage of these was that they consisted of three adjoining units, like a row of terraced houses, but with connecting hatches built into the party walls. The hatches could be left open to create one large aviary, or they could be closed to produce two or three separate units. Unfortunately, there was, though, a drawback: the whole construction, consisting of rough sawn timber, wire netting and corrugated plastic walls and roofs, was extensive and somewhat ramshackle in appearance, leading one neighbour to christen it, with no thought of political correctness, 'Soweto'.

My plan for the use of this set-up was simple: to place Carrie and the Scottish bird in adjoining units, each with their own nest box, leaving the intervening hatch open and allowing the birds, if they so wished, to interact. If they could not, or would not, get on, I would simply separate them by sliding the hatch cover back into place. The first few days of this experiment proved to be a very tense period – for me, at least. Although they spent some time together in the same aviary during the day, the birds habitually returned to their own nest boxes at night in a kind of 'his 'n hers' arrangement. Although various shrieks and other cries would occasionally issue from the units during the night, no serious disputes seemed to be breaking out. Left alone as much as possible and subject only to covert surveillance, the apparently platonic relationship between the birds gradually blossomed. By late October, they were regularly cohabiting, making use of only one aviary and a single nest box. Benign indifference to their occasional squabbling seemed to have worked a treat.

14   Back on the farm

While my two latest acquisitions were getting acquainted, I continued to make daily trips to the farm with a bag of food for the pair I now called The Hartleys, named after the farmers. In early spring, a trip along the lane to the farm often proved a delight, particularly when I chose to go on foot. Swallows, swifts and martins would hawk for insects overhead, whilst bank voles scurried amongst the gnarled and twisted tree roots that helped to retain the earth embankments of the cutting through which the lane meandered. Occasionally, there were even little adventures, such as rescuing a sheep from its entanglement in a bramble bush, my expertise in such matters well-honed by my childhood in the Lakes. But the winter months made for much less pleasurable experiences: freezing cold winds, lashing rain and pitch darkness. Even the use of the car couldn't prevent my night-time feeding routine becoming much more of a chore than a pleasure. Occasionally, the ladder that I'd left carefully propped against the wall the previous night was no longer there. This would invariably coincide with the farm being deserted, my forgetting to bring a torch and the ground being awash with a mixture of squelchy, cloying mud and liquid cowshit. Slipping and sliding about in the dark, cursing foully as my leg encountered unseen obstructions – a gate left half-open here, a wheelbarrow abandoned there – I might eventually locate the ladder by a combination of touch and sheer luck.

Even when found, the ladder had to be carted back across the yard, manoeuvred into position against the internal wall and then scaled to reach the loft above. Fortunately, there was a feeble source of illumination in this part of the building – a single, dusty light bulb – so my ascent and descent were not quite as hazardous as they would have been in complete darkness. For the job I had to do – place a handful of chicks on the feeding platform just inside the loft door – I had to make a disproportionately tremendous effort. Even these hardships were surpassed when the muddy ground was frozen, moulded into a moonscape of rock-hard miniature peaks, surrounding hoof-sized depressions, each with its own filling of frozen slurry. This unpredictable surface was, I soon found, virtually impossible to traverse in the dark whilst bracing myself against a gale and carrying a long, heavy ladder. I invariably tottered, unbalanced, on the peaks, or got a foot wedged in one of the hollows, the diameter of a cow's hoof, I discovered, being just slightly smaller than the width of my size tens. In such conditions, instead of the customary squelch across sodden ground, I made clumsy jerking movements, backwards and forwards, with the ladder held at shoulder height in an attempt to aid balance, so that, from a distance, I must have looked like an incompetent tightrope walker, or, more likely, a very drunken would-be burglar. At least there's no-one around, I would think, cursing loudly at every involuntary stumble and lurch.

Although, as a considerate fellow, my usual rule was to put the ladder back where I had found it when the job was done, I must confess that, in weather conditions such as these, I would simply lay it down at the foot of the inner wall, or even fling it into the nearest corner if I'd had a particularly trying time, and hope that no-one would notice that it had mysteriously moved in the night. My priority then was to get back to the warming comfort of home as quickly as I could possibly manage.

Compensation for all my hard, and occasionally hazardous, work finally came in late spring. From time to time throughout the previous months, I'd not only left food for the owls but also dragged the ladder in after me, like a mountaineer pulling up his rope, and set it against the beam from which the nest box was strung. Climbing up as quietly as I could, I would peep briefly into the box to check on the owls' progress. Only too well aware of Jane Ratcliffe's dire warnings, I was always extremely careful not to disturb the birds by being overly intrusive. I did linger, though, on one warm evening in early May, stunned and over-joyed to be staring at six clean and shiny white eggs formed into a rough circle towards the back of the box, the adult owls standing immediately behind their precious clutch, blinking with bewilderment at my sudden appearance. The whole scene was reassuringly familiar: just what I had found when I had looked in on the owls at home.

'Great! Well done!' I declared, like some visiting VIP congratulating a scout troop on their success at knot tying. As I spoke, though, I sped down the ladder and out of the loft in my fastest time ever. Over the next few days, I continued to make only the most fleeting of visits, and even these were conducted with all the care and skill of a cat burglar. I eased up latches, positioned ladders, unfastened padlocks and crept into the loft with the speed and deliberation of movement that would have been the envy of any sloth. Thankfully, there was never any sign of the farmer or his family, so I wasn't called upon to explain my strange lapse into slow motion.

Jeff and his son, Philip, were typical working farmers, all soiled overalls, mucky hands, big boots and uncombed hair. I think this unkempt world was all part of the attraction for someone like me, who spent all his working days encased in a suit and tie. Philip's wife, though, was quite a different matter. Jenny was a curvaceous blonde, who would occasionally appear at the farmhouse door, dressed in spotless, tight blue jeans and an equally figure-hugging top, to totter, on shiny black stilettos, the few feet to her sporty, bright red BMW, zooming off down the lane towards the sophisticated – and expensive – attractions of nearby Knutsford, or Wilmslow. These visions, regrettably rare, were a taste of what I thought it might be like to bump, metaphorically speaking, into Madonna or Kylie Minogue in a local Cheshire pub. The effects would doubtless be similar – a jaw-dropping inability to continue whatever conversation I was having at the time, coupled with a surreptitious eyeing- up of the vision that was unexpectedly before me. However hard I tried to control my involuntary reactions whenever Jenny hove into view, inwardly I still felt like one of those cartoon characters whose eyes pop out on stalks and whose tongues drool uncontrollably when faced with an equally exciting stimulus. It was soon to become apparent, however, that my lascivious thoughts had not gone entirely unnoticed.

Like many farmers, isolated from outside human contact for much of the working day, Philip was always hungry for conversation whenever our paths happened to cross. The subject matter, usually of his choosing rather than mine, was often mundane stuff about the

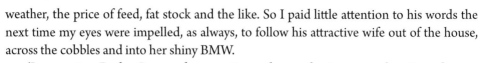

weather, the price of feed, fat stock and the like. So I paid little attention to his words the next time my eyes were impelled, as always, to follow his attractive wife out of the house, across the cobbles and into her shiny BMW.

'I was saying, Paul… I remember, one time, when we having some alterations done to the farmhouse'. There was a faint hint of irritation in his voice at having to repeat his opening scene-setter. The follow-up was hardly gripping either. 'We lived in a caravan in the yard, but if we needed to use the bathroom in the night, we had to go across to the house'.

He was still failing to attract my attention, which was by now focused on the little red sports car as it disappeared in a cloud of dust down the lane.

'There was never anyone about, of course, so Jenny would just wander across there without a stitch on – except for her wellies, of course!'

Now Philip *had* caught my attention – and he knew it. As I involuntarily glanced around the yard, with the image of an incredibly attractive blonde wearing only rubber boots and caught in soft-focus torchlight now stuck immovably in my mind, I surreptitiously sought out signs of ongoing building work, or even a caravan in a corner somewhere, that I hadn't spotted before. Perhaps, I thought, I could time my visits for somewhat later in the evenings? Sadly for me, the building alterations had clearly come to an end and there was not the slightest sign of a mobile home anywhere on the farm. To my horror, I realised that Philip was reading my thoughts. He said nothing, but a sly smile played on his lips as he shrugged his shoulders and sauntered knowingly into his workshop. As he obviously knew, not one of my visits to his farm would coincide with a naked romp around the yard by his wife, or anyone else. But he also realised that the image had been successfully planted in my mind, and the forlorn hope of an exciting encounter would doubtless remain to torment me.

Fortunately for me, there were other, less risky, sights in the vicinity to distract the frustrated voyeur.

15 Farm-bred success

In the nearby wood lay the biggest, most extensive, and probably the oldest badger sett that I have ever seen. It was Jeff who'd first mentioned it, telling me how, one day, he'd seen men digging in the wood and, suspecting what they were up to, called the police. Sure enough, before they could do much damage, the men were arrested for badger digging, a crime which involves forcibly removing the animals and carrying them off in sacks, so that they can be used elsewhere for the barbaric 'sport' of baiting with dogs. Unrepentant, the small gang was marched, alternately cursing and protesting their innocence, through Jeff's farm yard to the waiting Cheshire Constabulary van. Jeff related how, as he passed a tractor parked in the yard, one of these thugs picked up a spade and thrust it vengefully through the windscreen, shattering the glass into tiny fragments.

'Cost me a fair bit to get that mended,' Jeff lamented. 'And I never got so much as a penny's compensation!'

'Still, you saved the badgers, and that's the important thing.'

To my mind, the replacement of a broken windscreen was a price well worth paying for preventing murderous cruelty to badgers. In my eagerness to express support for Jeff's actions, though, I'd overlooked the one, constant obsession of farmers the world over: money. Even Jeff, normally the most mild-mannered and friendly of individuals, felt obliged to respond to my incomprehensible statement of priorities with a scowl. I had committed the cardinal sin of elevating an intangible consideration above the pre-eminence in the farmer's mind of good, honest, reassuring cash. As he wandered off, without a further word, I felt sure that our exchange would be the subject of bemused discussion at the local farmers' club that night.

When I first saw the woodland sett, I was amazed by its size and complexity. Taking the experts, Jane and Teddy, to view it one day, I received instant confirmation that it must have been used by countless generations of badgers. The main, and most visible, section consisted of a large, flattish dome, formed within a rough circle of mature trees. Numerous tunnels, large and small, had been excavated in the dome, the best of them lying in and around the substantial root systems of the surrounding wood, which provided a natural frame or skeleton to the whole construction. The red Cheshire soil lay outside these excavations in loose heaps, and also covered the dome in a kind of protective clay crust formed by the impact of countless padded feet over the years. Other signs of occupation were everywhere to be seen – scratching posts, where claws were sharpened and polished, rotten logs, shredded like paper to expose the insects and grubs hiding within, numerous narrow tracks, criss-crossing the whole area and, of course, badger latrines – dung pits dug singly or in groups.

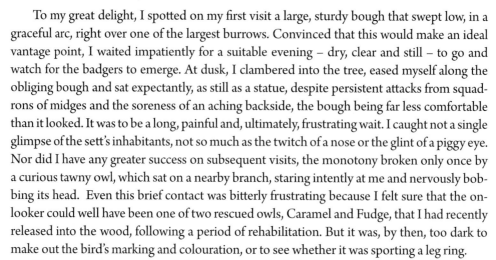

To my great delight, I spotted on my first visit a large, sturdy bough that swept low, in a graceful arc, right over one of the largest burrows. Convinced that this would make an ideal vantage point, I waited impatiently for a suitable evening – dry, clear and still – to go and watch for the badgers to emerge. At dusk, I clambered into the tree, eased myself along the obliging bough and sat expectantly, as still as a statue, despite persistent attacks from squadrons of midges and the soreness of an aching backside, the bough being far less comfortable than it looked. It was to be a long, painful and, ultimately, frustrating wait. I caught not a single glimpse of the sett's inhabitants, not so much as the twitch of a nose or the glint of a piggy eye. Nor did I have any greater success on subsequent visits, the monotony broken only once by a curious tawny owl, which sat on a nearby branch, staring intently at me and nervously bobbing its head. Even this brief contact was bitterly frustrating because I felt sure that the onlooker could well have been one of two rescued owls, Caramel and Fudge, that I had recently released into the wood, following a period of rehabilitation. But it was, by then, too dark to make out the bird's marking and colouration, or to see whether it was sporting a leg ring.

Having failed to spot a single badger, it was clearly high time for a change of plan.

On one side of the dome, I'd noticed that the land sloped quite steeply down to a small stream, meandering sluggishly through the lower woodland. The slope itself was peppered with the unmistakable signs of badger activity: although secretive by nature, the animals' behaviour is often boisterous and unrestrained, leaving behind clearly visible evidence of their activities. I had noticed that a large, apparently well-used burrow lay close to a bend in the stream so, on my next visit, decided to forsake the bough and plump instead for a waterside location. In my new position, I once again sat stock still, eyes and ears straining to catch the slightest hint of activity.

By the time I'd lurked for the best part of an hour in my new location, the light had begun to fade. Familiar nocturnal sounds – the low hoot of a tawny owl, emerging for a night's hunting; the 'pink pink pink' of a blackbird eagerly seeking out its favourite roost – provided reassurance that all was well with the wood. I tried hard to convince myself that this had to be a good night for badger watching. I was being totally irrational, of course, simply willing success on my enterprise and pretending that the omens were favourable. In reality, the conditions that night were no different from all the other badger-starved nights that I'd spent suspended, painfully, above the sett.

Stealth is not one of the badger's qualities. Blundering is. Like other members of the mustelid family – stoats, weasels and otters – a badger's eyesight is poor, so its normal hunting technique involves wandering around in an apparently aimless manner, hoovering up anything vaguely edible that it happens to stumble across. The nightly 'bag', understandably, contains large quantities of worms – sucked up noisily, like a messy child swallowing strands of spaghetti – beetles and grubs. This apparently random approach, however, conceals the part played by the animal's acute sense of smell. Although painfully short-sighted, any mustelid worthy of the name will bolt for cover the instant it catches the slightest whiff of human scent. I had therefore taken the precaution of testing for the wind direction, using the old moistened-finger-in-the-air technique, and satisfied myself that I was definitely downwind of the sett.

The light had, by now, all but gone. The silence was suddenly broken by a loud crashing of undergrowth, followed by a low groan, a series of snuffling noises and further sounds of a creature trundling through the tangle of brambles and ferns to my right. I tensed – the sounds were originating from very close by. I half expected the badger – it could only be a badger – to blunder right into me. I wondered, for a moment, which of us would be the more scared. Fortunately, my speculation wasn't put to the test, as I heard the creature move, unhurriedly, away from my position. For a brief moment its whiffling stopped, then came a splash, followed by the instantly recognisable sound of a furry animal shaking dry its coat, before continuing on its way. Maybe under the influence of my heightened senses – my heart was thumping, my eyes and ears straining – I convinced myself that this was a boar badger, simply because the sounds seemed to be emanating from something large, and the male badger is significantly bigger than the female. I tracked him going round behind me, not daring even to turn my head towards the sounds, whilst the grunting, wheezing and shuffling, as if made by some old codger on his nocturnal ramblings, slowly moved round to my left and eventually faded completely away.

Once again, I'd seen nothing of the badgers, but simply prompted a determined detour by a member of the sett, out on one of his nightly excursions. I was beginning to give up hope – this beautiful, ancient and accessible site seemed determined to deny me even the slightest glimpse of its fascinating inhabitants.

You might quite reasonably ask yourself why anyone should want to sit for several hours in gross discomfort, in a dark wood, assailed by swarms of biting midges, without any guarantee of success in their mission. Your curiosity might be even more aroused were you to look up in a dictionary the animal that is the object of such interest. The *Concise Oxford Dictionary*, for example, defines badger as: 'grey-coated strong-jawed nocturnal hibernating plantigrade between weasels and bears' ('plantigrade', incidentally, means an animal that walks on its soles). Knowing that many perfectly sane people do go badger watching – and enjoy rather more success than I had so far managed - I decided to abandon my efforts for the time being.

Throughout my unsuccessful badger-seeking forays, attending to the barn owls remained, of course, my daily priority. By mid-May, the tell-tale sound of faint chittering noises could be heard from outside the nest box, although the heifers in the yard below would often do their best to drown out the feeble sounds with their throaty bellowing. Sure enough, when Jeff and I peered carefully into the box, using the old torch and mirror technique, we could clearly make out two small owlets, as well as two rather dirty, and seemingly discarded, eggs. I was particularly surprised to see several mounds of food stockpiled around the nest area. Keen that this surplus should not be left to rot or, worse still, be fed to the youngsters after it had gone off, I reached in and removed several handfuls of chicks which, it soon became clear, were in various stages of decomposition. Even Jeff the farmer screwed up his face in disgust at the stench.

'I'd better reduce the daily feed,' I whispered to him as we retreated from the loft and down the ladder.

Food storage, or caching, is not unusual in birds. For many years, I kept a tame magpie, called Pica, who regularly secreted titbits around his aviary, skilfully inserting small lumps of mince into any available crevice, such as the joints between the rough poles that formed the framework. Most extreme was the behaviour of the disabled little owl I kept, which, I discovered, had lined its entire nest box with surplus food, so that, when inside, it was cocooned within a ball of desiccated chick carcasses. To prevent similar excesses on the part

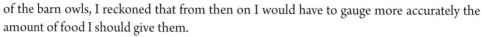

of the barn owls, I reckoned that from then on I would have to gauge more accurately the amount of food I should give them.

Although it was essential not to over-feed the birds, it was equally important to provide the owlets, in particular, with enough food to satisfy their appetites and sustain normal development. As I wasn't even sure how many owlets there were – I'd originally seen six eggs, yet Jeff and I had spotted only two young and two discarded eggs – getting it right would be tricky. I knew, from my own limited experience and from background reading, that when the young owls reach four to five weeks of age, they need three or four food items per day to fuel their development. It would be essential for me to know when these owlets reached that stage. I therefore decided, somewhat reluctantly, that I must be more interventionist in my approach from now on. Over the next few days, I peered into the nest box at regular intervals, noting that all seemed well, and confirming that the brood consisted of only two chicks. About three weeks after I'd first heard the owlets, I decided to take an even closer look. At first sight, there seemed to be no cause for alarm. One fairly large, well-developed youngster was trying to hide, none too successfully, behind its parents, who were standing like sentries at the back of the box. However, my eyes were then drawn to the smaller sibling who was resting closer to me, near the entrance to the box. Seizing my chance, I fished this youngster out for a more detailed examination. Still covered in thick white down, the owlet felt plump and warm but also, I sensed, strangely lethargic, with eyes that seemed milky in colour instead of the expected shiny jet-black.

'Is there something wrong with you, little one?' I murmured as I cupped my hands gently around the downy creature. There was certainly no obvious sign of injury or malnourishment, although my mind was racing with half-remembered scraps of information about competition amongst siblings for food, cannibalism and Jane Ratcliffe's claim that young owlets might be killed by their parents in mistake for day-old chicks. Unable to reach a definite conclusion about the owlet's state of health, I decided to operate my golden rule: when in doubt, leave well alone. In other words, the youngster's future – good or bad – lay with its parents, rather than with being removed to be poked and prodded by a vet, and perhaps raised by me in captivity. So I carefully replaced the owlet in the nest box and was instantly thrilled to see it scramble eagerly to its feet and shuffle noisily towards its parents, who were still standing defiantly to attention at the rear of the box. I was now even more certain that I had made the right decision, but I certainly approached the next day's inspection with a degree of trepidation.

As if to underline how unpredictable any creature can be, the owl parents on this occasion reacted aggressively, striking out fiercely with their feet and hissing loudly, when I peered into their box. The youngsters, too, seemed to have learned from the previous day's experience, as they huddled together behind their parents' impressive defensive wall. Greatly reassured by this display of family unity, I could only think that the young owlet's behaviour of the previous day had been a combination of being taken by surprise, and a deliberate attempt to play possum. I've experienced this with wild tawny owls held in captivity, which will feign unconsciousness at first, but appear perfectly lively once they think they're no longer being observed. I decided to keep my fingers crossed that the barn owl youngster had indeed been misleading me and that it would now continue with its normal development.

16   *An unexpected treat*

Although my judgement as to the amount of food to provide had improved as time went on, I still occasionally arrived in the loft to find two or three chicks left totally untouched on the feeding platform. Because of the warm weather, I always removed these leftovers and replaced them with fresh food. Most raptors, in fact, have remarkably strong stomachs, like vultures, seemingly able to cope with well-rotted carrion.

It was Jeff who, one day, suggested how I might dispose of the surplus food.

'Why don't you put 'em out for the badgers?'

'That's a good idea. I will.' I was reluctant to speculate openly about who might actually reap the benefits of this bounty, should the badgers choose not to take advantage of it. There are two common species, both on the increase, which are despised by all farmers, Jeff included: the brown rat, and the magpie.

'There's too many magpies these days!' was a complaint I heard from townies and country-dwellers alike, the former convinced that these handsome crows have been responsible for seeing off all their beloved garden birds. Like the rat, however, the magpie has proved a resourceful and adaptable creature, no longer the 'shy woodland bird' described in the older bird books, but an opportunist raider, equally adept at surviving in urban and rural surroundings. I was convinced that, unless they were quick, the badgers would be beaten to the surplus chicks by the local 'vermin'. Needless to say, I refrained from sharing these thoughts with farmer Jeff.

More often than not, after a long day in the office or the courtroom, I would find myself visiting the farm fairly late in the evening. I couldn't always be bothered to navigate my way through the obstacle course of gates, randomly parked farm machinery and barbed wire fences that stood between me and that part of the wood in which the badger sett lay. Instead, having gathered up two or three untouched chicks from the loft, I would position myself within range of the wood and hurl them, one by one, in the general direction of the sett. Although this was great fun, I prayed that no-one was around to spot my bizarre behaviour, as they would no doubt think I was practising for the world chick-chucking championships.

One warm, sunny evening, arriving home unusually early, I decided to effect a door-to-door (or loft-to-sett) delivery service. Crossing the farmyard and scrambling through the rickety barbed wire fence that bordered the wood, I didn't, as I would normally have done, test the wind direction by moistening my index finger and sticking it into the air, nor did I tread carefully through the tangled twigs and leaf litter that carpeted the woodland floor. Although managing, just, to refrain from whistling a happy tune as I went, I took no precautions whatsoever against being detected. After all, I reasoned, I was delivering food,

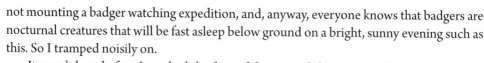

not mounting a badger watching expedition, and, anyway, everyone knows that badgers are nocturnal creatures that will be fast asleep below ground on a bright, sunny evening such as this. So I tramped noisily on.

It wasn't long before I reached the foot of the mound that contained the sett. Its main entrance holes were clustered around the top, and I was keen to leave my food offerings right outside the badgers' 'front door', so as to minimise the opportunities for other scavengers to get a free feed. But, as I took the few paces to the crest of the mound, I was stopped in my tracks by the very last sight I had expected to see: right in front of me, close enough to touch and, it seemed, totally oblivious to my presence, was a group of four badgers. Partly out of stunned surprise, partly out of an instinct to minimise the intrusion, I sank slowly to my knees on the spot, only just managing to suppress a gasp of delight. The movement had no noticeable effect on the animals' behaviour. They simply continued to snuffle about on the flattened earth surrounding the holes, occasionally communicating with each other in little grunts and squeals. Despite having thick blue-grey coats extending down over their short, powerful legs, giving them the appearance of animated hearth rugs, the badgers clearly displayed the sinuous, rippling run so typical of the mustelid family, as they began to career around more excitedly. By now, I was convinced that these were well-grown cubs, making the most of a sunny afternoon to indulge in a spot of play. As I watched, transfixed by their boisterous antics, one youngster bolted down a hole, only to appear, a second or two later, from the hole nearest to where I still knelt like a supplicant at a holy shrine. A broad black-and-white striped furry head, topped with white-tipped, pointed ears was now thrust out so close to me that I could have reached out and touched it. A pair of dark, piggy eyes blinked in the bright light and a broad, moist black nose twitched rapidly as the animal, somewhat belatedly, tried to work out whether this strange new lump represented any kind of threat. I could resist the urge to reach out my arm but, overcome with emotion, I couldn't stop myself from uttering one simple word.

'Hello,' I whispered, in the friendly tones I would have used to reassure a nervous puppy.

The effect was both inevitable and instantaneous. Quick as a flash, the cub disappeared backwards down the hole, as if yanked back by an invisible rope. Almost simultaneously, the other three animals, still bustling about on the surface, shot down the holes nearest to them. I knew they would not now reappear for a good hour or more. So, kicking myself for behaving so impulsively, I deposited the chicks I had brought near one of the holes and headed back towards the farm. As I wandered slowly along, I couldn't help reflecting on the irony of the evening's events. As so often seems to happen with wildlife, my best piece of badger-watching, by far, had occurred by accident. In fact, because I'd not expected to see them, I'd casually done lots of things – ignored the wind direction, crashed through the woods and walked directly up to the sett – that should have ensured a badger-free visit. All my deliberate attempts to badger-watch, following the rules to the letter, had resulted in nothing more than many uncomfortable nights spent in a tree, and the distant sounds of a badger taking evasive action during a nocturnal excursion. I began to think that accidental encounters might offer much greater prospects of success than highly-organised, purposeful expeditions. In other words, I should let the wildlife come to me, rather than go to the wildlife.

17   *Free to come and go at last*

By mid-June, it was clear that decision-time was fast approaching. The adult pair release method advocated by Jane and Teddy provided for only a very narrow window of opportunity to let the birds fly free. As unfledged offspring provide adults with a powerful incentive to return and fulfil their parental duties, the best time to open up the barn was when the young had reached five or six weeks of age. At this point, there was minimal risk of the adults simply clearing off.

It was easy enough to understand the theory, but extremely difficult, I thought, to accept its practical implications. A host of unpleasant possibilities flashed through my mind, from the obvious risk of a parental disappearing act to the rather more fanciful notion that the owlets could be stolen by a human intruder. Baby barn owls, I'd been told, could change hands for quite a lot of money on the black market. Still, I told myself, you can't keep accumulating captive barn owls. The whole point, after all, was to release them into the wild.

Having determined to bite the bullet, I arranged for the owlets to be ringed. Once again, Martin and Chris were happy to do the honours, and I knew now that I had passed the point of no return – the rules prohibited me from keeping ringed birds in captivity without good reason.

As we ferreted about in the nest box, capturing the youngsters, I discovered a rather discoloured egg. Not only was it now far too late for this to hatch, but it was also badly cracked, presumably as a result of several weeks spent as a football being kicked around the floor of the box. It was now impossible to tell what could have happened to the fourth egg, which I'd clearly seen on one of my daily visits. There was not a trace of it to be found. The ringing completed, we retreated smartly from the loft.

'I'll let you know when I open up the barn,' I told Martin and Chris. 'It'll probably be in two or three days' time'.

I was keen to give the whole family time to recover from their disturbing experience. Sure enough, on the next suitably fine and sunny afternoon, I entered the loft and, as quietly as humanly possible, removed the various ramshackle barricades that I'd constructed six months before to seal off all possible escape routes. Finishing with the large circular opening, I eventually tip-toed away, greatly relieved that the owls were showing no obvious signs of disturbance. As a parting thought, I placed a handful of fresh chicks on the feeding shelf as I eased my way through the door and down the ladder.

After an anxious wait of several hours, I returned to the farm that evening with great trepidation. I climbed the ladder stealthily and crept into the loft through the little door, as

I had done so many times before. There was no sign of the parent birds, although I couldn't be certain that, despite my precautions, they hadn't heard me coming and shot out through the circular opening. I knew that barn owls, like any wild creature, will react to disturbance by escaping if they can, unseen and away from the source of any unfamiliar sound. I'd once been given a vivid display of this ability to disappear. While visiting Jane and Teddy, they'd offered to show me a potential release site where they'd previously seen barn owls roosting. As we approached the classic Lakeland limestone barn, walking in single file with me bringing up the rear, I was the only one of the party to spot a solitary owl shoot silently from the far corner of the building, ride the gusting breeze like a surfer on the waves, and float high and wide around the barn to plummet into a small stand of trees to our right. The whole aerial manoeuvre had finished before I could utter a sound, so I simply smiled to myself at the ease with which the bird had evaded detection, even by two such acknowledged experts.

During this first visit after opening up the barn, I noticed that two chicks had been taken from the feeding shelf and realised that this must have been the work of the adult birds, since their young were still unable to fly. To be sure that the owlets ate that night, I took the remaining food items and placed them just inside the nest box. The same pattern continued for several more nights, although on one late visit I spotted the parent birds in the fields and woods behind the farm, so they were certainly around. But, increasingly fearful of losing my nerve and abandoning the whole enterprise, I decided to contact Jane and Teddy.

'Oh, the parents will certainly be about!' Jane proclaimed when I expressed my anxieties to her. 'Just keep providing food for them in the usual place - they'll take it if they need it. You can hack the owlets back, anyway'.

She was very matter-of-fact, and although my original intention had been to establish a breeding pair on the farm, I knew that the juvenile release method, known as 'hacking back', was also a tried and tested technique. It had not taken me long, in fact, to discover that the respective merits of the two methods, and indeed the value of breeding-and-release as a conservation measure at all, were hotly disputed amongst naturalists, with claim and counter-claim flying between their various proponents. I decided to follow

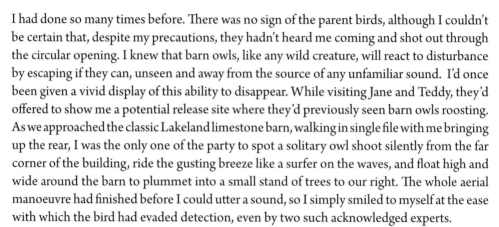

BALTERLEY GREEN

29.5.1988. Young ringed by David & me. Nick also present. Adult pair flushed out while young being removed from nest box. Female disappeared so thoroughly we thought she may have escaped. In fact, she was hiding in the cavity between two bricks in the gable wall opposite the nest box. Decided to open barn up, if weather OK, on 31.5.88.

1.6.1988. Barn opened up. Watched with Nick that evening. Parents seen inside barn taking food up to nest box, apparently not realising they were free to leave. After an hour, both adults began to look nervously out through the windows & pop-hole. Eventually, one came out, hovered over yard & perched on roofs of various buildings around yard. Then flew over roof of nesting barn & seemed to disappear, probably into trees beyond barn. Subsequent visits showed chicks being taken...

Jane's advice whilst keeping an open mind and was, above all, anxious to avoid doing, or not doing, anything that might harm any of the birds. At least I now had a chance to try out both release methods on the same site.

Over the next few weeks, it was to be a case of good news and bad news. Whereas the still-unfledged owlets seemed to thrive on their regular diet of chicks, leavened from time to time with more wholesome rodents, their parents were unfortunately nowhere to be seen, their food left untouched on the feeding shelf. Extensive searches in the surrounding area produced no sign of the absent parents, although I was hardly surprised by this, given the barn owl's famed talent for concealment. Instead, I had to console myself with incidental encounters with other wildlife during my searches, the highlight being the evening when I spotted a total of four badgers and a fox. And, of course, I still had my role of surrogate parent to perform.

It was during this nerve-racking period, when I was assailed by self-doubt, that Martin, one of the ringers, telephoned me to suggest that I should listen to a local radio station, which was due to broadcast a programme called *The Outsiders*. My appetite whetted, I duly tuned in to hear two members of a local conservation trust, Doug and Stuart, describe how they were releasing young barn owls, by the juvenile release method, in their part of the county. Even more impressive was their track record. They told their listeners how they'd first become involved when the owner of a factory unit in Trafford Park, the old industrial heart of south Manchester – the very place in which my dad had served his apprenticeship, and from which he'd subsequently been so keen to escape – had finally discovered why he was regularly being called out to his premises late at night to attend to suspected break-ins. It turned out that his burglar alarm was being triggered by barn owls breaking an infra-red beam on their way to and from a metal ventilation shaft positioned on the roof of the building. Having been called in to investigate, Doug and Stuart had been amazed to find five unfledged, but completely healthy, owlets sitting contentedly at the base of the shaft. Needless to say, the factory owner had been unimpressed by the birds' nocturnal activities, and the two conservationists had been given the task of removing the youngsters and relocating them to a more suitable site. They reported, with a well-deserved sense of self-satisfaction, that they had successfully hacked back the owlets, without their parents.

I was fascinated by their story for a number of reasons. Most striking, to my eyes, was the apparent ability of the parent birds to raise a large family in a place that was so totally different from the ideal barn owl nesting sites that I'd read about and studied. Not for them, it would seem, the bucolic charms of a ramshackle English farmyard; instead, they'd plumped for the exceedingly dismal industrial environment that my parents had so often referred to in the most unflattering terms. As for food, I could only imagine that they had been living off an abundant supply of rodents that must have infested the so-called Park. The tale also reassured me that the disappearance of parent birds, whether because of disturbance or through their own choice, did not necessarily spell the end of the release project for my youngsters. Greatly heartened by these thoughts, I decided to continue my release along the lines I was already following.

18   Working with Chester Zoo

I never did, to my knowledge, see my adult owls again, despite undertaking many nocturnal searches and stake-outs. For a while, I left sufficient food for the owlets in their nest box, and additional chicks on the feeding shelf should the adults return. Not one item was taken from the shelf, and by the time the owlets were themselves flapping around the loft, I decided to stop duplicating the food supplies.

Now that the two owlets were flying, I could monitor their progress like the proud parent I felt I had become. At first, I found that if I crept up the ladder extremely quietly and opened the door just a crack, I could catch a glimpse of them sitting on the landing platform at the front of their nest box, or on one of the various perches close by. A few visits later, I would discover that they'd ventured further from the box, perhaps sitting high up on one of the oak beams, crouched tight under the slope of the roof. For these first few weeks, wherever they were at first, the slightest sound from me would send them hurtling for the safety and security of their tea chest home. Inevitably, though, there came a time when this ceased to be the case, and I would open the door only to see one or both owls shoot not into their nest box, but straight out of the loft through the circular opening. They really are entering the big, wide world now, I thought.

In the early days, I could find them easily following one of their rapid exits. One might be trying to sit on a tractor in the farm yard, flapping its wings furiously and skidding about on the unfamiliar metal surface, finally regaining its balance to find a feature that could be gripped to serve as a perch, while the other owlet, perhaps the older and more experienced of the two, might be spotted in a nearby tree, going in for a leisurely bit of preening. During this stage, I noticed that the owlets always stayed within clear sight of the loft, to which they could retreat if alarmed. After a few more days, though, I began to see them at greater distances from the farm, hedge-hopping along the lane or, on one occasion, standing apparently bewildered in the middle of the carriageway. Such sightings began to worry me immensely, as if I had teenage offspring who were trying to make sense of the world whilst being assailed by its many dangers and temptations. I could only console myself with the knowledge that both birds were now, self-evidently, strong flyers and that they still had a back-up food supply that I was continuing to leave in the loft for them each day.

For a short period, during the summer, the owls regularly visited my back garden, drawn there by the captive birds in their aviaries. As time went by, though, not only did these visits cease, but their presence on and around the farm became increasingly difficult to verify. They stopped taking the food that I supplied and didn't seem to be using the nest box. In an effort to check up on them, I took to scouring the farm yard for pellets that I could dissect for evidence of the prey that they were catching. After a while, even chance sightings by the farmers tailed off. Unable to find any sign of their presence around Greenwood Farm, I was forced to assume that my owls had probably gone for good. Yet on one of my regular recces, I was to learn a valuable lesson about barn owl elusiveness.

'Hullo!' Jeff's voice startled me as I emerged from a barn one day, deep in thought after yet another fruitless search for clues. Sitting on a tractor, the elderly farmer appeared keen to have a natter with me.

'Not seen any sign of the owls, have you, Jeff?' I asked, trying hard not to sound quite as despondent as I felt.

'Can't say I 'ave'. Jeff confirmed my suspicions. If anyone were to see them about, it would be the farmers, out and about in the early hours of the morning or late at night.

'I think they've cleared off!' he added, somewhat unnecessarily, I thought.

No sooner had Jeff uttered his gloomy verdict than, as if pre-arranged and with the precision of a Red Arrows flying display, two beautiful white owls, gleaming in the bright afternoon sunshine, zoomed round the corner of the barn, shot a few feet over his head and plunged into the nearby woods.

'D..did you see that?' I stuttered, gesticulating wildly towards the trees. 'B..barn owls!' I cried in the astonished tones that a marooned sailor might use when spotting a passing ship.

Jeff had neither seen nor heard them, of course. With his back turned towards them and his attention focused on me, he'd been totally unaware of the owls' swift and silent fly-past. Nor, I think, did he believe me, though he was too polite to say so.

'Ah well, better be gettin' on'. With those few words, and a shrug of the shoulders, he chugged away on his tractor.

As he went, I thought what a pity it was that he hadn't been able to share my almost ecstatic feelings of joy and relief at seeing that the owls were fit and well. Later, in conversation with his son, Philip, I learned how proud of 'his' barn owls Jeff really was.

ROSE COTTAGE

31.8.1987. Birds placed in box @ Rose Cottage. Entrance/exit to box to be kept covered (with see-through board) until weekend.

7.10.1987. Visited M.B. Three birds still present. Seeing them around a lot. M.B. is keeping a daily diary (must get a photocopy!) Birds roosting often in empty water tank in part of barn where dog sleeps. M.B. has analysed some pellets, but no sign of rodent prey yet.

16.11.1987. Phoned – not taking food (stopped doing this 4 – 5 weeks ago). M.B. is still putting three chicks per night out. Thinks she is hearing them & says that under large ash tree near house there are a lot of white droppings like owls left in barn. Also reported speaking to man two weeks ago who lives near farm. He had been startled @ about 10.30 p.m. one night by a white owl sitting on his car when he went out of the house.

9.12.1987. Visited M.B. Still putting food out but none being taken. Had a look in loft - no sign of recent occupation. NB: M.B. did analyse pellets while owls were still resident and found shrew skull in one.

30.1.1988. M.B. phoned to say she was hearing barn owls around – large splashes of white on trees in garden. I advised her to clean out the nest box so that she could tell if they were using it & to put food out.

20.2.1988. M.B. phoned - hearing barn owls around on both sides of cottage (probably setting up territories). Has cleared out nest box as suggested.

'He tells everybody down at the club about them'. Philip smiled. 'It'll not be long before they'll all want some on their farms'.

Little did we know how accurate his prediction would prove to be.

Whilst offspring were being bred and raised down on the farm, the owls in my back garden certainly weren't inactive. By the end of the summer, Carrie and Mr McKay, the wild male owl from the Scottish Borders, had produced three young. (They went on to produce another brood, of six, and then many more young for release in subsequent years). The original brood of three were a fierce bunch and never failed to impress anyone who encountered them. One Dutch visitor to my house was particularly puzzled when, without explanation, I produced a cardboard box, its lid in place to conceal the contents. Although the occupants could not be seen, they could certainly be heard as they kept up a continuous series of loud hissings, which, the Dutchman reasoned, could only be coming from a nest of particularly angry snakes. When I set down the box and carefully drew back the lid, he peered nervously in from the safe distance to which he'd retreated and exclaimed, over and over again, 'Oh, vat boodiful leedle creatures!' It must have been his great sense of relief at not being confronted by venomous reptiles that prompted these somewhat inappropriate comments. The owlets – scrawny and shedding clouds of grubby-white down – were certainly not 'boodiful' and neither could they – or more particularly their feet and talons – be described as little, striking out viciously whenever the owls felt the slightest bit threatened.

'They're all males,' I volunteered above the din, as if to explain their aggression. In reality, I was far from sure, my experience of barn owl gender assignment still being rather limited. I didn't know it at the time, but I would soon be getting some intensive practice in the subject.

Out of the blue one morning, I received a telephone call from Chester Zoo (or, to give it its proper title, the North of England Zoological Society). It was the Curator

MR McKAY

14.10.1984. Male barn owl received from Jane Ratcliffe. She had received bird from a lady in Dumfries who had had it for three years. Bird had had fractured wing, which had received no treatment & had therefore healed wrongly. Bird placed in shed while middle aviary prepared.

Mid-October 1984. Bird placed in middle aviary. Box provided. After several days, bird allowed access to small aviary containing (?) female owl received from P.S. Birds seen together on one or two occasions (i.e. in same aviary). Appeared to roost in own boxes (separate aviaries).

28.10.1984. Birds sharing male's box at times but a great deal of shrieking/crying heard from both those aviaries & the open flight next to the shed. In evening, birds seen together in box in small aviary.

29.10.1984. Birds again seen together in box in small aviary.

Week commencing 17.3.1985. Female bird appeared to be sitting as if on eggs.

21.3.1985. At least two eggs seen in nest box.

8.5.1985. Two good-sized owlets (partly/thinly covered in down) seen by me. They can be heard "chittering" quite a lot.

12.5.1985. Two owlets plus one much smaller owlet seen.

20.5.1985. Saw three similar-sized owlets. 14 – 16 decapitated chicks being fed (& taken) per day.

1.6.1985. Definitely three owlets in box. One standing up.

2.6.1985. Three owlets seen again - one has patches of adult plumage on head and wings.

18.6.1985. I inadvertently disturbed birds by shovelling soiled gravel out of aviary. Looked in nest box and saw new (clean & white) egg!

of Birds on the other end of the line, who'd somehow heard of my breeding and release scheme and was, it turned out, making huge assumptions about my experience and expertise in the field.

'We've got a pair of barn owls, here at the zoo,' he disclosed, 'but we just don't seem to be able to breed from them. They've got as far as laying eggs, which we've candled and found to be infertile'.

'Hmm.' I tried to sound quietly self-confident. 'Are you sure they're a pair?'

The curator, Robert, sounded slightly irritated.

'Well, we were certainly told they were by the zoo we got them from. One of them has been surgically sexed by the vet ('a quick inspection of the gonads,' I mused), and is definitely female'. He paused.

'I was wondering if you'd mind coming and having a look at them?'

Mind? I couldn't have been more delighted if David Attenborough had personally invited me to help him make a natural history programme for the BBC. When I was a child, we would quite often, as a family, go to stay with those of our relatives who had chosen to remain in Manchester rather than flee to the countryside as our parents had. After a day or two of gamely entertaining three boisterous boys (well in advance of our arrival, one grandma would pointedly move out of harm's way all her fragile ornaments), the harassed relatives would, sooner or later, feel forced to pop the question: 'What would you like to do today?' And without hesitation, or the need to confer, we would cry out in unison: 'Go to Chester Zoo!' As our choice was usually indulged, we had become very familiar with the place over the years, with feeding times for the lions, tigers and sea lions being some of our favourite events. Another major draw was the polar bear pit, now long gone, whose inhabitants paced restlessly up and down the stained concrete surface or floated listlessly in water the colour of pea soup, while we speculated wildly about the probable fate of anyone who was careless, or unlucky, enough to tumble over the low wall skirting the enclosure.

'What would happen, Dad?' we pestered relentlessly.

'They'd make mincemeat of you!' came the terse reply. Fortunately, however often we and other young visitors clambered up the wall to get a better view, Dad's gory prediction was never put to the test.

Wrenching my thoughts from memories of childhood visits, I tried not to sound childishly enthusiastic at Robert's unexpected request, though my heart was racing at the prospect of going to the zoo as something more than just an ordinary punter.

'Er, yes, OK', I replied nonchalantly.

Robert seemed pleased, and we agreed to meet the following Saturday.

'Come to the time office, not the main entrance, and ask for me when you arrive'.

The time office turned out not to be some Tardis-like structure from *Dr Who*, but a boringly ordinary building in which zoo staff clocked on and clocked off, and where visitors like me, and delivery van drivers, were signed in and out. Any attempt at security seemed nominal, at best, and as I waited for Robert to appear, I began to wonder whether the story I'd heard many times about a schoolboy smuggling a penguin out of the zoo in his duffle bag was quite the urban myth I'd always assumed it to be.

Robert's arrival broke in upon my musings. He turned out to be a jolly, down-to-earth character, not at all the academic type, despite the PhD which, he later confided, had

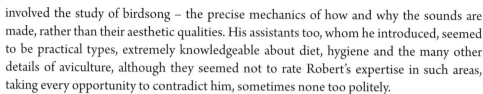

involved the study of birdsong – the precise mechanics of how and why the sounds are made, rather than their aesthetic qualities. His assistants too, whom he introduced, seemed to be practical types, extremely knowledgeable about diet, hygiene and the many other details of aviculture, although they seemed not to rate Robert's expertise in such areas, taking every opportunity to contradict him, sometimes none too politely.

From the outset, it was clear that Robert was passionate about birds, but possibly little else. Talking volubly, but exclusively about owls, and gesticulating in all directions, he promptly marched me past enclosures containing wapiti, kudu and even an enchanting pair of Asian otters, without a moment's pause to let me stand and gawp at them. Finally, having reached the Owls Section, built, he said, on the site of the old Elephant House, he gestured towards one aviary in particular.

By chance, or possibly because of its location in a dark and gloomy area behind a main toilet block, this part of the zoo was empty of visitors. Many of the owls – snowy, great grey, spectacled – were therefore sitting out, rather than skulking in their nests. The barn owls were no exception, although they flew towards the back of the aviary as soon as we approached.

Startled by what I had just observed, I couldn't stop myself from blurting out my verdict there and then.

'I'm not surprised they're laying infertile eggs – both birds are female!'

'Are you sure?' Robert eyed me suspiciously, perhaps beginning already to regret his invitation. I realised, too, that he was anxious not to be shown up in front of his keepers, some of whose faces were already beginning to betray signs of incipient knowing smirks.

Robert's tone was now a mixture of incredulity and exasperation. 'We know one of them is female, but they were transferred to us as a definite breeding pair'.

I resisted making the obvious retort that he'd been 'done' and launching into a learned exposition on plumage differences between the male and female barn owl. Instead, I grasped at a solution that would enable Robert to save face – temporarily, at least – and save me from changing, in an instant, from an especially valued expert visitor to *persona non grata* at my favourite zoo.

'You could test it out' I suggested. 'I happen to have a couple of spare males at home'. This made me sound like a real expert. 'Why don't you put your two birds in separate aviaries and introduce one of my males to each of them? We'll soon see whether I'm right!'

Of course, I also had an ulterior motive: my own aviary accommodation was becoming increasingly overcrowded, so lodging a couple of owls somewhere else had real attractions.

Despite his obvious scepticism, Robert agreed to try my plan, assuring me, with a malevolent grin in the direction of his insubordinate staff, that a vacant aviary next to the barn owls could be thoroughly cleaned and kitted out with a suitable nest box and other fittings by no later than the following weekend. Within a few days, I was back at the zoo, this time with my two boxed-up surplus males.

19   The decline of the barn owl in Britain

As before, there were no visitors in the area behind the toilets and it was an easy task to release the birds into their separate aviaries. In both cases, as I entered with my mysterious package, the female bird promptly disappeared into her nest box. Once released, each male briefly flapped around to get his bearings, before diving into the nearest dark hole, the nest box, to be greeted by shrieks and screams of alarm from the female occupant.

'They'll settle down,' I pronounced confidently, as we moved rapidly away from the immediate vicinity of the aviaries.

'Let me know how they go on – or if you want me to take them back'. I wasn't so sanguine about the outcome as to be sure he wouldn't.

Within a few weeks, Robert was on the telephone with a simple announcement.

'Both pairs are on eggs!'

'Oh, great!' I wasn't sure which of us was the more relieved, or surprised, by this news.

'Whatever you do now, don't interfere with them', I warned, emboldened by my apparent success in solving the zoo's problem. I was also very suspicious of what I'd learned of the zoo-keepers' propensity for manipulation, whether by candling eggs, artificially incubating them, or even just carrying out regular inspections.

'I'd just leave the birds to get on with it'. I wanted to reinforce the message, which was firmly based on my own experience, but my fingers were tightly crossed against the possibility that these clutches would also turn out to be infertile, thus undermining any credibility I had so far managed to gain.

A little over two months later, an elated Robert rang me again, this time reporting that both pairs had newly-hatched young.

'You were right!' He seemed genuinely impressed by the accuracy of my prediction.

'But it's even more important that you don't disturb them now,' I replied. Once again, although I was sure that he would accept my judgment, I was far from convinced that my strictures against interference would be effectively passed on down the line, let alone followed. After all, I thought, these guys often rear their charges by hand, which doesn't matter so much if they're being kept in the zoo, but would be disastrous for an individual that is to be released into the wild. The example of Barney came vividly to mind.

On one of my visits, I'd been thrilled to get a glimpse behind the scenes at the artificial incubation units, food preparation areas and all the other modern, hi-tech facilities that were at the keepers' disposal. With that lot, how could they possibly resist the temptation to meddle? I'd even met some of the successful output of the hands-on approach. Once I was taken to an indoor walled enclosure housing a couple of dozen juvenile penguins, whose portly bodies, covered in fluffy brown down, short legs and webbed feet, combined to produce jerky movements reminiscent of an old Keystone Kops movie, as they careered excitedly, en masse, around their pen. The pungent stench of stale fish and guano emanating from these cute youngsters was, however, so overpowering that I just had to turn away. As I did so, I spotted something else of interest in a caged area on the opposite side of the room. Curious as to its identity, I moved nearer, but all I could make out was a downy, brown mass, the size of an armchair and devoid of any recognisable features. From the rhythmic rising and falling movements, I was certain, at least, that this amorphous lump was a living creature of some sort.

'Oh, that's Lucy.' Robert had followed my gaze. As he spoke, a long, sinuous neck slowly extended from amongst the mass of down, and a beady black eye, set in a small, bullet-shaped head, blinked as it emerged into the harsh artificial light of the room. Most striking of all was the beak, shaped like a billhook and almost the same length as the creature's head, which it now held on one side as it stared up at us.

'She's our griffon vulture,' Robert continued. 'We raised her from an egg and she now eats thirty rats a day'. He beamed with paternal self-satisfaction.

Being without a spare rat on my person, and wary of the bird's vicious-looking bill, I instantly took several steps back. Now out of striking distance, I could study Lucy in more detail. She was certainly an impressive specimen, though apparently oversized and ungainly as she began to lope around her quarters, like some hapless exhibit in a freak show.

'The adult male keeps smashing the eggs,' Robert added, 'but we don't know why'.

I couldn't resist the uncharitable thought that the male vandalised the eggs because he knew what was going to emerge from them. But that was unkind, and also inaccurate. In their natural element, vultures, and their cousins the condors, are marvellously graceful flyers, riding the thermal air currents so as to minimise energy expenditure, and homing in on carrion across vast distances. Perhaps, I thought, it is really only their unpleasant feeding habits, dismembering carcasses and gorging themselves on the bloody flesh, that make vultures seem so repulsive to human beings.

At first, I was elated that the zoo owls had so dramatically proved my point by producing young. I'd double-checked the accuracy of Robert's claim by arranging to stand quietly beside each nest box and listen for the telltale chittering noises made by recently-hatched owlets. My next feeling was one of panic. With my own owls breeding, and now two sets of youngsters at the zoo, I was going to have to undertake a number of releases. If I didn't, I could see more and more captive adults producing an ever-increasing number of offspring. Robert had made it clear to me that the zoo was prepared to breed barn owls, now that they knew how to, but had neither the time nor the resources to carry out a controlled release programme.

It was then that I remembered the Trafford Park Two, Doug and Stuart, who already had a successful track record of juvenile releases. Contacting them via the local wildlife trust, I discovered to my relief and delight that they had found a number of ideal release sites, but had no owlets to place in them, whilst I had the owlets but no sites. It seemed that a collaboration had been born. Doug and Stuart came to see my aviaries and talk barn owls, and I accompanied them, still talking barn owls, to the farms they'd already surveyed. Several of them lay on Carrington Moss, near Dunham Massey, a flat and fertile agricultural area southwest of Manchester, not unlike The Fylde, on the Lancashire coast, where barn owls still thrive in relatively large numbers.

As at Greenwood Farm, a number of qualities were common to the sites that Doug and Stuart took me to see. Above all was the undoubted enthusiasm and commitment of the owners. Almost without exception, they'd reminisce that, as children growing up on the property, they'd been very familiar with barn owls as part of their everyday life. Every farm, it seemed, had been home to one. Usually, of course, there would have been a pair, breeding year after year on a ledge in a barn, in a gap between bales of hay, or deep down in a hollow tree. But no more. The landowners would, without exception, lament the birds' passing, usually telling me that, long ago, one of the pair had suddenly disappeared, that its partner had hung around the breeding ground forlornly for a year or so and then, itself, disappeared. What these stories proved to me was that, when natural wastage occurred, perhaps due to an accident befalling one bird, there were no surplus wild birds present in the general population to take its place. The single surviving bird, unable to attract a mate to its traditional nesting site, would be forced to leave and face the hazards of searching for a partner and a new territory, neither of which it would be likely to find.

This theory tied in with my own observations. When I was a child in the Lake District, barn owls had hardly been a common sight, but were also not particularly unusual. However, the number of sightings I made, or heard about from family and friends, steadily declined throughout the 1960s and 1970s. By the time I began my breeding and release scheme, various explanations for the decline were being mooted by interested parties, including the loss of nesting sites, through the demolition or conversion of barns, or the felling of dead trees; changes in farming practices, known as 'prairie farming', and involving the grubbing-up of hedgerows, the amalgamation of small farms, and the use of machinery to facilitate monocultures, leading to fewer prey-rich foraging areas; climate changes, bringing about generally wetter weather; and ever busier roads, where barn owls – not strong fliers at the best of times – would end up in collisions with fast-moving vehicles. Sadly, the only encounters with barn owls that many people have been able to recount to me have involved nothing better than roadside near-misses or fatalities: a true sign of the times. In one tale, the bird was even blamed for causing an accident.

Hearing about what I did, over dinner at a friend's house, a rather aristocratic lady told me that some acquaintances of hers had overturned their car as a result of swerving to avoid a barn owl, thus being forced to miss their engagement.

'The explanation they gave,' the lady told me, 'was that they'd narrowly missed being killed by a barn owl!' My response was, perhaps, unnecessarily tart.

'In my opinion,' I replied, 'they did exactly the right thing'.

Many of the farmers and other landowners I met had their own, somewhat surprising, explanation for the barn owl's decline.

'There's too many chemicals been used on the land,' they would suggest.

This always struck me as odd, coming from landowners, since they seemed to be the main – or even the only – culprits, if excessive use of chemicals was to blame. Or were they perhaps suggesting that they had been forced, or persuaded, to cover their land in pesticides and fertilisers? Out of sheer cowardice, I never challenged the statement directly, but simply tried to steer the owners of all the release sites away from an over-reliance on 'chemicals', whether to control rodents or to clear every patch of rough grassland on their holdings so that it could be dedicated to producing yet more agricultural yield.

20   An early setback

Meeting up with Doug and Stuart at their first visit to a site on Carrington Moss, I was relieved to find that it was a small, mixed-farming enterprise, reminiscent of Yewdale near Kendal, with its jumble of buildings, untidy yard and general lack of up-to-date, high-tech farm machinery. The owners, too, seemed highly motivated, and had clearly been fully instructed by Doug and Stuart on the practicalities of the juvenile release method. Having inspected the nest box which they'd fastened in position in one of the barns, I promised to return with some owlets as soon as they were the right age.

Within a fortnight I was back, with three plump young owls from my back garden aviaries. All fitted with their unique BTO rings, they were between five and six weeks old, and scrambled strongly to the back of the nest box when gently placed inside. I went over the practicalities, such as regular food, vitamin supplements and fresh water, with Terry, the farmer's son, and John, a volunteer conservation warden, who together would be looking after the birds, and only then did it strike me that this would be my first true juvenile release. At Greenwood Farm, I had been in control and close at hand, and had also felt sure that the parent birds had never in fact moved far from the release site. Now, I was entrusting 'my' precious chicks to the care of comparative strangers and, just like a parent racked with anxieties about how their teenage child will cope with living away from home for the first time, my mind was filled with vivid images of the hazards my owlets might face – cats, rats, thieves and murderers! Despite suffering from what might be called 'precious owlet syndrome', I eventually dragged myself away, assuring everyone that I would return to check on progress as soon as possible. In the event, it was nearly three weeks before I was able to visit the farm again, where I was met by Terry's dad.

'Ah'm afraid we've 'ad a casualty.' His opening words made my heart sink.

Anxious to appear neither shocked nor insensitive, I replied blandly 'Oh, right' and gently took the dead owl from his outstretched hands. Inside, though, I was in a turmoil of sadness and self-doubt.

'Are the other two OK?' I asked in as steady a voice as I could manage, still determined not to betray any hint of anxiety.

We decided to go and have a look in the barn, as the farmers had not checked the nest box since the previous night. To everyone's great relief, we found both the survivors alive and well, perched high up in the rafters. By now, Terry and his mum had joined us, together with John, the warden, and they all confirmed that they were regularly seeing the young owls fluttering around the farmyard, just as I'd been able to watch the birds at Greenwood Farm exploring their environment at a similar stage.

Wanting to be completely open with everyone, I took the sad little corpse over to a large square opening in the barn wall, so that I could examine it in clearer light. Spreading the bird's wings, I demonstrated to my audience that the youngster was fully fledged, with only the occasional wisp of down to be seen amongst the feathers. Conducting a methodical examination, I eventually discovered some superficial damage around the bird's left eye socket, but otherwise the body appeared to be in pristine condition. As I ran my fingers through the deep, soft plumage of the owl's head, I strongly suspected, although I was certainly no expert, that it had suffered a broken neck. Conscious that the farmers, in particular, were as anxious as I was for an explanation, I decided to share my theory with the assembled onlookers.

'I think it may have been taking its maiden flight,' I suggested, 'exited the barn through this opening, where we're standing, glided down towards the byre,' – I pointed to where I'd been told the body had been found – 'but misjudged its course and collided with something solid – a piece of machinery, a beam or suchlike.' My proposition was as shaky as the denouement of an Agatha Christie crime novel, but I was pleasantly surprised when the farmer volunteered a piece of circumstantial evidence that lent some credibility to my speculation.

'We've certainly been 'aving some strong, gusting winds over the last few nights. They could've blown it off course'.

'Well, whatever the cause, there's nothing anyone could have done,' I responded, in an attempt to soften the sense of disappointment and distress that all around were clearly feeling. But I was also keen to forestall any suggestion that the two survivors should now be removed to the safety of an aviary.

'Owlets are incredibly vulnerable at this stage, and I think that this one,' I nodded towards the corpse that I was still cradling in my palms, 'must just have been unlucky'.

If anyone had asked me, I would have been forced to admit that my words were designed as much to console myself as to provide comfort and reassurance to my audience. However, struggling to set my self-doubt on one side, I tried to concentrate on playing the role of knowledgeable expert, rather than that of keen beginner. I detailed Terry to inform the BTO of the young bird's demise, giving full details of place, date and circumstances, and suggested that for the next few days, whilst the remaining birds were practising their flying and other life skills, everyone should be extra vigilant about potential dangers. At least, I thought, this would make them feel they were doing something useful even if, in reality, they weren't. Certainly, I would be keeping my fingers very tightly crossed over the days and weeks to come.

To my great relief, the two survivors continued to flourish and were seen around the farm for many months afterwards. Despite the traumatic setback in the early stages, my first attempt at a juvenile release appeared to have been a success. Little did I realise, though, that this was also to be my first taste of wildlife crime detection, trying to find and piece together evidence in cases of disappearance, injury and death in a whole host of unusual circumstances.

21   Back at the zoo

Over the next couple of summers, more juvenile releases followed, the raw material in the form of owlets being provided by my own, and the zoo's, captive breeding pairs. Once established, all the pairs seemed remarkably fecund, some occasionally producing more than one brood per summer. Fortunately, a ready supply of suitable release sites was found and prepared by my co-workers, allowing me to concentrate on monitoring the owlets' progress and removing them from their parents at just the right age. To my great delight, these activities involved me in frequent forays to Chester Zoo, to which I continued to have free access via the Time Office. As often as not, once I'd checked on the barn owls by peering into the nest boxes, designed with hinged sides specifically for the purpose, I'd be free to wander round the zoo at my leisure, before heading off for home.

After years of childhood visits, I could only view these freebies as the best possible reward for my help in releasing the zoo-bred owlets. I noticed with wry amusement that the zoo was not slow to exploit the release scheme for positive publicity, attaching signs to the owls' aviaries, shortly after I started work with them, explaining that they were part of a conservation project. I also realised that, as is the norm in large and complex organisations, the aspirations of the zoo's PR department were not always matched by the efforts of the staff on the ground. Except when they were ogling scantily-clad female visitors, the male keepers, in particular, would invariably ignore the zoo's paying customers, marching through the crowds of people as if there was no-one there. Sometimes, they even seemed to take a malicious delight in some unsavoury incident that they could easily have prevented. As we entered an aviary, curious visitors would, naturally enough, rush forward to peer at us through the netting. Predictably, our presence in their territory would flush the adult barn owls out of their nest box, which they would exit at

BATE WOOD

15.5.1987. Three oldest birds (approx. five weeks old) removed from pair in aviary next to spectacled owls at Chester Zoo…Taken to Prestbury …and ringed there by Chris … Taken to (release site) and placed in nest box (4 p.m. – 5 p.m.)

7.6.1987. C.K. (site owner) phoned to say one of birds missing from box. Had looked in loft but couldn't find it. I told him to put some food on a hay bale & cause as little disturbance as possible.

9.6.1987. Phoned C.K. Has not seen first owlet to leave box, but has observed that the other two are leaving & returning to the nest box. Unlikely to be leaving barn itself yet. Told him to disturb as little as possible.

17.6.1987. Spoke to C.K. Still seeing two owls in loft but all are obviously flying in and out. Saw one flying round farmyard on 12 June. Irregular pattern of food being taken – some nights only one chick, others eight. Told him to continue feeding eight, or at least six, per night.

3.7.1987. Phoned C.K. 2 owls still being seen regularly. No sign of third one. Sometimes, 4/5 chicks taken, other times, only two.

1.9.1987. Spoke to Mrs K. Seeing one or two (never three) owls regularly until about one week ago. Advised her to keep feeding (perhaps every other day) & vary amount according to how much being taken. Asked her to keep pellets for me to analyse. Apparently, birds seen regularly down near S Hall (marshy brook area).

21.9.1987. Spoke to Mrs K. about a little owl she is looking after. She mentioned that the barn owls were still being seen and heard around her farm. Still feeding, but not much per day.

31.10.1987. Mrs K. phoned. One barn owl roosting in Dutch barn. Advised her to leave food near its roost & in the original nest box (both without disturbing it). She reckons there are plenty of mice about @ the moment. Two subsequently present. Last time, December 1988. Opposite side of (main road).

29.11.1989. Chris informed me of casualty. Owl found dead on 11.4.1989 - railway casualty. Had moved 9 km and 295 degrees from release site and survived for 695 days since release.

28.5.2005. Letter received from Mrs K. in response to my written survey: "Thank you for your letter & survey concerning the barn owls. Ours have been most successful and make it worthwhile writing to you. They have nested and reared young for each of the last eight or nine years, first in a hollow tree site subsequently blown out in a gale, and thereafter in one of two boxes we erected pre-empting this. One is a pole and one an apex tree box and both have been used; they seem intent on the latter this time."

speed, flying towards the netting and clutching on at the highest point, from where they would immediately expel a great jet of evil-smelling white faeces all over the watching crowd. These aerial bombardments prompted no discernible reaction from the keepers, who watched impassively as the more observant of the spectators managed narrowly to avoid the noxious stream, whilst the less nimble ended up dabbing at soiled clothing and possessions with anything that came to hand. Regardless of whether they escaped or were caught out, the spectators would invariably greet the shit stream with a loud chorus of disgust: 'Urrgh!'

Somewhat disconcerted by the keepers' apparent indifference, I always made a point, as we entered the aviaries, of warning the assembled crowds that they should, perhaps, stand back a little. Usually, most people would reluctantly shuffle backwards, receiving within a couple of seconds a vivid demonstration of the reason why. Seeing the squirt of liquid fall short of where they stood, they would still let out an involuntary 'Urgh', but at least, I thought, they had been spared any unpleasantly messy results.

In addition to protection from airborne hazards, I felt strongly that zoo visitors deserved some indication of what we were up to and why, particularly when young birds were being removed from their agitated parents, stuffed into a cardboard box and carted off. So, to the obvious irritation of the keepers, I would always stop outside the aviary and reel off a short spiel, which went something like this:

'It's part of a conservation project'…'We're moving the youngsters out to a new home'… 'The parents are fed up with them by this stage'… 'Just like a mum and dad with a teenager' (this always raised a laugh) … 'We're helping to repopulate the wild'… 'Would you like to have a look?'

Children in particular would crowd around as I gently opened the box to reveal several hissing owlets, rocking menacingly from side to side, or lying on their backs and striking out fiercely with their sharp talons. I thought, somewhat self-righteously, that not only was I doing my bit for education, but that it would do the owlets no harm at all to feel frightened by such close encounters with human beings. So I applied the same reasoning when it came to relocating the owlets at the chosen release site. I encouraged all comers – the site owner's children, friends, Great Aunt Bertha, anyone – to watch me handle and ring the birds, take photographs and even touch them, provided, I emphasised, that this was the first and last time that they should come into such close contact with humans, apart from, of course, in an emergency.

Human curiosity, I found, was not the only hazard to be negotiated when collecting the zoo owlets. One pair of barn owls was accommodated for a time in an aviary that was sandwiched between two others. The only way in and out lay through a large unit that was home to a pair of snowy owls. These large, powerful birds live on the Arctic tundra, where they nest on the ground and prey on an abundant supply of lemmings.

'You'll need to take a bucket in with you,' the keeper, Richard, muttered as he unlocked the door to the snowy owls' aviary.

I frowned, trying to work out why such an item should be necessary since I was already holding my trusty box for transporting the owlets.

'It's for the snowies – one of them put me out of action for three days last year'.

Richard briefly explained how his shoulder had been badly lacerated in an owl attack.

But why a bucket, I wondered: was I meant to use it as a makeshift helmet in case of attack, or to catch a hostile owl and keep it trapped in the upturned receptacle?

Richard could see I was still puzzled.

'Watch, I'll show you'. He grabbed a large black plastic bucket and marched into the aviary. In an instant, one of the inhabitants swooped at speed, hitting the bucket – bang! – with its outstretched feet.

The owl dropped to the ground, then, as Richard held the bucket at shin level, leapt up and attempted several more times to seize the object in its talons.

Bang! Bang! Bang!

Shuffling along behind the keeper, I was beginning to appreciate how powerfully the owl was armed, and how thankful I was not to be a lemming. Once we'd completed our business with the barn owls, the whole performance was repeated as we made our way out of the aviary complex.

'It's a territorial thing,' Richard explained casually. 'The bucket acts as a super stimulus, a focus for the owl's aggression'.

I was certainly glad that I worked with the gentle barn owl, whose reaction to threats was definitely flight, rather than the snowy's obvious determination to stay and fight.

22   Money problems

Up to this point, apart from the occasional unsolicited small donation from a well-wisher, I had been financing the breeding and release scheme from my own resources. But, as the number of owlets and releases grew, so did the demand on my finite income. So, against my better judgement – I had never wanted to feel beholden to anyone in return for their financial support – I decided to start applying for grants and awards.

My initiative, by chance, happened to coincide with a period when institutions of all kinds were falling over themselves to establish their green credentials by bankrolling wildlife conservation projects. To my surprise, therefore, I soon found that money was fairly easy to come by, provided that I was prepared to fill in lengthy forms –something of a busman's holiday for a lawyer – and agree to abide by the various conditions that were imposed. Predictably, these often involved publicity opportunities for the would-be donors. It wasn't long before I found myself penning items for house magazines such as Shell UK's *Shellman*, in which my project was sandwiched between a feature on the lucky winner of a readers' competition – 'Now the proud owner of a Tomos moped!' – and a report on the fourth annual Shell/Trust Forte Welcome Break 'Shell Shine' awards ceremony, which apparently extolled the virtues of various motorway service stations. There were spin-off demands, too, including local and regional radio broadcasts.

Whenever visual media were involved, Barney proved a very useful prop indeed. Whether sitting on my shoulder or held in my hands, she showed her accustomed tolerance. Despite the pleas of interviewers and photographers, though, I never trusted my tame owl sufficiently to allow her complete freedom in the open air. I was convinced that an unexpected event, such as a passing car or a visitor to the house, would spook her and send her flying off into the nearest tree, where she would soon fall prey to gangs of mobbing magpies or crows. She was such an innocent soul that she would not survive if driven away from her home. In the early days, I'd tried several times, always half-heartedly, to fit aylmeri, (pliable leather anklets through which jesses, or lines, can be threaded) to Barney's legs, but she had always resisted furiously, pulling sharply and indiscriminately at the leather, as well as at my fingers.

Given that I was never really that keen on my owl being encumbered by such ugly trappings, I soon abandoned the idea, and insisted from then on that any photo shoots would have to take place either in an escape-proof place, such as an aviary, or with Barney held firmly in my grip.

It soon became apparent that the effort needed to satisfy the ever-hungry PR machine far outweighed the small financial benefits that I was gaining, although these amounts were helpful contributions towards my outlay on materials for aviary or nest box construction.

At least they reduced the continual drain on the domestic finances. On the point of reverting to the completely self-supporting option, I happened one day to be spending my lunch break at home. Eating my sandwiches whilst flicking idly through the pages of a newspaper and half-listening to the TV, my attention was grabbed as the words 'conservation awards' suddenly emerged from the sea of inane chat which seemed to be this particular programme's speciality. Dropping a half-eaten sandwich onto the plate and flinging aside the newspaper, I gave the TV screen my full attention.

'Yes! Over the next few weeks, we'll be **giving away** prize money of up to **£6,000** to the five best conservation projects in our region. All **you** have to do is **write** and tell us about your project!'

So far, so good – I was definitely interested. The excitable presenter's clumsy delivery went on.

'…and, if you **win,** help us make a short **film** about it'.

Well, perhaps not so good, I thought, with my initial enthusiasm now rapidly evaporating at the prospect of yet again wrestling with Barney and my other owls for the benefit of the cameras. On the other hand, I argued to myself, a cash injection of several thousand pounds would mean that my finances wouldn't take any more hits for a while, nor would I need to apply for any more small grants. By now, I had convinced myself to go for it, strongly suspecting that I was in with a good chance simply because of the photogenic qualities of the barn owl. It certainly seemed to have worked before. I was sure that no TV producer would turn down the opportunity, particularly if I stressed, as I fully intended to, that I had a tame owl, suitable for close-ups. Barney had already proved herself to be a star, completely unfazed by cameras and friendly – sometimes over-friendly - towards photographers. A photo in *Shellman* had shown her in typical pose, sitting unconcernedly on my shoulder like a sort of bleached parrot, whilst I discussed my project with the man from the Shell Better Britain Campaign. Although she would never, thank goodness, be up to squawking 'Pieces of eight!' she did manage to utter soft and contented chirruping noises whenever she became the centre of such close attention.

Within weeks of submitting an entry, my hunch proved correct. A letter from the BBC told me that the project had won its 'natural world' category and that I would shortly be receiving a cheque for £1,000, as well as being entered in the grand final, which carried a prize of a further £5,000. Predictably, though, the sting came in the tail.

'We would now like to discuss with you in detail the arrangements for filming your project in action' the letter continued.

I had absolutely no experience of film-making. My interactions with the media had always involved still photography of captive subjects. I had, though, heard lots of horror stories from those who had got caught up in the world of moving pictures. Jane Ratcliffe's tales of being asked to repeat particular sequences over and over again ('Can you just get the badger to go through the tunnel one more time, please?') confirmed my fears. As Jane had replied, no doubt with great forcefulness: 'You simply can't do that with wild creatures. They're not performers in a circus!' Another friend found to her dismay that her ideas, as the writer of a screenplay based on one of her novels, were sometimes very different from those of the director and film crew. Her first experience of such a venture had therefore turned out to be her last.

With these troubling thoughts in mind, I decided to try, diplomatically, to manage as much of the process as I could. It soon became apparent that this would take a great deal of effort, not least in co-ordinating other people's contributions.

My first call was to Robert at the zoo. Needless to say, he was delighted at the news, particularly because of the positive publicity a film would generate.

'Of course you can film at the zoo,' he oozed. 'But we will have to involve our PR people, I'm afraid'. The latter comment, uttered in lowered tones, appeared a little more tentative.

It was a similar story at one of that year's release sites – a farm on a country estate run by the local county council – where, I was told, the farm manager must be present throughout any filming. Although I felt that some unnecessary complications were being added in, I found to my great relief that I could, at least, insist that the film locations remain secret. I was utterly paranoid about this, knowing how vulnerable any release can be during its early stages, when unfledged birds are easily hurt or stolen.

Because I hadn't yet gained my own licence to ring from the BTO, I also needed to secure the co-operation of my friend, Chris, if the ringing process was to be captured on film. Like the other organisations involved, the BTO would stand to gain some incidental publicity.

Finally, many telephone calls later, I had completed my itinerary. Starting at my house, there would first be an opportunity to film Barney and talk about the project; then we would drive to a release site where there was an adult release in progress, and film the owlets being checked and ringed. From there, we would head over to Chester Zoo to remove owlets from the aviaries and, finally, everyone would meet at a second release site to witness the zoo owlets being checked, ringed and placed in their nest box.

By my estimate, all this activity would probably take the best part of a day – if it went according to plan, that is. Timing was critical for other reasons too. Not only would we be restricted to the exact two weeks when all the owlets were between four and six weeks' old, but this window of opportunity would have to coincide for both the young from the adult release and those collected from the zoo. Otherwise, we would all be faced with two filming expeditions instead of one.

Having taken the precaution of checking up on the progress of all the owlets, I picked up the telephone with great trepidation and rang the BBC. Carefully, and in considerable detail, I ran my proposed itinerary past the programme's assistant producer.

'Er, yes'. She sounded more positive than I'd expected, but clearly had some reservations.

'I was just wondering…'

I waited tensely for the one point I hadn't anticipated that would throw all my careful plans into complete disarray.

'…what are the arrangements for lunch?'

'Well…' I had to think quickly, completely wrong-footed by the question, to which I hadn't given a moment's thought.

'…there are lots of lovely Cheshire pubs in the areas we'll be visiting – if you think that will be OK'.

'Oh yes, splendid!' The prospect of dining on pub food in the cosy inglenook of a half-timbered Cheshire hostelry had obviously struck a distinctly positive note.

'That's fine,' she burbled. 'Everything's arranged then!'

And with that, I was dismissed.

23   A barn owl "shoot" (part one)

The one great imponderable was, of course, the weather. But when the day of the shoot dawned, it turned out to be warm and sunny, with a cloudless blue sky. The film crew arrived mob-handed. Four of them – director, assistant producer, cameraman and sound engineer rolled up in a large silver estate car weighed down with loads of expensive-looking gear.

'Right, where to first?' asked Martin, the director, a man whose credentials for making a wildlife conservation film turned out to be some experience 'doing *Gardeners' World*'.

'Haven't you read the itinerary?' I groaned inwardly, convinced now that it was going to turn into a very long day. Contrary to my gloomy forebodings, however, the shoot began well. Once we'd all crammed into Barney's aviary – even the assistant producer insisted on being in there – I explained, to camera, as succinctly as possible the details of the project, while Barney performed to her audience as though every move had been carefully choreographed and endlessly rehearsed for days beforehand. We were treated to her entire repertoire of cute chirruping noises, head bobbing, pelvis wiggling and feather ruffling. To the delight of the film crew, she hopped gracefully from my shoulder to sit on the camera's lens and gaze unashamedly into the eyes of each of them in turn, like the most attention-seeking of fashion models. If she'd possessed any, she would no doubt have fluttered her eyelashes at them too.

With this footage in the can we headed off in a convoy of vehicles, with me leading the way, to the first of the two release sites on our itinerary. This was a working farm attached to a large estate in the custodianship of the National Trust, where I was using the adult pair release method that I'd first tried at Greenwood Farm. Provided that my calculations were correct, the owlets should by now have reached just the right age for ringing. My ringer friend, Chris, and the farm manager, Tom, met us at the site and, after brief introductions, I insisted on first going alone into the loft to check on the situation. The last thing I wanted was to discover, in the presence of my expanding retinue, that some tragedy had occurred, such as the escape of the parent birds or the deaths of one or more young. So, despite Tom's assurances that all was well, I ascended the vertical ladder set into the wall, opened the hatch above my head and clambered into the loft. To my great relief, a quick peep into the nest box confirmed that all was well. Hurrying back down the ladder, taking great care to close the hatch behind me, I addressed the assembled throng, who by now were laughing and joking as they got to know each other. I spoke in the hushed tones of a librarian attempting to maintain the required ambience whilst giving directions to a lost reader.

'Everything's OK – but we must be as quiet as possible to minimise any disturbance'.

The plan was for Chris and me to be filmed removing the owlets from the nest box, giving them a quick visual check up, attaching rings to their legs and then returning them to their parents' care. All these were procedures that we would have been carrying out at this time in any event, though not in the presence of a BBC film crew.

Unfortunately, just as in a library, my request for silence appeared to have fallen on deaf ears. It seemed that the entire contents of the estate car just had to be taken up into the loft. This was no easy task, as the crew's luggage consisted of a number of bulky metallic cases that were doubtless relatively easy to manhandle in normal circumstances, but were certainly not easy to transport up a ten-foot high vertical ladder and in through a narrow hatchway. The whole exercise was therefore conducted to an accompaniment of wheezes, groans and curses, as the crew hoisted their luggage aloft with all the finesse of a gang of baggage handlers at a busy airport terminal. No matter how many times I shushed them, or begged them, please, to try and be quiet, it made no difference. I could only keep my fingers crossed that the owls and their young would not be unduly disturbed. Although it might make a good piece of film, the last thing I wanted was for the parents to effect an escape, right under our noses, through the open hatchway. I came to the conclusion that experience of working with gardeners and their plants – not noted for being easily frightened – was poor preparation for filming wild creatures, with their readiness to depart the scene at the slightest provocation.

At last, after an eternity of banging and crashing about, we were all finally assembled in the loft, surrounded by the crew's precious equipment.

'Right,' announced Malcolm, the director, 'I'd first like to film Paul and Chris entering through the trapdoor'.

'What, you mean we have to back down again?' By now, I was feeling more than a little peevish.

'Not only that, but we'll probably need several takes before we get the light levels right'.

In a maddeningly casual way, Malcolm explained that, although Chris and I were, in theory, to be filmed entering a pitch black loft illuminated only by torchlight, he would need to create a fairly high ambient light level in order to capture anything on film. To my utter dismay, and with Tom and Chris pulling faces at the prospect of further disturbance for the owls, the crew promptly began to crash about even more noisily than before, unpacking and assembling their reflectors, recording equipment, cameras and numerous smaller gadgets. As I watched, in an alternating state of dismay and bewilderment, I noted wryly that the clumsiest and noisiest individual of all was the sound man, a scruffy, wheezing, unfit-looking chap who seemed to me as if he might not last out the day.

Finally, everything was ready and all it took was for Chris and I to clamber in and out of the highly-illuminated loft a couple of times, shining our torch around as if entering the blackest of caves, for Malcolm to be satisfied that he had a suitable take.

'We'll get the owlets out for ringing now,' I whispered, adding sarcastically 'There'll be no point asking us to repeat that: once the rings are on, there's no way of getting them off again'.

In the event, the whole procedure went very smoothly, the more feisty of the owlets hissing and struggling, whilst the others lay quiet and still, allowing the film crew to get plenty of varied footage. Unfortunately the same would not be true of the next session.

Having placed the ringed owlets back in their nest box, checked on the location of the adults, who were hiding high up in the rafters, and heaved all the equipment back down the ladder, we gathered together in the cobbled farmyard below. Malcolm explained that he would now like me to do a short piece-to-camera, explaining the release method in use at this site. The set-up seemed ideal: bright morning sunshine, a picturesque backdrop of old-fashioned red-brick farm buildings and a camera ready to roll. I even knew what to say, having been thoroughly prepped by the assistant director/producer. What we had all overlooked, though, was that this was a busy, working farm that also happened to lie under the flight path of a major international airport. No sooner had I begun, or begun again, my carefully-rehearsed speech than I was drowned out by the roar of a passing jumbo jet, or the deep, sonorous lowing of a nearby herd of cattle. Each time, the interference was met with a scowl and an oath from the sound engineer, who was listening through his headphones, furiously twiddling knobs on the tape recorder slung from his shoulder with one hand and clumsily manoeuvring his long microphone boom with the other. Eventually, the strain of this performance got the better of him when yet another attempted take was ruined by the raucous intervention of a particularly enthusiastic cockerel.

'Fucking thing!' he screamed, setting off, at a run, across the farmyard in pursuit of the noisy fowl. As the rest of us dissolved into fits of laughter, the ungainly figure of the enraged engineer, struggling vainly to control the erratic movements of the tape recorder and the sound boom as he went, disappeared from view behind a farm building, preceded by his more fleet-footed tormentor. We waited expectantly to hear either the final squawks of the cornered bird or, more likely, a volley of expletives from its pursuer as he lost his footing and crashed in a tangled heap onto the unforgiving cobbles. We heard neither squawks nor swearing, and the sound engineer soon reappeared looking a little shamefaced and even more dishevelled than ever. With his equipment still mercifully intact, we tried, and finally succeeded in achieving, one last take. Of the cockerel, though, there was neither sight nor sound.

24   *A barn owl "shoot" (part two)*

Next, it was off to the zoo, where we were due to talk barn owls and conservation over cups of coffee before proceeding to collect the young from one of the resident breeding pairs. Robert was there to greet us in the impressive Oak Tree restaurant, housed in an ornate redbrick villa that stands incongruously in the zoo grounds. Here he introduced various other members of the zoo's administration, including the Head of Public Relations, a corporate-looking woman sporting a dark business suit, long painted nails and a carefully arranged hairdo. Over coffee and biscuits a lively conversation took place, with various people contributing tales of their encounters with owls, from the exotic varieties seen by Robert, an avid twitcher, on one of his many foreign trips, to childhood memories of finding owls' pellets. Throughout these noisy exchanges, the Head of PR sat ostentatiously making copious notes in her leather-bound Filofax, no doubt for a forthcoming piece in the zoo's newsletter.

She eventually seized on a lull in the conversation. 'Excuse me. Can I just clarify something?' Her tone was smoothly professional. 'These pellets you all keep talking about – where do you get them from?' Everyone – even the *Gardeners' World* contingent – looked nonplussed. Wasn't it obvious? Lying about wherever an owl has spent a bit of time.

The Head of PR, puzzled by the quizzical looks her question had prompted, pressed on.

'I mean, the owls obviously take a lot of feeding, so someone must supply the zoo with pellets'. She was probably thinking of a potential sponsorship deal.

There followed an embarrassed silence, as everyone except the Head of PR herself recognised the clanger she'd just dropped. The lady had clearly got hold of the wrong end of the owl's digestive process – the inputs, instead of the outputs, as it were. Amid smirks and the odd guffaw from our audience, I had to explain patiently that raptors could not be fed on the carnivore's equivalent of cattle-cake, but needed whole food – meat, bones, fur, the lot. Some of the components were indigestible, although vital as roughage, and were therefore regurgitated in neat little packages known as pellets, or castings. 'By collecting and analysing these, we can work out what they've been preying on,' I explained.

As I outlined to the embarrassed PR lady the technique of soaking the pellets in water, then gently teasing them apart to extract skulls, jaws, shoulder blades and a host of other tiny bones from the tangle of fur that enveloped them, I couldn't help thinking of similarly unfortunate misunderstandings I'd come across. Sitting round a campfire one night, a group of adolescent boy scouts had been puzzled when one of their number kept chipping into the conversation with some very unusual contributions. Strangely, perhaps, for a fireside

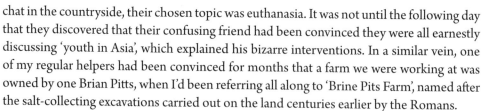

chat in the countryside, their chosen topic was euthanasia. It was not until the following day that they discovered that their confusing friend had been convinced they were all earnestly discussing 'youth in Asia', which explained his bizarre interventions. In a similar vein, one of my regular helpers had been convinced for months that a farm we were working at was owned by one Brian Pitts, when I'd been referring all along to 'Brine Pits Farm', named after the salt-collecting excavations carried out on the land centuries earlier by the Romans.

Though thanking me politely for my run-through of the avian digestive process, the Head of PR was clearly unconvinced by my project's potential to be turned into a good news story for the zoo's newsletter. No sooner had I announced that our next stop was the aviary, where we would be collecting some owlets, than she made her excuses and left, muttering something about 'another appointment' and how she would 'be in touch'.

The next stage, removal of the young, went smoothly, the presence of a BBC film crew in the aviary producing a larger than usual gaggle of onlookers. I did my customary bit to explain what we were doing, and showed the four downy owlets both to camera and also to the watching crowd, before placing them gently into the carrying box.

After a long and exhausting morning, the shoot was at last entering its final phase. I wasn't the only one beginning to feel the strain. It wasn't quite a move to down tools, but the cameraman and sound engineer were making it pretty clear, by a shuffling of feet and general air of inactivity, that they were in urgent need of sustenance.

'Right, lunch time!' announced the assistant producer peremptorily, having cannily read the cues and consulted her clipboard.

It was immediately clear that Chris and I were not going to figure on the crew's expense account – or if we did, our appearance might be a purely fictitious one. Arranging to meet up with us again close to the release site, they sped off in their laden-down vehicle in search of that idyllic Cheshire hostelry. With the owlets safely stowed in their carrying box, Chris and I sought out more modest fare in one of the zoo's many cafes. In truth, we were glad of the respite from the TV people's manic demands.

To my surprise, the crew managed to turn up at the rendezvous on time. They'd clearly feasted well and were therefore in much better spirits than when we'd parted. Even the sound engineer had perked up. He was less scruffy in appearance (well, he'd combed his hair) and even began to make positive comments about the forthcoming, final stage of filming.

'Surprising what a good lunch and a few beers can do,' I muttered sarcastically to Chris as we all departed for the release site.

Nor did the crew seem to mind when they had to unpack all their bulky equipment and heave it, once again, up on to the first floor of another barn. Because this was to be a juvenile release and there were therefore no adult birds to disturb here, we could all bang and crash about as much as we liked. There was no need for me to hiss '*Please* be quiet' at the sound man, or fuss about the hatchway door not being closed. So the whole experience was a lot more relaxing for me, too.

The site owner, Joe, a pig farmer, was keen to get his first glimpse of the owlets. I let him hold them one by one in his big, calloused hands and watched with amusement as they struck out with their needle claws at his sausage-like fingers. So hardened were his great mitts from years of physical toil that strikes which would definitely have drawn blood from my own soft office-worker's skin simply bounced off his, like darts off an elephant's hide. As he held them, carefully but firmly, and the cameras rolled, Chris fitted a BTO ring to each bird's leg. All went swimmingly, and surprisingly swiftly, with no unreasonable requests for retakes.

'Right, that's it,' declared Malcolm as the last owlet scrambled to the back of the nest box. Thanking us profusely for our help, his crew packed away their gear in double-quick time, aiming to find the nearest motorway junction before the rush hour got underway. Just before they zoomed off, I had sufficient presence of mind to enquire, of no-one in particular, when the programme was due to be broadcast.

Either no-one knew or, more likely, they weren't prepared to delay their departure for a moment longer. My question was simply left unanswered, hanging in midair as the car disappeared up the farm track in a great cloud of red, sandy dust.

As the next few months proved particularly hectic on the barn owl release front, I barely gave the film another thought.

There was also something else of great significance to preoccupy me. Just when invasive fertility treatment had seemed to be the only remaining option for us to pursue if we wanted our own offspring, my wife and I discovered that she was pregnant. As any parent-to-be, particularly a first-timer, will know, the prospect of producing and looking after a 'nestling' of your own tends to prompt a reassessment of what is important in life and a preoccupation, if not obsession, with getting things ready for the great event. So I soon found that there were relatives and friends to inform, rooms to prepare, equipment to be acquired, and the inevitable moments of panic ('what have we *done*?') to be overcome: in many ways, very much like the barn owl project.

So for a short time at least, I was forced to swap the fitting out of barns for the preparation of a nursery; the converting of tea chests into nest boxes for the assembling of crib and cot; and the studying of Warburton *et al.* on the barn owl for the works of Dr Spock in an attempt to find out how best to bring up baby.

Perhaps my greatest worry was the layer of complexity that this long-sought, but previously elusive, experience would add to our already frantically busy working and home lives. I eventually realised, though, that there was really no alternative to taking it in our stride. Throughout their childhoods, the boys (a second one appeared five years after the first) were completely involved in the barn owl project. In the early days, they could safely be left to doze in a parked car or be strapped into a bouncy chair, content to watch the manic activity going on around them. In extremis, I would plonk a toddler in a papoose carrier and cart him round on my back. As they grew older, they could be distracted from any unsuitable task I had to perform by being taken off to see the farm animals or machinery, or be plied with biscuits and cups of fruit juice. Eventually they would become useful, helping with the more interesting jobs such as emptying small mammal traps or ringing unfledged owlets. And, literally following in their father's footsteps, they would enjoy many a free visit to Chester Zoo.

25   *The price of success*

One day, months after filming the barn owl releases, I was brought up with a start whilst idly watching TV.

'The BBC has just announced that it is to discontinue the popular daytime show, *Pebble Mill at One*. It was the very programme that had commissioned the barn owl film.

'That's a pity,' I thought, disappointed by the likelihood that my efforts to tell the barn owl conservation story would never see the light of day. I then began to feel somewhat resentful of the amount of time and effort I'd put into the whole thing, which would now have been a waste.

'Bloody typical,' I grumbled, before consoling myself with the sudden recollection that I had at least received the initial prize money, through the post, in the form of an extremely acceptable cheque. The more I thought about it, the less unfair it seemed. I simply regarded the money as my fee for arranging the shoot – it was up to the BBC what they did with the resulting footage.

The BBC, or perhaps it was the sponsors, turned out not to be as willing to write off its investment as I'd assumed. A letter soon arrived from the Birmingham studios reassuring me that, despite the demise of *Pebble Mill at One*, the barn owl film would be used when an appropriate slot could be found in the TV schedules. As the letter also reminded me, similar films had been made of four other prize-winning conservation projects and further cash was up for grabs by the 'winner of winners'. The TV people were clearly not going to give up on the programme, as I had been beginning to hope, so I had no choice but to await further developments. In the meantime, there were other things on my mind: our child was due in a few weeks' time. I therefore pushed all memory of the whole filming experience firmly to the back of my mind once again.

It was the following year before I was summoned to the TV studios. My only previous experience of such places had been years before, when I and a group of fellow sixth-formers had been taken by coach to Border Television's headquarters in Carlisle. There we were to join the audience for a recording by The Settlers (a folk band that, somewhat unfortunately but perhaps appropriately, shared its name with a proprietary cure for indigestion). The whole experience had proved depressingly short on the anticipated glamour. Seen up close, the set looked small and grubby, and the most exciting part of the visit was when a rumour began circulating that the recording had been delayed because of a bomb scare. This was truly incredible – a less likely target for a terrorist attack than Border TV Studios was almost impossible to imagine. With this limited experience behind me, I was not in a particularly positive frame of mind when I entered the TV studios in Birmingham.

Regrettably, much of the day was to live down to my expectations. For a start, there were seemingly endless bouts of waiting around in spartan rooms, punctuated by occasional offers of hospitality ('Would you like another cup of coffee?'), or desultory conversations with other contestants. From time to time, one of us would be whisked away to be prepped, or one of the judges – a TV naturalist and a representative of the sponsors, a national building society – would be ushered in to shake our hands and, with a hint of awkwardness, wish us all well. The fabled green room treatment it certainly wasn't.

This was all taking place in the days when judges on TV shows at least pretended to be fair, long before the current fashion for the open criticism and humiliation of contestants. The most challenging moment came when we each had to face a grilling by a moderately well-known female presenter, Paula. Each session, we were told, was to be recorded, as was the final session, when we would all be present to learn the judges' verdict.

When my turn came, I was guided to the recording studio and motioned over to the interviewee's black leather chair. I sank down and looked about me. Paula was nowhere to be seen, and no-one paid me the slightest attention, going about their various tasks in a matter-of-fact, highly efficient, way. Feeling completely superfluous, I sought to distract myself by watching the multifarious activities going on around the studio. Someone, I noticed, was checking camera angles, whilst a colleague fiddled with the lighting, or moved a chair fractionally to one side. Others buzzed about with headphones and clipboards, waving their arms around and occasionally shouting out instructions. A few rushed in and out of the studio, apparently at random. It all had the feel and appearance of the opening night of a school play.

All of a sudden, I was roused from my daydreams by a man's voice barking urgently

'He'll need make-up! Get him to make-up, quick!'

At first, I looked round, wondering who on earth he might be referring to. Then, as an attractive young female assistant beckoned, I realised that the person deemed to be in need of urgent facial treatment was, in fact, me.

Still, make-up, I mused, seduced by the thought of the assistant undertaking extensive work on my features to bring out the best in them. As I was ushered into the make-up room, I spotted Paula sitting in front of an enormous mirror, obviously having just been given the full works. My turn next, I thought, as I eased myself into the newly-vacated chair, fully prepared to be pampered and groomed at the BBC's expense. Sinking back in complete relaxation, I was suddenly roused by the sight of a man bearing down on me, an enormous pink powder puff in his hand. Without a word, he dabbed it twice on my forehead in the general area of my receding hairline, before retreating from view as rapidly as he'd appeared.

'I-is that it?' I spluttered, bobbing my head about in front of the mirror, trying hard to discern even the slightest beneficial effect from the application of powder with the big pink puff. There was no need for an answer to my question. It was obvious that they'd finished with me in make-up – in two seconds flat – so I slunk sheepishly back to the interviewee's chair. Sensing my disappointment, the attractive young assistant, who'd witnessed the whole scene, attempted to soften the blow.

'It's just to stop these strong lights making your head look shiny,' she volunteered. I smiled feebly in response, sensitive to any reference to my prematurely-balding pate. The

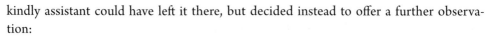

kindly assistant could have left it there, but decided instead to offer a further observation:

'We get the same problem when we have Neil Kinnock in the studio.'

At a stroke she demolished what little was left by then of my self-esteem, likening my scalp to the smoothly-glistening bonce of a man I considered old enough to be my father. These remarks, coming on top of all the time-wasting and waiting around I'd endured, guaranteed that I was not in the best of moods when Paula shimmied into position to begin her interrogation.

Not surprisingly, as this was an uncontroversial 'green' programme, the questions were only moderately challenging: 'Don't you worry that you might be releasing birds into the wild that are unable to fend for themselves?' and 'What will you do with the money if you win the overall prize?' Unfortunately, I was in no mood to put on an act, and therefore found myself slipping inexorably into professional mode. Trained, as a lawyer, to answer only the question that is put, to do so sparingly and with precision, my replies to Paula were brief and factual, delivered in the slow, measured and unemotional tones best suited to the courtroom. Despite several takes, my forensic approach didn't change, and a shrug of the director's shoulders indicated that my session was now at an end. He clearly thought that it was the best he was going to get from me. As I stepped down from the interview seat, I felt sure that my muted performance would be attributed to an attack of stage fright, rather than to the intense irritation I was feeling with the whole exercise.

Only when the assembled contestants were given a preview of the interviews did I realise quite how stilted my performance had been. My interview contrasted most starkly with the one given by a contestant from Northern Ireland. When asked his questions, he simply oozed enthusiasm, his arms and legs flailing all over the place as he peppered his replies with words like 'morvellous', 'unberlievable' and 'brilliant'.

Sure enough, his histrionics carried the day, with his project being judged the overall winner, and he repeated the whole performance as the prize money was handed over by the grey little man from the building society.

Chastened by the experience, and convinced that I was incapable of communicating my passion for wildlife conservation in the animated way demanded by television, I departed for home determined never to apply for any more grants or prizes. Instead, I vowed, I would do without the money – and the publicity – and go back to funding the barn owl project from my own meagre resources.

I was soon to find that the effects of publicity wouldn't necessarily wear off quite so easily. Determined, almost schizophrenically so, to keep my working and private life separate, I said next to nothing to office colleagues about my conservation activities. By now, I was working in central Birmingham, heading up a small team of public lawyers engaged on processing compulsory purchase orders, traffic regulation orders, and similarly dull, but undoubtedly worthy, tasks. As a suitable occasion never arose, and I certainly didn't intend to create one, I never got round to mentioning my impending TV appearance, even though I had by then been informed by the Beeb of the date and time of transmission.

On the day after the broadcast, which I'd stayed at home to watch, I marched into the team's office, as usual, to view the morning's post. I still had no intention of mentioning my new-found celebrity status. But at least one member of the team was not going to let me get away with it so lightly.

'Oy got a terribul shock yesterdye!' The junior legal clerk, Lauren, owner of a broad Brummie accent which she delivered in a squeaky, high-pitched tone, was addressing no-one in particular, but the office in general.

As this was a common occurrence, I paid little attention, instead burying my nose even deeper in the contents of the post basket.

'Oy was at howme', she continued, 'on study leave. Oy put the telly on at lunchtoime, and oo should oi sey?'

There followed a pregnant pause – several minutes long, it seemed – as the speaker stared meaningfully at me and I fought to avoid her gaze.

'Oy didn't know you were intow conservaishun'. Her tone of voice now bore a slightly accusatory tone, and she had certainly managed to gain her colleagues' full attention.

'Oh, er, yes,' I spluttered, now well and truly put on the spot. 'Barn owls... breeding and release scheme... spare time... needed funding... had to agree to be filmed... extra prize... four thousand pounds... Pebble Mill... must go now – lots of things to do'. And I shot through the door and quickly down the corridor to my own office, leaving my interrogator to provide a more coherent account of my television appearance to her bewildered colleagues.

It was a considerable time later that day before I set foot again in my team's office. I was relieved to find that they were all still speaking to me, my unexplained secretiveness not seeming to have offended anyone, although I was perhaps slightly miffed that my new national profile hadn't prompted them to treat me any differently. A slight touch of hero worship would not have gone amiss, I thought. However, I did eventually get my comeuppance at my team's hands, although I'm sure it was inadvertent.

About a year after the TV incident, on my last day in Birmingham before moving to another job, I was forced to undergo the ritual leaving presentation. After enduring a few kind words from my boss, receiving the usual collection of 'Good Luck' cards, book tokens and gift vouchers, and responding with what I hoped was wit and sincerity, I was approached by none other than Lauren.

'We also got yow this,' she said, holding forth a small, brightly-wrapped package.

'Oh, thank you'. This time, the surprise and delight was truly genuine. 'What can this be?'

Tearing off the wrapping paper, I suddenly began to wish that I hadn't been quite so enthusiastic, but had instead deployed an old evasion technique of my dad's ('I won't open it now; I'll save it for later!') I could now see all too clearly what was coming. The small cardboard box contained a pottery owl figurine, cheap, tacky, and crudely painted. It was even the wrong species. If the colour and shape reminded me of anything, it was a tawny rather than a barn owl, but it was difficult to tell what, if anything, the manufacturer had had in mind when producing this dreadful creation. With a forced smile, I thanked everyone for their kindness and beat a hasty retreat towards home. I'm sorry to say that the pottery owl figurine certainly did not achieve pride of place on my mantelpiece.

26   Finding release sites

Absolutely determined to leave behind the glitz and glamour of showbiz, I spent the next few months finding and checking out suitable release sites for the forthcoming crop of owlets, in between caring for my own baby. Sam had had the good sense to arrive in mid-August, just after the height of the year's releasing activities. I was fortunate to learn of many potential sites by word of mouth. If I used a site, word soon spread in the locality and the presence of barn owls on a farm seemed to become something of a status symbol. I could certainly imagine some farmers of my acquaintance boasting loudly down at their local pub or club about the qualities of their landholding which made it uniquely suitable for barn owl releases: 'Least it shows that mar land's healthy. The amount of them chimicals yer put on yours, ah'm surprised yer mange ter grow anythin' at all!'

Up to a point, such conversations weren't unhelpful. I had learned early on that a good way of producing sustainable breeding pairs was to carry out several juvenile releases, using unrelated clutches, within an area of a few square miles. Two or three seasons' work seemed consistently to result in at least one pairing off within the release area and the eventual establishment of a breeding pair.

The word-of-mouth approach had another distinct advantage. Farmers and other landowners keen to play host to some barn owls, could be more easily persuaded to adopt owl-friendly practices when managing their land. They would listen to advice on the use of rodenticides, some of which are less harmful than others to raptors swallowing poisoned rats and mice, and often agreed to leave uncut margins around fields and woodland edges to provide habitat for prey species such as voles and shrews. These strips, perhaps no more than a couple of metres wide, mimicked the headlands that existed in the days when ploughs were drawn by horses and provided a space in which they could turn. The most enthusiastic of the landowners would wholeheartedly embrace the Government's set-aside scheme, under which they would be paid to leave some of their land unused or only minimally cultivated. As I explained whenever I got the chance, the effect of these measures – whether intentional or incidental – was to provide much prey-rich foraging territory for barn owls and other predators.

The most challenging part of these interactions was, without doubt, the site visit. Whenever a site was recommended to me, provided it was not in an obviously unsuitable place, such as close to a motorway or other major road, I would first send the owner a set of leaflets describing habitats, nest box provision and release methods. The owners were asked to get back to me if, after studying the leaflets, they still felt that their site fulfilled the necessary criteria. A few I never heard from again but I was usually invited to carry out a visit. Armed with more leaflets and a set of photos illustrating various stages in the release process, such as the fitting of BTO rings, I would arrive at the site fully prepared for all eventualities – or so I thought.

Physical inspection usually proved to be the easy bit. A highly-organised, mechanised enterprise, centred around a spotless tarmac farm yard, suggested that I'd find fields that were prairie-farmed, where hedgerows had long since been grubbed out leaving only a solitary old tree, like a lonely beacon, in a green sea of cultivation. By contrast, some of the smaller outfits I visited were mixed farms, where a higgledy-piggledy collection of farm buildings seemed more at ease with the surrounding small fields bounded by untidy hedgerows, ragged woodland edges, muddy lanes and rough dry-stone walls. The whiff of nostalgia, the good earthy smells I recalled from Yewdale Farm, as well as the country sights and sounds, all played strongly on my emotions whenever I encountered 'real' farms such as these. But I had to curb these warm feelings and work methodically and objectively through my checklist of questions: the decision whether or not to use a site was far too important to be left to instinct alone. I would quiz the owners on which buildings could be used to house nest boxes, whether I could be allowed to check for prey availability by small mammal trapping, and how they would cope with the required daily feeding routine.

There was also one absolute killer question, one that caused me endless trouble, but which it was vital to have answered: 'Are there any wild barn owls on or around your land?' Somewhat disconcertingly, the vast majority of my interviewees – predominantly farmers – would immediately say that there were. It was at this point that my task began to get difficult. I knew, both from my own observations and from published information, that barn owls in Staffordshire and Cheshire were few and far between, with no more than a handful of breeding pairs, at most. And yet, here I was, consistently being assured that they were a common sight. It just didn't add up, so I would probe more deeply. A typical conversation would go something like this:

> Me: 'Have you seen any barn owls round here recently?'
> Farmer: 'Oh, aye, I saw one only last week/month/year.'
> Me: 'Really? What colour would you say it was?'
> Farmer (hesitating): 'Well, sort of brownish, I suppose.'
> Me: 'Can't have been a barn owl then – much more likely to have been a tawny.'
> Farmer (displaying slight signs of irritation): 'Well I saw it in my barn. It wasn't a tawny owl. I know what they look like.'
> Me (trying a different tack): 'Well have you heard owls round here at all?'
> Farmer (triumphant): 'Oh yes, I hear 'em hooting all the time.'
> Me (more assertively): 'It's tawnies that hoot. Barn owls screech and hiss.'
> Farmer (distinctly sceptical): 'I've only heard 'em hooting.'
> Me (convinced I'm right): I think that what you've seen and heard are tawny owls – some people call them brown owls – and not barn owls, which are also known as white owls.'
> Farmer (mounting high horse): 'How can you be so sure? I know what I've seen. I've lived on a farm all my life ... .'

It was at this point that I would reach for my photos. Producing them with a flourish, I would lay the full set, illustrating clearly the barn owl's various stages from egg to adult, before the obstinate farmer. In an instant, his attitude would change completely, with a grudging admission that the birds he'd been seeing hadn't looked anything like the ones in my photos, so they couldn't have been barn owls. So striking and consistent was this transformation in attitude that it set me thinking: was I simply being tested out? Did the persistent voicing of a contrary opinion arise out of a deep-rooted scepticism that would have been turned on anyone who knocked on the farm door claiming to be an expert? In other words, I was just asking for a hard time, as surely as if I'd turned up trying to sell a different brand of animal feed or fertilizer. Robustly challenging the new was all part of a great farming ritual.

Even when I succeeded at these mind games, I would insist on double-checking for the presence of barn owls by inspecting all the likely roosting places on the property. Fortunately, not every site visit was quite as taxing as I'm suggesting. One summer weekend, I decided to take advantage of an unexpected break in a spell of wet weather to make three visits within a particular locality in Cheshire. The only drawback was that I had also agreed to spend that very weekend entertaining one of my wife's colleagues, an eminent Spanish scientist. Fortunately, I knew Miguel well enough to believe that he would enjoy experiencing some of the English countryside, or at least be polite enough not to say that he wouldn't. He was also reasonably clued up on my barn-owling activities, so there would be no need to make long and complicated explanations to someone whose English was not too good.

We started our tour at a typical, small Cheshire dairy farm, where the yard – and, indeed, the farmers – were caked in a mixture of mud and cow dung, still liquid but bearing a deceptively thin crust. A personal army of flies buzzed around each beast and each farmer, clearly enlivened by the warm, dank atmosphere. The farmers, husband and wife, were both madly enthusiastic about a possible release being made from their ramshackle premises and, having gone through my standard routine with them, I marked the site down for potential future use.

I reflected on how unfamiliar this scene must be to Miguel. He was from Salamanca in Castilla y León, set in a picturesque, spacious environment of dry and dusty heat, where white haciendas with their bright, orange-tiled roofs gleam in the sun, their chimney stacks providing ready-made platforms for the large, untidy nests of white storks. As for agriculture, sleek black bulls destined for the ring are raised amongst pleasant groves of cork oaks. I wondered what my guest could possibly be making of lush, rural Cheshire.

With little time to ponder such questions, we arrived at our next site. It was, in fact, one that I had used before, and I simply wanted to check that it was no longer inhabited by the released birds. By contrast with the previous site, any resemblance between this property and an agricultural enterprise began and ended with the inclusion in its postal address of the word 'farm' – apart, I suppose, from the fact that the kitchen window looked out onto a neighbour's flock of well-groomed sheep. It was the large, detached stone barn that I was interested in, though, rather than the ugly modern 'farmhouse'. As I led Miguel over to this building in the company of the owners, Jim and Betty, I noticed that he seemed a little reluctant to proceed. Following his gaze, I could see that he was looking somewhat askance, first at the steep wooden steps that ran up the barn's gable end to a doorway at first floor level, and then at what lay beneath them. As I had discovered on previous visits, Jim and Betty were involved in animal rearing, and this was the nerve centre of the operation. Immediately beneath the steps and extending to cover a good proportion of the yard was a large, stoutly-fenced area, the preserve of the couple's beloved dogs. These were no ordinary mutts, but pedigree Rottweilers, a breed of fearsome reputation, alleged to have been used by the Romans to drive cattle north into Germany and herd gangs of slaves on the return journey. To access the barn, it was necessary to climb the steps, which had no more than a flimsy handrail on their open side, and pass directly over the dog-infested enclosure. Needless to say, the Rottweilers were irritated by this intrusion into their territory and duly gave vent to their feelings, barking and snarling incessantly in a ferocious manner. One false step, I thought, and I would suffer the same fate as the hapless chieftain in the old Hollywood film *The Vikings,* who ended up being tossed into a pit full of vicious, ravening wolves and promptly torn to pieces.

Having survived both ascent and descent, clinging nervously to the wall, we were invited into the house for a drink – something, I thought, that would perhaps have been of more use prior to our ordeal. As on previous occasions, I expected that the hospitality on offer would consist of a mug of coffee and, perhaps, a biscuit, served in the glisteningly-clean modern kitchen. I was therefore surprised to be ushered, instead, beyond the kitchen and into a spacious lounge. This special treatment had, I supposed, something to do with the presence of my exotic companion. Neither room bore the slightest resemblance to the many real farmhouses that I'd visited over the years. In sympathy with the kitchen decor, the lounge was brightly decorated and expensively furnished, with a glitzy, purpose-built bar extending along half the length of the room. As our hosts generously offered us drinks from the vast and varied array on offer and motioned us towards a couple of luxurious armchairs, I could see that Miguel, a self-confessed epicure, was hugely impressed. However, I was anxious that he didn't get the wrong impression.

'This isn't typical, you know,' I hissed, as soon as Jim and Betty were out of earshot. But, despite his experience of the previous site, Miguel's response - a polite but enigmatic smile - told me that he was far from convinced. No doubt, I thought, he assumes that my conservation project consists of little more than bowling round the countryside and visiting properties whose owners ply me with refreshments and engage me in cosy chats, all in comfortable surroundings. I hoped that our next, and final, visit of the day would firmly disabuse him of such notions.

After stopping off for lunch – steak and kidney pudding, chips and peas – at a traditional Cheshire pub, a short car journey took us to somewhere called Ashton Grange. Centuries old, its walls bearing a mantle of ancient ivy, the building was more solid than spectacular, its elderly inhabitants giving every impression of ageing in situ in total sympathy with their dwelling. There was no sign of a glitzy drinks cabinet here, but we were warmly invited to partake of tea or home-made lemonade and sticky-sweet cakes, served outdoors on the well-kept lawn. So genteel did our hosts, Mr and Mrs Whiting, appear that I half expected one or other of them to faint at the mention of dead day-old chicks or any of the other less savoury, though necessary, aspects of carrying out a barn owl release. On the contrary, however, as our conversation wore on, it became increasingly apparent that these were true country types, who wouldn't turn a hair at the prospect of a bit of fish gutting or pheasant plucking. On learning that barn owls don't generally dine on rabbits ('They're too big,' I pointed out), Mrs Whiting volunteered to produce 'nice fillets' for the owls from any rabbits that might come her way.

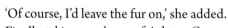

'Of course, I'd leave the fur on,' she added.

Finally taking our leave of Ashton Grange, our visiting finished for the day, I noticed that Miguel, normally an ebullient character, was uncharacteristically quiet. After a while, driving along the picturesque country lanes, I decided to break the silence.

'You know, Miguel,' I began, 'you've seen a pretty good cross-section of English rural society today. Quite by chance, we've met peasant farmers, representatives of the nouveaux riches and old county squires, in that order'.

'Oh yes, yes,' he murmured with a wry smile. And that was all. I rather think that the whole day's activities, including my interactions with the people we met, had taught my friend far more about the English class system – clearly alive and well in rural Cheshire – than about conservation of the British barn owl.

Growing Barn Owls in my Garden

*The demolition or conversion to housing of many traditional barns has
been a major factor in the barn owl's decline*

*Collisions with vehicles on fast, straight roads account for an estimated
3,000 – 5,000 barn owl deaths each year*

Above: Intensive cereal crop production, resulting in large, open fields and grubbed-out hedgerows, has significantly reduced the amount of foraging habitat available to barn owls

Left: My first breeding female barn owl. In contrast with the male (see opposite), note the sandy colouration and the distinct black spotting of her breast feathers, which also extended under her wings, and the darker edging to her facial disc

My first breeding male barn owl. Note the absence of markings on his underwing and breast, and the white edging feathers of his facial disc

A close-up of the barn owl's upper wing with barring and distinctive teardrop markings clearly visible

The Tawny Owl – often mistaken for the Barn Owl, particularly after dark

The first aviary I built for the captive breeding of barn owls

'Mr McKay' an injured bird from the Scottish Borders

Left: Barn Owl in full threat display, intended to deter a would-be attacker

Below: It worked! Inside the aviary nest box, the female barn owl stands over her clutch of eggs whilst the male (Mr McKay) glares back defiantly. A close look shows that his tongue is extended as he makes clicking sounds to intimidate the intruder

The eggs of (l. – r.) domestic hen, tawny owl and barn owl

Barn owl chick (top) and tawny owl chick (bottom), both of which failed to hatch. Note the difference in size and the egg tooth, particularly on the tawny owl chick's beak

The barn owl family in the nest box: adult male on the left and female on the right. Note the obvious difference in age, particularly between the youngster on the left, with its well-developed facial disc, and the smallest bird, still showing a largely featherless pink face

The view from a barn window at a potential release site

Fixing a nest box in position in the chosen barn

The release site must have a plentiful supply of wild prey, such as this field vole (Microtus agrestis)

Wood mouse (Apodemus sylvaticus)

Left: Common shrew
(Sorex araneus)

Below: House mouse
(Mus domesticus)

Bottom of page: Three young
birds ready for release

In addition to my own captive-bred birds, barn owls were collected from the
aviaries at Chester Zoo. Here, the keeper has flushed the adult male from the
nest box (above) in order to remove the young (below)

Above: Before being placed at the release site, the young birds are fitted with leg rings issued by the British Trust for Ornithology (BTO)

Below: The rings are fitted with a special pair of pliers and do not in any way constrict the bird's leg

Left: Daily visits to the barn to provide food are essential until the birds are flying free and able to fend for themselves

Below: The ideal location for a successful release – remote, undisturbed and surrounded by prey-rich habitat

What it's all about!
Barn owl hunting
for prey

Left: Barney, who lived with me for over 15 years. She never bred, despite plenty of opportunity, but helped my conservation project in countless other ways

Below: The author holding Barney

Bottom of page: Barney

27   Public presentations

Another good way of finding release sites was through talks that I gave to groups and societies. Having effectively hung up my boots as far as broadcasting was concerned, I was still determined to spread the message as widely as I could by other means. I travelled far and wide throughout the region giving illustrated lectures in return for my petrol money and a (usually modest) yield from an end-of-show collection. Sometimes I felt that I was simply entertaining a bunch of armchair naturalists, but at other times I quickly realised that I was addressing a knowledgeable group of active conservationists. Whatever the audience, I would invariably end with an invitation to anyone interested to take away some leaflets and get in touch with me later if they thought they had a suitable release site to offer. I certainly made a few useful contacts this way, although some of the reactions to my talks were totally unexpected, ranging from the humorous to the downright scary.

I saw a classic case of over-enthusiasm one evening when, after the talk, a short, fat, bald man burst through the small group clustering around me to get more information or just have a chat.

'This is just what I've always wanted to do!' the latecomer proclaimed, like a zealot who has just seen the light.

Sweeping up a fistful of leaflets in his sweaty hand, he careered towards the exit, shouting 'I'll be back in touch!'

I never saw or heard from him again.

On other occasions, it would be the questions that were odd. After the first few sessions, I felt equipped to respond to most points with a seemingly authoritative answer, but just occasionally would be stumped for a suitable riposte.

'Have you ever come across a recipe for cooking barn owls?'

This must surely have been the most bizarre question to ask someone who had just spent the best part of an hour extolling the merits of conserving the species. All I could bring myself to do was respond tartly: 'No, and I don't think they'd taste very nice,' which at least raised a titter amongst the saner members of the audience.

I was also once asked whether I had any spare barn owl wings – detached from their owners, of course. The enquiry came from the curator of a well-known country house, who'd read that the owl's wing was by far the best tool for dusting stuffed specimens, of which she had plenty. As it happened, I did have a spare pair of wings in my freezer that had come from a road casualty, so I promptly dispatched them to the curator. Within days she telephoned me to say how absolutely marvellous they were at doing the job.

It would sometimes be me who opened my mouth only to put my foot in it. One

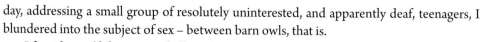

day, addressing a small group of resolutely uninterested, and apparently deaf, teenagers, I blundered into the subject of sex – between barn owls, that is.

I found myself absent-mindedly reeling off my standard presentation.

'I've been breeding now for about ten years'.

As soon as I'd uttered the words, I wished I hadn't.

As though shocked into life by a sudden electric charge, my audience instantly dropped their disdainful poses and bored expressions, leaned forward and began to exchange knowing looks and sly grins. Unable to retrieve the situation, and too rattled to try, I simply ploughed on, seeking desperately to avoid making any further embarrassing gaffes. Like predators who know that they have their prey cornered, the teenagers now played a waiting game, judging the optimum moment to strike. The final blow came when I least expected it. Having hastily wrapped up the session, I began to withdraw gratefully towards the sanctuary of my car. Unfortunately, my route was blocked by the gaggle of youngsters who were now hanging around in an apparently desultory manner awaiting the arrival of their own transport. Passing through the throng, I sought to disarm them with a weak, somewhat defensive smile. But they were not to be put off the scent so easily. As my pace quickened, I was pursued by a volley of snorts and sniggers that soon broke into a chorus of raucous laughter, and then some only-too-clear words of encouragement, delivered in a sneering, sardonic tone:

'Good luck with the breeding, sir!'

As I sped away, not once looking back, I consoled myself with the thought that I'd at least managed to stimulate some interest, even if in the wrong subject.

Having Barney with me at a talk usually went down well. I'd been to talks given by other people, such as Tony Warburton, a well-known naturalist based in west Cumbria, and seen how well the audience reacted to a live owl. I'd also been to at least one other talk where the best that could be offered was a dried owl skin mounted on a stick, like a museum specimen, which didn't really inspire the audience. I reasoned that it was important for people to see the real thing, not least to prevent confusion in their minds between barn owls and other owls – fully-grown little owls, for instance, are often mistaken for baby barn owls. As I'd never managed to fit Barney with jesses, and couldn't therefore control her movements, I always took a roomy cage for her to sit in. Being so thoroughly imprinted, Barney loved to appear before an audience. Like the magician's beautiful young assistant, her job was to draw the eye and gaze admiringly at the performer (me). Without any need for training – or, for that matter, a sparkly, figure-hugging costume – Barney played her role to perfection, staring fixedly in my direction, her adoring liquid-black eyes wide open, occasionally chirruping sweetly to the obvious delight of the audience.

At the end of each talk, I would gently remove my assistant from her cage and invite members of the audience to come forward to get a closer view, or even to touch her if they wished. Cradled in my hands, she was completely unperturbed at this close-up examination by complete strangers, or by having her head stroked. The strokers would remark how soft and deep her feathering felt, and I would point out that an owl's head is made up of a variety of carefully arranged feathers, performing purely practical purposes such as sound gathering, whilst its underlying skull shape is similar to that of other raptors. In other words, the large round head that we find so attractive is just a clever illusion.

One question that I was regularly asked at this point in the proceedings always mystified me. Almost without fail, someone would pipe up, 'Isn't it cruel to hold her like that?'

Resisting the temptation to snap back that I wouldn't be doing it if I thought Barney didn't like it, I would instead carefully explain that, because she was a tame bird, she was completely at ease. This was absolutely true. I could feel how relaxed she was, resting in my cupped hands, with her legs dangling between my fingers, like someone lolling in a hammock, idly trailing a limb or two over the side. Barney's steady heart beat, which contrasted with the frantically pulsating breast of every wild bird I'd ever handled, was a clear indication of her relaxed state.

'An owl that isn't tame,' I explained, 'would be struggling to escape, lashing out with its piercing talons and attempting to bite the hands that were holding it, however gentle they might be'.

As I continued to field questions – trying hard, at times, to contain my sense of irritation – Barney maintained her charming ways, like the old trouper she was. Rather than playing a supporting part, she came instead to fill the starring role.

My talks certainly bore fruit in terms of producing good sites and site-owners keen to help with my project. But there were also the time-wasters, like the chap who insisted that he had the perfect place on the outskirts of Macclesfield. He was so persistent, ringing me every day, that I felt obliged, despite serious misgivings, to go and have a look. Sure enough, his proposed release site turned out to be a suburban park with a nest box installed in a disused storehouse for garden tools. My tormentor turned out to be one of the gardeners. Furious though I was – the man had clearly not read the leaflets I'd sent him – I was unable, even then, to let fly with my true feelings. Instead, I decided to let him down gently.

'I'm afraid it's not suitable for barn owls,' I told him, 'as there's too much traffic, no suitable hunting areas, human interference. But I'm sure you'll have tawny owls in a place like this, with lots of big, old trees. You might even get long-eared owls here, particularly in winter time. You could try putting up some nest boxes'.

The reason why I was so restrained in such trying circumstances was because I wanted to encourage, rather than put off, anyone interested in wildlife conservation, however misguided they might be.

The Macclesfield gardener, though clearly disappointed with my verdict, seemed to accept my explanation. As time went on, I found that, unfortunately, he was not unusual – someone who got a bee in his or her bonnet about conservation, wanted to do something about it, but had totally unrealistic expectations about what it involved. I strongly suspected that some of these characters might try an alternative way of indulging their interest, and indeed one or two of them said as much, hinting darkly that there were 'other sources' who would supply owls 'with no questions asked'. By this they meant unscrupulous owl-breeders who would have no qualms about birds being released in a totally uncontrolled way. So alarmed was I about the lack of regulation governing breeding and release activities – it was clearly the lawyer in me coming out – that I wrote an article for a magazine advocating the setting-up of a licensing system. Little did I know what would eventually come to pass.

Sometimes the offers I had were tempting, but impractical, such as the suggestion made by its constable that I use his Welsh castle (which was, regrettably, too far away), or

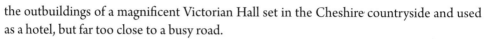

the outbuildings of a magnificent Victorian Hall set in the Cheshire countryside and used as a hotel, but far too close to a busy road.

Over the years, I became used to strange approaches of various kinds. Quite often there would be enquiries about adverts seen in a local newspaper, offering barn owls for sale.

'Isn't that illegal?' I'd be asked, and had to reply that, in fact, it wasn't. Provided breeders follow certain rules, they are as free to buy and sell barn owls as they are zebra finches or budgerigars. Once, I even had to share a corner of a farm building at an agricultural show with such an enterprise: while I was telling visitors to my stand how rare the bird is and trying to interest them in its conservation, my neighbour was extolling the barn owl's virtues as a pet and taking customer orders. I was greatly relieved when he failed to turn up for the second day of the show. Sadly, there are probably more barn owls in captivity in this country, being kept as totally unsuitable pets, than there are in the wild.

Easily the most bizarre approach I had came completely out of the blue, and long before the advent of cold-calling.

'Hello, is that Paul Hackney?' a polite male voice enquired. 'I'm ringing on behalf of the Central Council for British Naturism…. no, please don't hang up,' he added, only just in time to stop me from announcing frostily; 'I'm not interested, thank you!'

'I have a serious offer to make,' he continued.

Contrary to my expectations, he was not touting free trial membership of his organisation, an introductory visit, or even a rundown of the bare essentials of naturism. Instead, it transpired, he wanted to talk to me about barn owl conservation.

The caller went on to explain that his group leased large tracts of land in the county where they could indulge their minority-interest activities. Resisting the temptation to congratulate them on their fortitude ('It isn't exactly the south coast around here'), I instead listened politely and agreed, as usual, to send off some leaflets.

'Do get in touch again if you still think your site is suitable.' I put down the phone and thought nothing more of the call.

A few weeks later, my parents, who both took a great interest in the project, came to stay with me. We were all sitting down to breakfast, chatting about this and that, when I heard the postman delivering the mail. Retrieving the envelopes from the door mat, I returned to the breakfast table, clutching the usual collection of bills, reminders and junk mail. One plain brown envelope, however, aroused my curiosity. Slitting it open, I slid the contents onto the table. There was an embarrassed silence, interrupted only by the noisy rattle of a dropped spoon as it ricocheted off the breakfast pots. There lay before us a glossy, full-colour leaflet, a far more professional job than my poorly-photocopied information sheets. It wasn't the quality, but the contents, that caught the eye: a brazen advertisement for the pleasures of naturism. Against a backdrop of improbably (or, in the case of Staffordshire, impossibly) blue sky and shimmering white sand dunes, there stood, bronzed and fit – and unashamedly stark naked – an extremely well-endowed young man and his voluptuous female partner, beneath the caption 'British Naturism'.

More images – modern, coloured versions of the sort of photographs previously available only in *Health and Efficiency* and similar illicit publications – could be found on the other pages. Closer scrutiny, purely in the interests of wildlife conservation, of course, revealed that the landscape apparently used by the naturists might indeed be suitable hunting terrain for barn owls. Having studied barn owl hunting techniques in action, however, there was no way that I could advocate lying 'tackle out' in the grass on a warm summer's evening whilst the birds foraged overhead for something plump and furry.

Taking a deep breath, I was about to embark on an explanation as convoluted and utterly unconvincing as one of Basil Fawlty's attempts to justify himself to Sybil. Although my mother was probably somewhat more relaxed about such matters, my father was far from being a libertarian where sex and nudity were concerned. Like Canute trying to hold back the waves, Dad spent much of his sons' teenage years attempting to shield us from the growing tide of sexual freedom that swept the country in the 1970s. The mere glimpse of a naked body – an uncovered breast here, a bare buttock there – or a lapse into 'bad language' would prompt him to stride across the living room (no zappers in those days) and summarily switch off the television, the words 'Bloody rubbish!', uttered with genuine venom, his only attempt at an explanation.

Fortunately, I was spared the agony of having to explain myself. Just in time, I noticed that another item had been tucked in the envelope with the leaflet; and, to my great relief, saw that it was a letter referring to the telephone conversation a few weeks earlier and inviting me to carry out some site inspections. Handing over the letter with a sigh of relief, I thought I had narrowly escaped a tricky situation. But I'd reckoned without my parents' mischievous sense of humour. Roaring with laughter (heightened, perhaps, by feelings of relief), they let fly a volley of less than helpful comments:

'You'll probably have to strip off before they'll let you in!'…'Watch out when you're climbing ladders!'…'Where will you keep your hankie and your car keys?'

Needless to say, with such a reaction from my own family, I instantly, and perhaps unfairly, dismissed as a non-starter any possibility of taking up the naturists' kind offer.

28   Equipping sites and trapping prey

Once a site had been inspected and approved, it was largely a matter of awaiting the arrival of a suitable crop of owlets to be placed there. In the meantime, it was vital to produce and erect nest boxes on the site, one, called a release box, for the owlets to inhabit while they fledged, and as many others as possible scattered on and around the site to act as potential roosting or nesting places.

The manufacture of owl nest boxes is an art in itself. Various designs have been published for both indoor and outdoor versions, the latter of course needing to be completely weatherproof. Because of the relative ease with which they could be made, I mainly preferred to adapt old tea chests for use inside buildings. The chests are roughly the right shape and size when laid on their sides, and then need only a front panel, with an entrance hole, and a landing platform. Because they are thrown together in a very rough-and-ready fashion, I have probably spent more time, over the years, removing bent, rusty nails and jagged lengths of metal edging from inside the chests than I have adding the two extra features. There was no way that I was going to risk my precious owlets suffering injury, and possible infection, by snagging themselves on these vicious barbs.

If knocking together nest boxes was fairly straightforward, fixing them in place could be an entirely different matter. When positioning a release box, I usually tried to achieve the best possible compromise between the needs of the owlets – to be safe from predators and sheltered from chilling winds – and the convenience of their human hosts, who had to be able to access the box daily to provide food and check on the inhabitants' wellbeing. Fastening the box directly onto a stout beam deep inside the building usually seemed the best bet. If the building had sound flooring at first floor level – quite a rarity, I found – the task was made all the easier. Otherwise, it was a case of heaving the box up a long ladder; no mean feat, thanks to its awkward shape, rather than to excessive weight. There was then the difficulty I'd first struggled with at the Hartleys' farm of driving several strong nails through the floor of the box and into the beam below. As time went on, my technique improved, particularly when I began to use a smaller hammer and nails so that I could get in a decent swing within the confines of the box.

On most occasions, though, a degree of improvisation was called for, particularly when siting the roosting/nesting boxes, which I was keen to fasten in the highest, most secretive places I could find. Sometimes, there would be no tie-beams, only longitudinal beams, supporting the barn roof. So, together with a volunteer, I would have to stretch planks of wood from one beam to the other, and fasten the box onto these. In some places, even this would not be an option, and we would end up suspending the box below a beam using an unsightly combination of vertical wooden battens, binder twine and any other material that came to hand. Provided that the end result was a dark, private and safe retreat, I didn't think it mattered that it was more Heath Robinson than Habitat in appearance. After all, it wasn't as though I'd been commissioned to construct a charming dovecote in the grounds of someone's picturesque country mansion.

Two of the most successful nest boxes that I came across had little or nothing to do with me at all. They were designed, created and installed by a farming friend, Ted, who turned out to have a pretty unconventional approach to life generally. Not least among his eccentricities was that, despite being extremely slight of build, he insisted on keeping a herd of enormous Charolais cattle. These large and powerfully-built animals have an unpleasant reputation for indulging in unpredictable violence, and the breed has a long record of making fatal attacks on farmers. Seeing Ted in amongst his beasts on a frequent basis, I felt sure that he must be pushing his luck. Despite his slight stature, however, he never appeared short of energy. Shortly after I'd first made contact, he outlined his plans to me one day and by the next had refloored and refurbished an old pigeon loft in the gable end of a barn and created a highly unusual nest box in another part of the building by hoisting up into the rafters an old kitchen unit, which he had fastened into position on its side.

'Hmm, the proof of the pudding will be in the eating, I suppose,' was my comment on being taken to see his handiwork. Little was I to know that this was only the start of Ted's unconventional barn-owling endeavours.

With a site visited and boxes installed (even if not used to release from, a fully-equipped site would be available to passing barn owls), a vital piece of assessment remained to be done: gauging the availability of food. Whilst still supported by ready meals of dead day-old chicks, the owlets would need to be able to learn to catch their own, live food. In time, of course, they would have to be capable of fending completely for themselves. Although the marked decline in barn owl population numbers in most areas of Britain has been attributed to a variety of factors, it goes without saying that a plentiful supply of prey in safe, convenient foraging grounds is a key ingredient for survival. Assessing the availability of small mammal prey in a release area was therefore crucial.

Many conservationists argue that we shouldn't be releasing top predators such as barn owls at all. Instead, conservation efforts should be focused on species like the field vole (the barn owl's favourite prey), wood mouse and various types of shrew. This, they say, would not only add to the general health and diversity of the countryside, but would also have a beneficial impact on species along the whole length of the food chain. Both nocturnal raptors, such as owls, and the 'day shift', diurnal species such as kestrels and buzzards, would ultimately benefit, their numbers increasing as a natural response to improved food supplies. Whatever the arguments amongst the experts, I felt that the data on small mammal populations was useful in itself, so a-hunting I would go!

There is nothing quite like setting, checking, emptying and re-setting one hundred traps twice a day for a period of up to one week. Perhaps that's as well. The traps, designed by a Mr Longworth to capture small mammals, without injury, and keep them alive until freed, are elaborate affairs consisting of two rectangular metal boxes, one slightly smaller than the other so that, when not in use, it can be slipped inside its larger counterpart, like one Russian doll inside another. However, when joined together, end to end, the smaller box forms a tunnel leading into a chamber created by the larger box, which is furnished with dry hay – to act as warm bedding – and baited with suitable food. As a hungry or inquisitive animal moves from the tunnel into the chamber, it passes over a sensitive trip wire which releases a top-hinged trap door at the tunnel entrance. Like a one-way cat flap, this prevents the animal from leaving by the way it came in. There is nothing for the animal to do other than tuck into the food supplies and curl up in a warm bed, safe from predators, to await release. For once in its inevitably short life, it is completely insulated from the outside world. The Longworth trap is, then, the Travelodge of the small mammal world.

Operating to a system is vital when trapping on such a scale. Every trap must be identifiable and therefore have its own number painted clearly on both sections, the traps must be set out in pairs, each pair located ten paces from the next, and the traps in each pair must be positioned so that they face in opposite directions. It is also vital that the larger box, in particular, slopes slightly downwards, towards the tunnel, so that any rainwater that does penetrate the structure runs out of the sleeping chamber rather than collecting within it, soaking the food and bedding. Traps are set each evening, checked very early the following morning, restocked with supplies and reset as necessary and then left for the day, with the procedure being repeated that evening.

The checking procedure involves examining each trap in turn to see whether the front door is closed, indicating that someone is in residence. If it is, the whole trap is lifted gently into a large plastic bag, where it can be taken apart and the contents carefully emptied out for identification. However many times I've carried out this delicate and time-consuming procedure, I've never lost the atavistic sense of the hunter examining his catch, a shiver of excitement running down my spine. Even the knowledge that the captive would, in all probability, be nothing more exciting than a vole, mouse or shrew, couldn't dampen my feelings of eager anticipation. Sometimes, there would be a big letdown.

'It's only a bloody slug!'

The trap mechanism is sufficiently sensitive to be triggered by an enterprising gastropod. At other times, my excitement levels would soar, as I reckoned that the unusually increased weight of a trap might mean I'd caught something really special. I'd read somewhere, for instance, that it wasn't unknown for a weasel to follow its quarry into a Longworth trap and for the trapper to get quite a surprise when a lively, well-fed mustelid tumbled out into the plastic bag. So far, though, I haven't managed to catch anything quite so exotic, the extra weight of a suspect trap usually being caused by a super-size vole, possibly a pregnant female.

Whatever the catch, it must be assiduously recorded, which can be easier said than done. You need to get a pretty close look at a vole to determine whether it is of the field or bank variety and, because of their small size (between 65 and 75 mm long, excluding tails), the various species of shrew can be difficult to distinguish. Some captives decide not to wait around long enough to be identified. Spotting its escape route, one creature shot up the sleeve of my companion's jacket as it was encased in the plastic bag, scampered in a trice across her shoulders and down her other sleeve before leaping to the ground below and freedom. It was an escape worthy of Edmond Dantes, the Count of Monte Cristo.

My companion, momentarily stunned, recovered sufficiently to make the all-important identification.

'*Apodemus sylvaticus* – wood mouse!' she cried, as a pair of skinny hind legs and a long tail disappeared into the undergrowth.

The university students who were with us could only stare, open-mouthed.

Although, as a piece of machinery, Mr Longworth's traps work superbly, I can't help thinking that he perhaps gave less thought to the practicalities of their use in the field. Made from sheet metal, their unchamfered edges, sharp corners and moving parts combine to bruise and scrape your hands so that, by the end of the day, they look as though you've been involved in a punch-up. These unpleasant effects are only made worse when your fingers are aching with cold and damp and you are faced, for the umpteenth time, with the task of emptying out the noxious contents of a trap that has been occupied for many hours by an incontinent animal. It may also have started to rain heavily. Too small for your whole hand, the main chamber has to be thoroughly cleaned of all the noxious detritus left by the previous tenant before being set up for reuse. Poking two or three fingers into the box commonly results in painful cuts to the sensitive web of skin between your fingers and, as often as not, some scraped knuckles for good measure. Even the bait adds to the discomfort: whilst hamster food is dry and slightly sweet-smelling, the casters (pupae of flies), needed to sustain any insectivorous shrews that might be caught, give off a powerful, nauseating stench of rotting flesh.

Both my sons, Sam and Peter, who have accompanied me on countless barn-owling trips from an early age, were completely unfazed by their various experiences, whether they involved clambering around rickety old farm buildings, handling owlets, tramping across the countryside to trap small mammals or sitting absolutely still and quiet at dead of night to watch the comings and goings at a nest site. There were, though, some more conventional fringe benefits too – the opportunity to meet farm animals, including less common varieties such as Vietnamese pot-bellied pigs, llamas, ornamental pheasants, peacocks and water fowl. There was also great fun to be had with some of the human characters we met. Farmers often provided us with rich sources of amusement.

One day, Sam and I went off to check out a potential release site on a farm in the uplands of northeast Staffordshire, an area notorious amongst the urbanites of the Potteries for the supposed eccentricities of its inhabitants. The allegations levelled against these good people were, I gathered, along the lines that it wouldn't be entirely surprising to learn that one or more of their number had, as the newspapers would coyly say, been caught in 'a compromising situation with a farm animal'. Not to put too fine a point on it, they were branded as sheep shaggers.

In the event, the family we were visiting turned out to be a very pleasant and hospitable bunch, although their appearance was something like the Peak District's answer to the Beverley Hillbillies, their trousers held up with string, their clothes crudely patched. Having passed the ritual initiation test – the customary exchange about the colour of the barn owl – I was invited into the farmhouse, Sam quietly sticking by my side. We would not, I knew from experience, get as far as the inner sanctum, the pristine sitting room with its old-fashioned polished wooden furniture, loudly ticking grandfather clock and glass-fronted cabinets full of dainty porcelain. Instead, we were ushered into the cavernous stone-flagged kitchen, the hub of any farm, heated by an ancient stove and furnished with battered settles ranged against the walls and covered in dozing cur dogs and farm labourers, who

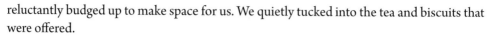

reluctantly budged up to make space for us. We quietly tucked into the tea and biscuits that were offered.

Here, in his kitchen, Mr Hayes, the farmer, was in his element, regaling us with farming stories and other agricultural goings-on – his dealings with a troublesome bull, the extent of his landholdings, inevitably involving some complicated, long-running feud with a neighbouring landowner, and the local fat stock prices. Most of what was said must have been pretty meaningless to young Sam, who just sat listening and stroking one of the cur dogs that had crept unobtrusively up by his side on the settle. As his monologue gathered pace, Mr Hayes became increasingly excited, jerking his arms and legs around in a disjointed fashion, like a puppet. Suddenly, perhaps because even he had realised that his audience's attention might have begun to drift, he leapt to his feet, seized a large air rifle from its cradle on one of the beams, and fired it twice into the plaster ceiling immediately above his head. Crack! Crack! Mrs Hayes gave forth an almighty shriek, the dogs leapt about barking furiously and poor Sam sat, open-mouthed and completely bemused by the whole chaotic scene. My immediate thought – why don't I just grab my son's hand and make a run for the back door? – was interrupted by Mr Hayes who, still holding the rifle, was now wishing to explain why great lumps of plaster weren't showering down upon his head.

'Dunner wurry,' he beamed, 't'weren't loaded!'

His wife's contribution was a little more to the point.

'Aw, tek ner notice,' she tutted, nodding at Sam, ''e were only showin' off t' t'lad'.

Not wishing to stay for a repeat performance from Wild Bill Hillbilly, I promised to get back in touch if and when I had some owlets to release. Shocked into utter silence until we were back in the car, Sam spent the entire journey chattering nonstop about our bizarre encounter with the hill folk of the wild and woolly uplands.

29   Monitoring release sites

Once a release site had been approved and appropriately furnished, it was simply a matter of awaiting the arrival of suitable birds: either a compatible pair, or a healthy brood. Before becoming fascinated by barn owl conservation, I had spent a number of years rescuing and rehabilitating various species of British wildlife, predominantly birds. Eventually, I became a Licensed Rehabilitation Keeper (LRK) under a scheme administered in accordance with the Wildlife and Countryside Act 1981 by the Department of the Environment, a government department that has since undergone a number of transmogrifications and is now known as the Department for Environment, Food and Rural Affairs, or Defra. One condition of being an LRK was that any rehabilitated bird being returned to the wild should first be fitted with a BTO ring. Ever since that first shag in the sand in my youth... perhaps I should re-phrase that ... Ever since finding the corpse of a green cormorant on a beach as a boy, I have been a passionate believer in the ringing scheme. My long-held belief in the necessity of ringing or tagging schemes was reinforced by hearing one day on the radio about various seal rescue centres located in coastal areas. Of the three or four enterprises featured, only one, based in Holland, used a mark/recovery scheme. As the interviewee pointed out, how can you stand any possible chance of knowing whether your work has been worthwhile unless you have some means of identifying released animals? Unlike the others, the Dutch operation had also banned visits to their facilities, as they were keen to ensure that their wild patients did not become habituated to human beings. Their whole approach chimed perfectly with my own ideas on rehabilitation and release. Too often, I had seen, heard or read of rescue efforts that were driven by sentimentality instead of hard-headed realism about the difficulties of carrying out successful releases.

Fortunately, wherever I operated, it didn't prove too difficult to find willing ringers. In Staffordshire, through a mutual contact, I came across David James. I knew I would get on well with him when, on our first encounter, I spotted that he was wearing a *Guardian* sweatshirt. I was more unsure about his reaction to me. Our first joint assignment was to ring two adult barn owls that I had confined in a barn loft.

'You catch the buggers and I'll ring 'em!' I warmed to David's no-nonsense approach.

If only they stay in their box, it'll be a piece of cake, I thought, as we climbed the wooden staircase to the loft. Seriously doubting that the birds would be quite so co-operative, I had visions of chasing them all round the large room, my arms flailing helplessly as they evaded capture whilst David looked on, wondering who this plonker was that he'd become involved with.

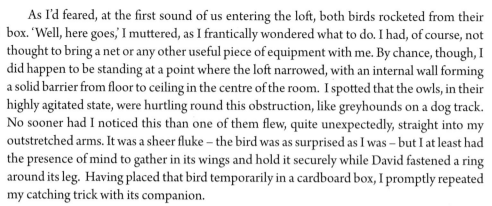

As I'd feared, at the first sound of us entering the loft, both birds rocketed from their box. 'Well, here goes,' I muttered, as I frantically wondered what to do. I had, of course, not thought to bring a net or any other useful piece of equipment with me. By chance, though, I did happen to be standing at a point where the loft narrowed, with an internal wall forming a solid barrier from floor to ceiling in the centre of the room. I spotted that the owls, in their highly agitated state, were hurtling round this obstruction, like greyhounds on a dog track. No sooner had I noticed this than one of them flew, quite unexpectedly, straight into my outstretched arms. It was a sheer fluke – the bird was as surprised as I was – but I at least had the presence of mind to gather in its wings and hold it securely while David fastened a ring around its leg. Having placed that bird temporarily in a cardboard box, I promptly repeated my catching trick with its companion.

'Well done! You're obviously an expert at this!' David cried, apparently much impressed by my skill.

'Oh, I'm sure there was a bit of luck involved,' I replied, somewhat disingenuously.

On the strength of this first, successful, ringing expedition, I was sure that David and I would get on famously.

Although my new-found friend was always very willing to ring my owls, this did depend on his availability. The window of opportunity, when the owlets were between four and six weeks old, was quite narrow, and would often coincide with one of the newly-retired David's many jaunts abroad. Equally, the reports on any ringed birds that were picked up (or 'recovered', to use the rather confusing technical term) would go to the ringer, and I therefore had to rely on receiving the details after David had seen them. Any delay in getting the information to me could be particularly unfortunate if, for instance, a live bird had been found with a non-fatal injury: the sooner I could take it into my care, I felt, the better its chances of successful rehabilitation would be. So I decided to find out about obtaining my own licence to ring.

Enquiries to the BTO revealed that this was possible, but only if I was suitably trained by an experienced ringer. With some trepidation, I popped the inevitable question and, to my great delight, David readily agreed to train me.

'I'll have to be present, anyway,' he pointed out, 'so I shan't miss any of the fun!'

Over the next few owling seasons, we reversed roles, with David holding the birds firmly while I fastened rings round their legs. He was the best of teachers, not least because his instructions were always brief and to the point.

'Watch out the little bugger doesn't grab you!' or 'Mind it doesn't shit all over us!' were typical pieces of guidance.

As I well knew, this was a man who had in his time ringed a huge range of birds, from puffins to spotted flycatchers, and had contributed a section on ringing techniques to the ringers' bible, *The Ringing Manual*. He was therefore a true expert and very little would faze him. He did always insist, though, that I should be the one to do any climbing up ladders. Just like me, David enjoyed immensely our encounters with different characters and the places they lived.

'Verrry Cheshire set,' he would mutter, as we wandered round an obsessively tidy hobby farm. 'What a bloody mess – cowshit everywhere!' came the cry as we squelched around the working variety.

'Shhh!' I was always worried that the owner might hear his comments, take offence and ask us to leave.

By far the most difficult and disconcerting aspect of the whole process was the element of mental stress involved. Over the years, as an LRK, I had handled many different bird species, including buzzards, sparrowhawks and kestrels, ducks, geese and guinea fowl, snipe, blue tits, swallows and swifts and most species of native owl. I'd learned to be firm but gentle, particularly with birds that were injured and in distress. I'd had to withstand feelings of nausea and revulsion at the sight – and smell – of an open wound crawling with maggots, or a bloodied and shattered bone protruding through tattered feathers. But none of this did I find quite so unnerving as holding a split metal ring, tight within the jaws of a pair of metal pliers, around such a delicate and vital structure as a barn owl's leg. In my first few attempts, the thought that, with one slip, the bird could be seriously injured, or even permanently maimed, threatened to prompt an attack of the trembles. Worse still, as I slowly but firmly increased the pressure on the ring to overcome its inbuilt resistance, there would be a sudden sharp click, which could easily be mistaken for the sound of a snapping tarsus. I noticed once or twice in the early days that onlookers would flinch at this point, doubtless assuming that my pliers had slipped and that I'd bungled the whole procedure. I began to make a habit of forestalling such misunderstandings by giving out a breezy explanation in advance:

'Now, you might hear a loud click as I tighten the ring – nothing to worry about, it's all part of the procedure. I'm not breaking the bird's leg!'

Some of the disapproving looks I attracted suggested that my jolly banter might not always be striking the right note. Indeed, some individuals occasionally queried the value of ringing at all, suggesting it was cruel. Although the BTO point out that metal rings have been safely used on birds for over one hundred years, they do emphasise the need for the proper closing of butt-fitting rings, so that there is no gap. Opponents, however, claim that hard metal rings, particularly when fitted to raptors, might cause damage to their legs and feet when they impact at speed on an unyielding surface. This is most likely to occur when they miss their prey and hit the ground, or a tree branch, instead. The nearest equivalent I could think of was when I occasionally caught the edge of my signet ring and forced its sharp edge deep into the skin at the base of my fingers, which certainly hurt.

So vehement could the anti-ringers be that I mischievously imagined they must be assuming I was wringing birds' necks, rather than ringing their legs. In the end, I dismissed the arguments by asserting that, even if occasional accidents did happen, the possible drawbacks for an individual were more than outweighed by the clear benefits produced by the ringing scheme, in terms of information and research that helped birds generally. Equally, I couldn't see how the outcome of any release could possibly be known unless the subject was marked in some way. I suspect, though, that however often I put these arguments, they cut no ice with determined anti-ringers.

The antipathy to breeding and release schemes was not, I found, confined to a few ill-informed individuals. Some of the most well-known conservation bodies were not exactly enthusiasts, although they rarely expressed open hostility. There were some inconsistencies in the stances they took. With my training as a lawyer, my first instinct is to look for evidence and frame arguments accordingly. And yet, without the benefit, it seemed, of any substantial research producing such evidence, some organisations would sound off about the futility of barn owl breeding and release schemes, whilst vociferously supporting the reintroduction of birds such as the sea eagle and the red kite. Although I thought at the time that these criticisms were subjective and unfair, I eventually began to suspect that they were based on a desire to promote professionalism, rather than to denigrate people's efforts for the hell of it. I was also beginning to realise that there was a lot of amateur involvement in the field that might not bear too close an examination. Hardly a month went by when I didn't read, or see on television, some item involving a well-intentioned individual who'd somehow come into possession of a pair of barn owls and thought it would be a good idea to 'set free' any offspring they might produce. Ringers would tell me tales ('I ringed five pulli [chicks] one time for a chap who was carrying out a release, and within a week they were all picked up dead on the surrounding roads') and an 'escaped' bird would occasionally be brought to me that I was sure had been the subject of a misguided release attempt. Frustrated by the absence of any control over such cruel and damaging activities, I wrote an article advocating the setting up of a licensing scheme along the lines of that operating for LRKs. It was published in *Environment Now*, a new 'green' magazine and, although I can't claim that my article had any great influence on events, it was pleasing to see an announcement some time later that the Department of the Environment intended to set up just such a scheme. In the meantime, I continued with both my breeding and release activities and close monitoring of individual release sites.

The monitoring regime that I adopted would vary during the course of, and after, a release. During the first few weeks, a close watch was kept by the landowner or the person providing the owls' daily meal. I was also much in evidence, stocking up the rapidly-disappearing food supplies on a regular basis. As the birds began to fly and explore their surroundings, pellet collection and analysis, in addition to visual observation, became a good way of keeping a check on the birds' wellbeing. In modern performance management jargon, this would constitute the monitoring of outputs, rather than inputs (which were assessed through trapping the birds' potential prey in the way I've described). As many a schoolchild knows, unpicking bird pellets is an art in itself. Depending on the age of the object – a freshly-regurgitated pellet is moist and shiny, whereas one that has been lying around for several days is more likely to have the consistency of concrete – the task can be reasonably easy, or hellishly difficult. At all costs, the pellet must be dissected so as to separate the tiny, delicate skeletal remains of the raptors' last meals from their shrouds of matted fur and feathers. Techniques vary, as do opinions on the best tools to use. Dry pellets can be soaked in water before dissection, but this does tend to produce some fairly noxious smells. Although scalpel and tweezers might seem the obvious choice of implement, I've always found a pair of needles or long pins much more useful in teasing apart the constituent parts.

As with any human endeavour, it seems, it is possible to pursue even pellet analysis to the nth degree, rummaging through the detritus to find the microscopic setae of earthworms, or the wing cases of beetles. For my purposes, however, it was sufficient to identify small mammal remains, primarily their skulls, and differentiate these from leftover bits of chick beak, feet and so on – which would indicate that the owls were still relying on the daily feed. Having first fished out all the cranial clues, you then need to identify them. Certain indicators are obvious: the insectivores, such as shrews, have red colouration to the tips of their teeth, as if indelibly stained by the blood of their victims; and the width and big eye sockets of some larger skulls are unmistakeably those of hapless voles. For more accurate attributions, a magnifying glass, a pair of tweezers and a specialised diagram are essential. How, for instance, would you distinguish between the skull of a long-tailed field mouse (*Apodemus sylvaticus*) and that of the common house mouse (*Mus domesticus*), assuming of course that you would ever want to? The answer is carefully to remove the first upper cheek tooth, using the tweezers, and then examine the resulting sockets with the magnifying glass. The number and arrangement of the sockets can finally be matched to the right species with the aid of the diagram – what you might call a 'root map'. Not only can different types of mice be identified in this way, but mouse can also be distinguished from rat. In fact, rat remains were a rare find in my experience, although my friend Ted's farm initially provided a rich supply until, to his great delight, the owls finally saw them all off.

My most startling find came when I caught sight of a particularly large pellet lying on the floor of a barn. There was something odd about its shape, too, and when I bent down to get a closer look I could see two broad, leathery-looking paws protruding from the object's side. They were unmistakeably the front feet of a mole, which looked as if they were about to emerge from the pellet, to be closely followed by the rest of the animal. But, alas, this was a mole that would burrow no more. Analysis of the pellet revealed its skull, twice the size of a shrew's, but the same long, narrow shape. The array of sharp teeth was clearly designed to make short work of its big, juicy earthworm prey.

Food preferences will obviously depend to a large extent on the local availability of prey. Some birds, having perhaps made a chance catch in the first place, may develop a taste for a less standard diet. I once cleared out a nest box on a Cheshire farm that, the farmer told me, had been used for many years by a pair of barn owls and their broods. Because it had been abandoned some years before, much of the nest detritus had become desiccated and dusty, but the bony skeletons survived. I removed half a dozen sacks full of the stuff, the overwhelming majority of the skulls being those of small birds, presumably sparrows and suchlike. Out of sheer generosity, I donated the sacks and their contents to Dr. Derek Yalden, a zoologist at Manchester University, as I thought he might be able to set a student to sifting through the material and coming up with a more detailed analysis than my 'small birds'. I suspect that it may have been too big a job, however, because I heard nothing further on the subject.

The barn owl's predation of birds is not confined to the smaller varieties. I was told by a reliable eyewitness that he'd once seen a cock bird drop onto a collared dove as it flew out of the shippen on which he was perched. The victim was quickly dispatched then taken to a nearby fence post and eaten.

By far the best, and most interesting, method of monitoring release sites is to do it myself. That way, I not only get the chance to observe the rare and beautiful barn owl, but I can spot other wildlife too – foxes, badgers and rabbits will wander quite close if you are sitting stock still in a field while you wait for the owls to emerge. Without the benefit of a pair of night-sight binoculars, enabling you to see in the dark, the crepuscular habits of the owls can be most frustrating, though. Timing their first appearance of the night to coincide with the precise moment when visibility has faded virtually to nil, an owl family will first spend ages announcing that they're all beginning to wake up. Like a disorganised, rumbustious human family, they'll interact with each other, snoring, screeching and staggering around as they come to and prepare to face a new day (or, in their case, a new night). There's a lot of flapping around, youngsters hissing at their parents because they're hungry and want their breakfasts, parents trying to ignore the persistent demands. They primp and preen themselves to prepare for the outdoors and, finally, driven to distraction, the harassed adults emerge from the family home, relieved to be setting off to the comparatively straightforward task of foraging and bringing back the family's meal. Prior to this sudden departure, only the briefest glimpses of the various family members can be caught as they flit past a window opening or some other gap in the brickwork. It's just like looking in on the occupants of a house as they go about their daily lives, unaware that they are under observation. Like human teenagers, juvenile barn owls that have become reasonably competent fliers spend a good deal of their time hanging around just outside the home, so if your timing is right it is possible to see an entire brood congregating on the barn roof or some other prominent place.

Of course, another way to monitor progress is to check with the on-site owner. Some, I found, were better (more observant, that is) than others. Ted, for instance, would watch his birds obsessively, having set up a nesting area in the gable end of a barn conveniently overlooked by his sitting-room window.

Other landowners, like Jeff Hartley, wrongly assumed that the owls had left because they hadn't seen them for a while. Farmers, though, are generally the best bet because of their tendency to be up and about at all hours, especially early in the morning. It is then that they are most likely to have surprise encounters, as Bert did.

Bert's farm was not one of my release sites, though it might well have made a perfect one. It was, in fact, within a short flying distance of several sites that I had used for juvenile releases. The owner of one of these other sites, Bill, a local vet, phoned me one day to say that he had heard reports of barn owls possibly breeding on Bert's farm. I promptly invited myself up there, having been warned that the farmer was a trifle eccentric. As I drove into the yard, I was instantly struck by what a glorious tip heap the place was. Bert seemed to be more a collector of scrap than a serious farmer. Vehicles and machinery had been left to rot where they stood, including an old-fashioned red post office van, which I half expected Postman Pat to clamber out of at any moment. The yard was strewn with untidy piles of pallets, crates and bags of God-knows-what. Inside the farmhouse was no better. Bert shooed out a smelly, off-white goat as I entered (it seemed to have been tucking into an old settee) and a large fuse box hung from the wall above the cooker as though blown off by some long-forgotten short circuit. Piles of dirty pots lay everywhere and, looking about, it didn't take me a second politely to decline Bert's kind offer of a cup of tea.

The man himself, though, turned out to be both knowledgeable about, and interested in, wildlife. Leading me through his disorganised enterprise, he explained excitedly how, in the early hours one morning, he'd wandered into his cowshed and it had 'seemed t' explode wi'owls!' He thought he'd spotted at least five birds, which flapped around wildly once they'd been disturbed. From his description, it seemed likely that at least some of them had been recently-fledged owls still hanging about and exploring their home environment. Bert had some even more exciting information to impart. Pointing upwards – by now we'd negotiated the obstacle course and reached the cowshed – he showed me a water cistern, hard up under the roof of the building where, he claimed, the female barn owl was brooding more eggs. Unfortunately, this cistern had already flooded once and he had called out a local naturalist to sort out the problem. Although he was sure that the breeding pair had returned, Bert was convinced that the cistern had flooded again.

Though looking the type who would soldier on forever, the elderly farmer was clearly reluctant to climb up to the cistern to find out what was, or was not, going on inside. So I volunteered. I knew it was a serious offence to disturb Schedule 1 birds without the appropriate licence, but I reckoned that if Bert was to be believed, this was an emergency. So I grabbed a ladder and up I climbed with a gang of curious steers milling around below me. Once I was up there, the cause of the problems was obvious. The arm of the ball cock had been roughly tied in position with baler twine, but the slightest touch brought a stream of icy cold water pouring into the tank. So sensitive was this mechanism that it could easily have been triggered as the owls – adults or young – brushed past it on their way in or out. Now came the tricky task of viewing the contents of the cistern. Leaving the flooding problem aside, the site was certainly well chosen. Not only did the shed's inhabitants generate some welcome heat, but there was also very little space between the top of the cistern and the roof above, making unwanted intrusion very difficult. Even benign interference, such as I intended, was well nigh impossible, and only with a great deal of twisting and turning did I eventually succeed in positioning my head so that I could look into the chamber whilst simultaneously shining my torch into its dark interior. To my great relief, I found no birds present. Instead, the floor of the cistern was awash with water, on which was floating a raft of soggy straw and pellets bearing two rather sad-looking, dirty white eggs. Contorting myself so as to reach in, I discovered that, not surprisingly, the eggs were stone cold. Reluctantly, I removed them and proceeded, with great difficulty, to clean the cistern of its remaining contents: water, sludge, straw and pellets. Then I dried out the container using handfuls of old rags and asked Bert to let me cut off the water supply completely. He took some persuading because, he said, he was concerned that his beasts should have access to a drink whenever they needed one. Eventually we compromised on diverting the water supply via a different piece of pipe, thus ensuring that the elevated tank would forever remain dry.

Despite my strenuous and well-intentioned efforts, it turned out to be too late in the season for the site to be used yet again that year. I consoled myself with the thought that at least three, possibly more, young had already been produced and the adults had even tried for a second brood, so the site must be a very good one. I was itching to discover what the main food sources were – a quick glance round the farm suggested strongly that vermin would figure prominently – but all pellets had either been soaked into a sludge or trodden into fragments on the floor of the shed. There was only one thing for it: having diverted the water supply and, as a belt-and-braces approach, tied up the ball cock more firmly than before, I lined the floor of the cistern with the mixture of dried peat and sawdust that I always kept handy. At least this was one plum(b) nesting site that would be available for the following year.

Bert's farm lay in a natural depression, like a large amphitheatre, where it was protected from the prevailing winds. This meant, according to Bert, that he enjoyed a milder climate than would otherwise be expected at such a height. Besides the newly-arrived barn owls, he delighted in telling me that he regularly saw little owls, short-eared owls and the more common moorland species such as skylark, peewit and curlew. I felt sure that the sudden appearance of Bert's barn owls was a direct result of the releases I had carried out in the area, but had no way of proving it. This was often the case – the evidence was purely circumstantial – but sometimes, I found, it was much easier to work out why barn owls had appeared at a particular site. This could be because people deliberately did not do what they were told to do, or because they accidentally did something out of the ordinary. I occasionally suspected that wilfulness played a part too. In the event, unconventional approaches could produce both good and bad results.

30   The secretive barn owl

One of the obvious disadvantages of the adult pair release method was the fact that the birds would be confined indoors, unnaturally, for several months before being released. Although netted-over windows and other openings gave them the opportunity to look out and familiarise themselves with their immediate surroundings, their lack of access to the outside world, which would have been available, for instance, in an aviary, may have inhibited the birds' feathering from becoming fully 'hardened off' by the effects of the weather. This could be overcome, to some extent, by providing sitting-out areas, fitting a small wire cage to the outside of the building, around an opening in the wall, for example. The theory, at least, was that the birds would expose themselves to fresh air, sunlight and even the occasional rain shower whilst enjoying the use of their enclosed balcony. Whether or not this particular drawback of the adult pair release method is more imagined than real, another identifiable risk does seem to be supported by clear evidence.

An acknowledged expert, Colin Shawyer, refers in his book *The Barn Owl* to drowning as the third-highest known cause of mortality in barn owls. Of the drowning reports he has received, sixty per cent have occurred in July, and all have involved female birds. Colin speculates that these fatalities occur primarily when the adult female birds emerge, heavily-soiled, from their nests, after spending a total of eight weeks incubating their eggs and brooding their young. Like a desert wanderer confronted by a sparkling oasis, the desperate bird heads for the nearest water – usually a cattle trough or water butt – and, plunging straight in, ends up literally dying for a bath. With her soft feathers soaking up the water like a sponge, she finds herself unable to gain a foothold on the sheer, smooth walls of the metal or plastic container, and is dragged slowly beneath the surface. I remember Jane Ratcliffe's fierce condemnation of these modern materials, which she compared unfavourably with the rough stone that was used in previous times to fashion shallower troughs, from which an owl would have at least some chance of scrambling.

'Tell the farmer either to cover his troughs completely with netting, or to float a big piece of wood in them to act as a life raft. The cattle will still be able to get at the water, and the precautions can be removed after a couple of weeks'.

I sensed that she would have little sympathy for the farmers' beasts, even if they did become desperate for a drink.

Whilst they were in captivity, the owls did of course have access to a clean water supply for drinking, or bathing, or both. I usually made this available in a cat litter tray or washing-up bowl filled to a depth of just one or two inches. This mod con was therefore completely safe and, while confined, the adult female and her mate could – and, judging by the discoloured state of the water and surrounding floor, did – make full use of the facility. It was therefore even more important to ensure that, once allowed her freedom, she didn't head to the nearest trough for a good, deep and probably fatal bath. I tried to make sure that Jane's temporary modifications to any nearby water tanks were followed to the letter. On most occasions, it seemed to work well. The human factor does, though, always have to be taken into account.

Nick, a friend I had met through the local badger conservation group, was also a keen ornithologist. He had found a perfect release site at a farm on the Cheshire-Staffordshire border, where he had sited a hide in the woods. The farmer, George, was only too happy to place a large, airy barn at our disposal and, with Nick's help, I kitted it out in the usual way. We soon introduced a pair of owls and the whole release process went like clockwork, first with the production and incubation of a clutch of eggs, then with the hatching and successful rearing of four young. All was going without a hitch until, one day, Nick telephoned out of the blue. Not one for pleasantries, he simply made a dreadful announcement:

'I think the adults have escaped!'

'Oh, shit!' It had all been going so well, with both the adults and their offspring thriving. 'Stay there, I'm on my way.'

In my car, driving out to the site, I speculated about what might have happened. I trusted Nick not to have dragged me out on a wild goose chase, and at least to have carried out a thorough search himself. If he hadn't been able to find the adults, how on earth could I be expected to? Someone must have left a door open, I thought, or perhaps we didn't block up all the possible exit holes.

By the time I pulled into the farmyard, I was in something of a lather.

'Still no sign?' I enquired anxiously as Nick and George hove into view. The grim looks on their faces answered my question without the need for words.

'We've looked everywhere', Nick muttered disconsolately.

'I'd better have a go anyway'. I tried hard to inject a note of optimism into my voice, but in reality my spirits were sinking fast. To have lost the adults after so many months of hard work would be truly devastating.

Nick and George, clearly disheartened, decided to leave me to it. Opening the door, I stared at the seemingly vast open space in front of me. A nugget of information that I had managed to get from Nick was that chicks were still being taken from the feeding platform up to the nest box, which meant that the owlets were thriving. Following Sherlock Holmes' advice to Dr Watson, to eliminate the impossible (the owlets, I knew, were too young to fly down to the feeding platform and back) and to accept whatever remains, however improbable (there was no sign of a break in, the door and windows were locked, and no adult birds had been seen flying outside the barn), I was driven inexorably, as Holmes might have said, to the conclusion that at least one of the parent birds was still present. Now to test my hypothesis. Like the great detective himself, I proceeded to conduct a detailed and systematic inspection of the scene. Rather than crawling about on all fours, magnifying glass in hand, my investigation involved climbing up and down ladders to peer or feel into gaps in the brickwork, or along the tops of walls where they met the slope of the roof. By the time I'd finished, I felt as if I knew intimately every brick in the building, every beam, ledge and recess. But nowhere at all could I find an owl. Apart from the odd stray feather, both birds seemed simply to have disappeared without a trace.

I now (sorry, Holmes) began to have serious doubts about my totally logical theory. Surely the owls couldn't suddenly have vanished. Utterly exasperated, my hands clasped tightly behind my head, I gazed heavenwards, not so much in search of inspiration as in an attempt to stretch my aching neck. It was only then that I noticed something that struck me as odd. At the very apex of the gable wall, where the topmost bricks met the roof, there were distinct and copious trails of white droppings, one set to the left and, almost in its mirror image, another set to the right. George, who had by now rejoined me, along with Nick, confirmed my supposition that this was a favourite sitting-place for the adult birds – 'Like a pair of book ends,' he volunteered. He also offered another vital clue, although none of us at first appreciated its significance. It turned out that the walls were double-skinned, having an inner and outer layer of bricks held together with metal ties set at intervals between the two.

As if a light switch had suddenly been flicked, an idea popped into my head. Remembering the barn owl's secretive tendencies – it's not uncommon for them to nest in the narrow gap between the floorboards of one storey and the ceiling of the storey below in derelict buildings – I began to wonder whether the owls might have eased themselves down from their perching places on the wall's apex and into the space between the two layers of brickwork. After all, Jane had always insisted that barn owls could squeeze through a gap just a couple of inches wide. Once again climbing my ladder, any feelings of weariness now forgotten in the renewed excitement of the search, I felt around in the gap between the brick skins, but, to my complete dismay, I found no sign of any owl. Descending to floor level again, I stared, mystified, at the unyielding brickwork. What had seemed such a good idea now felt like a piece of wild and hopeless speculation.

'Well, I don't know,' I sighed, 'perhaps they have escaped after all'.

Just as I uttered these despairing words, an unusual noise caught my attention.

'Did you hear that?' I motioned to the right, towards the point at which the sloping gable wall met the vertical side wall. Again, there came a brief scrabbling sound, like a cat scratching at a door. Thinking that there must be a pigeon, or even a rodent, scrambling about in the rafters, I rushed forward to investigate. Shining my torch at the point in the wall from which the sounds had come, I noticed that there were several small holes where the mortar had fallen away from between the bricks, and peeping in through one of these, I was amazed to see the golden, tear-dropped plumage of an adult barn owl. I trembled with excitement as I tried to work out whether the bird was dead or alive, healthy or, possibly, injured. My mind raced as I remembered the trauma we'd all suffered when my young son's hamster, Harriet, had become trapped in the cavity walls of our family home. For several days, we'd been able to track her movements around the house by the weird scratching noises she made day and night. It was as though we had rodents living behind the skirting boards, just as Beatrix Potter describes in *The Tale of Samuel Whiskers*. The only way we could think of extricating poor Harriet was to knock a hole through an inner skin of breeze blocks, within the confined area of the cupboard under the stairs, where our cats couldn't get at her, and set a good old Longworth trap, baited with chocolate and other goodies. After two anxious days, I staggered downstairs at breakfast time to find the trap door shut. Rushing back upstairs in triumph, trap in hand, I separated the two halves with a flourish, to see a very dusty and bedraggled pet hamster emerge. As I recalled this incident, I began to wonder whether I could hope for a similarly happy ending from the current situation.

Directing my torch beam as I peered into the crevices in the brickwork, I started as the light reflected off a shiny, jet-black eye staring straight back at me. Its owner was clearly very much alive, and irritated, as the rapid blinking response demonstrated. There the owl sat, like a recusant cleric walled up in a tiny priest-hole.

'I've found one!' I cried, turning round to see that I was telling only myself, as Nick and George had once again crept quietly out of the barn, abandoning me to my quest.

'I wonder … ?' Again talking to myself, I moved along the gable wall to examine the corresponding point at the opposite end. Sure enough, my hunch was right: behind the brickwork, like a second fugitive priest, lurked another adult barn owl, the mirror image of the first. It seemed like a clear case of 'his 'n' hers', with the birds sitting on their own separate bricks atop the gable wall, and retreating down separate tunnels whenever they felt the need to disappear or simply to be alone. Perhaps this behaviour should have come as no surprise. I knew, after all, that barn owls have a liking for holes in trees or man-made substitutes, such a chimneys, or even ventilation shafts on industrial estates, as had happened at Trafford Park. The thing that did impress me, though, was that the birds had not only squeezed down through such long, narrow shafts, but had also managed to turn round on reaching the bottom and had apparently made themselves perfectly comfortable.

Once I'd shown Nick and George my amazing discovery, only one concern remained: despite their obvious caving skills, would the owls, like my son's hamster, need any help to extricate themselves from their hidey-holes? In other words, would I again need to deploy hammer and chisel to remove a brick or two and create an easy escape route? Explaining these worries to Nick, I was greatly relieved when he volunteered to monitor closely the goings-on in the barn. A few days later, my mind was finally put at rest when he reported that all was well, as he'd seen the parent owls emerge from the cavity wall as easily as they'd tucked themselves away in the first place.

Sadly, having weathered this particular storm, the same release site was to demonstrate how easily triumph can turn to disaster. Several weeks after the parent birds' disappearing act, their four healthy offspring were fitted with BTO rings and, a couple of days later, the barn quietly opened up. Between us, George, Nick and I intensively monitored the site, seeing the adult male and female venture cautiously into the outside world and checking that they continued to feed their still-unfledged young. For a month following the opening of the barn – the period, I thought, of the greatest danger – all appeared to be proceeding according to plan.

It was early July and I left for a short holiday in Scotland. The weather had turned particularly hot at the time and, looking back, I should perhaps have reinforced the message about keeping cattle troughs covered. But I didn't. In the middle of my holiday, I received the chilling news from a very upset Nick that the adult female owl had been found dead in a cattle trough on the farm. They could tell it was her, even without checking the ring number, because of the distinctive brood patch on her underside, an area devoid of feathers in which a sitting female can keep her eggs and young secure and warm. One of the stockmen, concerned about his cattle's increased need to drink in the hot weather, had apparently removed the netting covering one of the troughs. It was soon found by the owl, who decided to take the thorough bath that was to prove fatal.

Keen to reassure Nick and George, despite my feelings of bitter disappointment, I suggested that they revert to providing food direct to the owlets by placing it on the ledge just outside the nest box. Although we all thought that the adult male bird would still be in the vicinity, we could not be sure what effect the sudden disappearance of his mate might have on his behaviour, particularly on his attitude to his new family.

'I suppose he might just bugger off now,' was my own gloomy assessment.

So over the next few weeks, we salvaged something from the disaster by following the juvenile release method for the rapidly-developing youngsters. Thanks to all our efforts, they fledged successfully and dispersed from the site in their own time and in the usual way.

31   A different approach

By the early 1990s, the bureaucratic machine that was the Department of the Environment had finally swung into action. A ban on releasing captive-bred barn owls without a licence was announced. Licences would be issued by the Department on application by would-be releasers. To encourage compliance, anyone carrying out a release without a licence would be guilty of a criminal offence.

In justifying its new licensing regime, the government used much the same reasoning as I had set out in my magazine article several years earlier: poor release practices leading to inadvertent cruelty, the need for habitat restoration to be undertaken in conjunction with releasing, and, according to some scientists, the damage that captive-bred birds might do to the remaining wild population, because of genetic differences between the two groups.

So far, so good, I thought. The intentions seemed to me to be sound, but would the design and implementation of the scheme match up? When the first set of forms dropped through my letter box, my heart sank. Like any good bureaucrat – and I should know, I'm one myself – the men (and women) from the ministry tend to judge a form by its length and its detail. The Application Form and accompanying Code of Practice Guidelines scored highly on both, as did the End of Year Report Form, to be completed and submitted for each site. There were the usual warnings about not deviating from the guidelines and complying with the conditions of any licence that the department granted.

Reluctantly, I had to accept that the price of proper regulation is almost always yet more paperwork. I was comforted by the thought that I was already keeping my own detailed records and doing the practical investigation work, such as conducting surveys and small mammal trapping, to gauge the suitability of any site that I was thinking of using. I was concerned, though, about the substantial form-filling that would now be needed, over and above the BTO's detailed requirements, and, most of all, about the practical application of the scheme. Not to put too fine a point on it, although the regime had been set up in consultation with experienced conservation organisations – I knew this because the paperwork said so – I was pretty sure that the administrative personnel administering it would behave in the classic bureaucratic manner, rigidly applying the rules and procedures without any in-depth knowledge of the subject. Whilst I could prepare and submit my applications for licences in good order and in what I thought would be plenty of time, I would never have real control over the timing or outcome of the efforts of my captive-breeding stock, who might for instance breed early or late in the year, depending on the weather, or have abnormally small or large broods, or produce more than one. The more I thought about it, the more I feared that the whole thing would turn into a nightmare of coordination. I almost began to suspect that the licensing scheme may have been cunningly devised to discourage even the most well-organised and reputable releasers from making applications in the first place.

Sometimes, a healthy disregard for rules and procedures such as the ones now being promulgated by the Department of the Environment can pay dividends, although it can also, of course, land you in the dock. Probably as a result of my working life in the law, I've always been a stickler for rules and precedents. My farming friend Ted – the one who constructed a nest box from a redundant kitchen unit – had no such inhibitions. He lived and worked on a traditional Staffordshire farm. The farmhouse, three storeys high, looked out over a large cobbled yard, on the far side of which stood an impressive range of solid, brick-built farm buildings.

'When I was a lad, I used to sit at my bedroom window for hours and watch the barn owls that lived up there.' Ted pointed to the gable of the main barn with its pop-hole close to the apex.

'They disappeared about twenty years ago,' he explained. 'I'd love to have some back.' His young daughter, standing by his side, nodded in agreement.

Making some vague promises along the lines of seeing what I could do (I had more sites than owls to release from them at the time), I pointed out that if there were still any wild owls around the area, they might choose Ted's site for themselves. In the meantime, I suggested, he could continue his practice of farming in an environmentally-friendly way and, if possible, create suitable foraging habitat which would help to attract barn owls and other raptors. But I obviously hadn't realised how keen and impatient my friend was to fulfil his dream of recreating his childhood experiences. Within a few weeks he was on the phone.

'Paul? I've got myself a barn owl. It's a hen, bred in captivity. I bought her off this bloke'.

Not a good start, I thought, bringing to mind all my self-imposed restrictions on buying and selling birds. But there was more to come.

'I've set her up in a flight in the yard,' Ted went on, 'and you'll never guess what – she's got a visitor already!'

Apparently, within a few days, a cock bird had come a-calling (proving there must be wild barn owls about) and, just as in the romantic tale of Pyramus and Thisbe, the pair's courtship was now being conducted from either side of the aviary wall. Seeing how desperate they were to consummate their relationship, Ted had a further proposition to make.

'I'm thinking of moving my bird up into the barn. I'm sure the cock will follow her – he seems very keen, visiting her every night!'

'Er, I'm not too sure about that.' I hesitated, all of a sudden becoming the cautious lawyer. 'Let me think about it and get back to you'.

Before I'd thought about it and got back to him, Ted was busily telling me in another phone call that he'd implemented his plan. Not only had he moved the hen bird, as intended, but the cock had reacted as he thought he would, pursuing her into the barn. Ah, the power of lust, I mused. That was not all he had to report: judging by the noises he was now hearing (described in the field guides as 'repeated staccato squeaking'), the pair were making up, with great frequency, for their previous frustrations. Such sounds were music to the ears of the livestock farmer, immersed in the fecund world of semen banks, A.I.D. and calving. To me, hidebound by rules and procedures, Ted's novel approach was rather disconcerting, but there was nothing for it, I decided, but to shrug my shoulders and see how things worked out.

Ted obviously possessed the farmer's equivalent of the gardener's green fingers because, within a few weeks, the unmistakeable chittering of recently-hatched owlets could clearly be heard. Mind you, the quarters he had created for them were little short of magnificent. One end of the barn, at first floor level, had been sectioned off with sheets of stout wire mesh attached to a sturdy wooden frame to create a large room, or flight, whilst up aloft, under the eaves and hard against the gable end, was a triangular wooden structure that looked something like an elevated dog kennel, with a hinged door facing into the room. The other end faced directly onto the pop-hole, from which an incoming owl would drop down a foot or two onto the kennel floor. Ted explained that, during the years when his farm had been without resident barn owls, this kennel area had been partitioned off as a home for ornamental pigeons, so he had simply refurbished the existing structure. The space thus created was large enough for a tea chest to be placed inside to provide a more sheltered nesting area. As well as fitting tree branches across the main flight, to ensure plenty of perching places, Ted had built up a great wall of hay bales in which the owls could find tunnels and crevices when they were feeling particularly unsociable. The absence of any windows meant that the whole room was half-dark, at best, so the entire set-up had the feel, and even the smell, of a traditional barn owl nest site from years before. Ted had come very close to recreating his happy childhood memories.

Technically, because the cock bird was wild-bred, the site now qualified for special protection under the Wildlife and Countryside Act. Ringing of the offspring would therefore have to be carried out by the holder of a Schedule 1 licence. This refers to many species of birds listed in the Act. It is an offence, carrying especially high penalties, intentionally to disturb any such bird while it is building a nest or is in, on or near a nest containing eggs or young. However, a licence could be granted (in those days by a body called the Nature Conservancy Council, now Natural England) to disturb even these species for the purpose of ringing or marking, or examining any ring or mark on them.

This, I thought, was clearly a mission for my friend David, the holder of a Schedule 1 licence, who, as ever, was only too happy to oblige. However, despite – or maybe because of - being the learned author of the BTO's guidance on physical risks involved in ringing activities, with sections on cliffs, quarries and trees, David steadfastly refused to do any clambering about above ground level. That was to be my job, as the ringer's apprentice. Having climbed the usual rickety wooden stairs to the first floor of the barn, and heeded Ted's advice to avoid certain places where the floorboards were 'a bit unsafe' (a euphemism for missing), we finally entered the area which he'd partitioned off. Ted followed close behind with a ladder he'd collected from the farmyard. Wedging one end firmly against a stout horizontal rail that had been fastened to the floor to form the base of the partition, we gently lowered the other end to rest on the kennel twenty feet or so above our heads.

'OK, here goes,' I murmured as I began my ascent, at a pace that would have tried the patience of a snail. My timid progress was slowed even more when Ted suddenly hissed: 'Watch out, there's one or two rungs missing!' His warning was only just in time – in the semi-darkness of the barn, I hadn't spotted the gaps I was heading for.

'Are you sure these bloody ladders are safe?' I snapped back, beginning to regret not checking them out in daylight.

'Oh yes,' came the unfazed reply, 'I fished them out of the river ages ago!'

I glanced down towards David standing at the foot of the wonky ladder and, although not able to see the look on his face, I knew exactly what he would be thinking – 'Tight bugger – too bloody mean to go out and buy a new set!'

Ignoring further distractions, I edged gingerly onwards and upwards towards the kennel. Once up there, I could see that it was a lot bigger than it seemed from down below, more Rottweiler than Yorkshire terrier. Sticking my head through the open door, I peered inside. It was certainly spacious – and cold, I noticed, as a chill wind whistled through the brickwork and struck me full in the face. Very sensibly, I thought, the young owls had left their converted tea chest, which would be far from windproof, and huddled together in a small group in the lee of the gable wall. Like penguins on an Antarctic ice field, their combined body heat would provide some protection from the howling gale that was being channelled through the pop-hole. There was a disadvantage, though, from my point of view: in this position, the owlets were impossible to reach unless I eased my shoulders through the opening and then squirmed on my belly into the kennel itself, leaving only my legs protruding from the entrance.

'I hope to God it's more solidly built than the rest of this farm,' I muttered darkly, thinking of the complex risk assessments I would have been required to carry out if I'd been on official business from work. Although the kennel seemed sound enough, I still had visions of tumbling suddenly onto the hay bales below, accompanied by shattered lengths of wood, a tea chest and several terrified owlets. Remarkably, the apparently jerry-built structure withstood my great weight long enough for me to capture the three plump youngsters, stuff them gently into a canvas bag, and retreat with them down the ladder, taking care to compensate once more for the missing rungs. The owlets were duly ringed by David and returned by me to their living quarters, where they immediately scuttled back to the shelter of their windbreak against the gable wall. Throughout the whole procedure, the parent birds had kept a determinedly low profile, skulking inside the wall of hay bales or squeezing into gaps in the brickwork.

Although, once settled, barn owl pairs tend to stay loyal to one nest site, this situation is much more difficult to achieve artificially. From the releaser's point of view, a site may seem ideal, with a sympathetic landowner, a plentiful supply of prey and safe nesting and roosting places. However desirable from a human perspective, though, it is more likely than not that the owls will find something not quite right about the site: perhaps it isn't quiet enough, or it might be too draughty. This pernicketiness was vividly illustrated by Ted's experience. Once he was certain that the youngsters were no longer dependent on their parents, he propped open the wire mesh door to the partitioned end of the barn, allowing the owls free range throughout the whole building, and access to the outside world.

'I thought they needed more room,' he told me (again, after the event) as we climbed the wooden steps to the first floor of his barn. 'Besides, I reckoned it might help with all the rats I'd got up here.'

'R-rats?' The question all but stuck in the back of my throat as a sudden feeling of panic began to take hold.

'Yes, terrible they were,' Ted continued, oblivious to the fact that I was about to bolt back down the steps at any moment. 'Look, this is rat damage.' He pointed to piles of what had once been tightly-packed bales of hay, but was now just a loose heap of material, like stuffing that had been violently pulled out of an old settee.

'It was that bad', he continued (quite unnecessarily, I thought), 'that I was too frightened to come up here. You could hear them after dark, rustling and squeaking all over the place'.

My head was on a swivel, my ears pricked more intently than any farmyard cat's, as I tried desperately to work out whether we were, at that very moment, surrounded by a pack of loathsome brown rats. One of my granddads, a veteran of the First World War, used to horrify my brothers and me with stories about 'rats as big as cats' that inhabited the Belgian barns where he and his comrades would sometimes spend the night. The soldiers could feel these rats running about on top of them as they lay, trying to get some sleep, in the pitch dark.

'Mind you,' – Ted was, regrettably, still on the unwelcome subject of *Rattus norvegicus* – 'within two weeks of setting the owls free, all the rats were gone. Not one left. I've never seen a trace of them up here since'.

He couldn't possibly have known how relieved I was to hear this. If a hard-bitten character like my friend admitted to being scared, then a townie such as me could surely be forgiven for reacting with a feeling that bordered on utter panic. Besides, I thought, he's only confirmed exactly what I've been telling landowners for years – that a resident family of feathered rat-catchers is just as effective as poison, and a damn sight more environmentally-friendly. Ted's cavalier attitude to rules and procedures certainly seemed to have paid off.

It didn't all go Ted's way, however. The following year, the pair chose their own nest site, abandoning the five-star luxury of the loft and plumping instead for the inner depths of the barn, where even less daylight could penetrate and the floors were peppered with holes. For the nest itself, they chose the disused kitchen unit that Ted had previously hoisted into the rafters. Clearly irritated by this perverse decision, akin to moving from a well-appointed detached home to a broken-down hovel, Ted and his wife and daughter still managed to enjoy plenty of barn owl sightings. It may not have been as comfortable as sitting in a warm room overlooking the barn gable, but he would proudly report on how he had waited quietly in his pick-up truck in the farm yard to watch the owls' comings and goings.

'One night,' he told me, 'I watched the cock bird bring back twenty one prey items in just over an hour. As soon as he'd delivered one, he was straight back out again.' This was at the height of the owlets' growing phase, when each bird could easily account for three or four small rodents, or their equivalent, per night. With demanding infants of my own, I knew exactly the pressures that the parent birds were under, though in my case I didn't need to resort to pursuing live prey.

32   *Some ups and downs*

Just as with the accidental drowning at George's farm, I had distinctly negative experiences at some release sites. As I frequently explained to would-be releasers and other interested folk, there were plenty of dangers to be faced, particularly by newly-fledged owlets when they struck out on their own.

'But don't you get attached to them?' I was often asked, as if the owls were pets, like cats or dogs. The truth was that I didn't, although I did at times suffer strong doubts about the usefulness of my breeding and release project. My worries were essentially twofold: firstly, whether captive breeding and release was an effective conservation measure, and secondly, even if it were, whether it was fair to the individual birds that I bred and released. As time went by and I read and heard about conservation efforts throughout the world – from the California condor and the black-footed ferret in the USA, to the return of the sea eagle to Scotland and the red kite to Wales – the more I realised that the facts and arguments on the subject were as intricate and interrelated as the reasons for the decline or disappearance of a species in the first place. Although that realisation, in itself, did not answer the underlying questions, every source I could consult suggested strongly to me that, given a fighting chance, life, in whatever manifestation, will find a way to flourish. My answer, therefore, to the critics and sceptics was that, properly undertaken, captive breeding and release schemes could help a depleted wild population to recover its numbers, or at least arrest further decline. Conversely, a badly-executed release can have disastrous consequences. So when a ringer volunteered to me at a conference that he'd once ringed five or six owlets on behalf of a release scheme and that within a couple of weeks they were all found dead on a nearby road, I replied that the answer was obvious. It wasn't that captive breeding and release schemes are inherently wrong, as he was implying, but that an unsuitable release site had been used in that instance.

My positive views about what I was doing were reinforced by the subsequent appearance of a nesting pair in many previously barn owl-free localities where I'd recently carried out releases. The fact that these pairs often didn't crop up until several years after my releases in that area made me doubt the usefulness of some of the information now being required from releasers by the Department of the Environment under its new licensing scheme. For instance, all the end-of-year reports had to be submitted by 1 December in the year of release and included questions such as whether any of the released birds were still on or around the site. There was no follow-up to find out what the situation was in subsequent years. What's more, a scientific study carried out by Keele University, which drew on data that I had supplied and fieldwork that I had taken part in, compared survival rates of

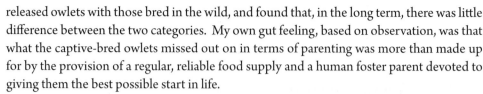

released owlets with those bred in the wild, and found that, in the long term, there was little difference between the two categories. My own gut feeling, based on observation, was that what the captive-bred owlets missed out on in terms of parenting was more than made up for by the provision of a regular, reliable food supply and a human foster parent devoted to giving them the best possible start in life.

Even so, there were plenty of downs to counteract the ups. More then once, newly-fledged owlets were almost certainly taken by foxes – in one case, all that remained of the unfortunate bird were a few chewed-off feathers and a BTO ring, which the fox had spat out. At another release site, a bird was found dead in suspicious circumstances. The releaser, David, was convinced that it had been shot, despite the absence of any sign of this on the carcass. Even a thorough post mortem, carried out by a vet friend of mine, failed to reassure David and he insisted that I remove the other owl because he feared that it would suffer the same fate. Other releasers were more sanguine about losses, accepting the statistic I trotted out that, in the wild, only one in three of a year's crop of owlets would be likely to survive its first winter and be alive to breed the following year.

And there were plenty of positive experiences. At one release site, the owner told me, he'd organised a pheasant shoot. When he'd bellowed at the shooters 'Watch out for my barn owls!' they'd all thought he was joking, until he pointed out that a pair had been breeding successfully on his land for the last few years. He'd left them in no doubt about the ferocity of his reaction if any harm should befall his beloved owls. Fortunately for all concerned, they failed to put in an appearance. By contrast, Derek, a pig farmer turned restaurateur, was regaling some guests at his home one evening with stories of how lucky they would be to catch sight of the owls we'd released there. These people, too, must have thought they were having their legs pulled. As Derek and his wife Kath later told me, no sooner had he uttered his pessimistic prediction than everyone present was treated to the most breathtaking aerial display by the adult owls. Right outside the house, as if performing a Red Arrows display, they twisted and turned at speed, one following closely behind the other as though linked by an invisible thread. As they flew hither and thither, they uttered a variety of rasping screeches and loud wailing noises, most unlike the friendly hooting sounds associated by many people with owls of any description.

'I'm sure our friends thought we'd staged it,' Derek remarked, 'but it was far better than any entertainment we could possibly have laid on'.

33 Fred's story

I knew that I wasn't the only one in the country, but I was happy enough to be referred to as 'the owl man'. Sometimes, that was exactly how I would introduce myself, particularly to people I'd met only once or twice before. So, depending on who answered the telephone, or opened the door, my stock greeting would be something along the lines of 'Hello – it's Paul Hackney, the owl man', or 'Please can you tell so-and-so it's the owl man?'

Not only did my reputation and nickname bring me many useful contacts, but they produced some totally unexpected encounters with owls. Although many of these incidents involved other species of owl – an 'orphaned' tawny that would have been perfectly safe left in its tree or that 'helpless baby' that turned out to be a fully-grown, well-armed and rather annoyed little owl – my main concern was always with the much rarer barn owl. Many referrals came via organisations such as the Hawk and Owl Trust or Chester Zoo, but others came from individuals, who'd perhaps seen one of my talks, or read about my conservation work. I wouldn't have wanted it any other way, because it was through such contacts that I had some of my most fascinating experiences.

One day the telephone rang at home.

'Hello, it's the PDSA here'.

Convinced that they must be trying to sell me something I didn't want, and unsure what PDSA stood for, I was about to reply politely that I wasn't interested and put down the phone, when the caller suddenly used the magic words: 'We've got a barn owl here – can you help?' Quickly ascertaining that the organisation was the People's Dispensary for Sick Animals – a charity that treats the pets of those who are unable to pay full vets' bills – I got directions and was on my way within minutes.

As with many such unexpected call-outs, I was ushered on my arrival towards a box-shaped object draped with a piece of cloth; in this case an old curtain. Gently pulling it away, I felt rather like a magician slowly revealing the contents of his top hat on stage, though I was far less confident about what might pop out. Given the surgery's location, in a run-down urban backstreet, I had a strong premonition that what I would be uncovering in my trick would be a common old tawny owl rather than a rare barn owl, as billed. I'd be like Tommy Cooper, producing a scruffy feral pigeon instead of a gleaming white dove. To my astonishment, however, the people at the People's Dispensary had got it right: *Tyto alba alba* it was.

'It's a male,' I announced self-assuredly to the little throng of white-coated staff who were crowding round. I reached carefully into the box to cup my hands gently around the bird's body. To my relief, there was no aggressive tongue clicking, no vicious pecking or frantic striking out with stiletto-sharp talons, but simply a contented chirrup and a long, mournful stare from two large, circular black eyes.

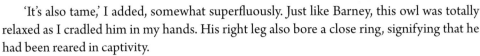

'It's also tame,' I added, somewhat superfluously. Just like Barney, this owl was totally relaxed as I cradled him in my hands. His right leg also bore a close ring, signifying that he had been reared in captivity.

Convinced by now that I was a genuine expert, my audience couldn't wait to tell me the owl's story. Apparently, he'd come to grief after colliding with a telephone wire whilst flying about the city's streets in broad daylight. I stressed that both this behaviour and the habitat he'd been found in were totally unnatural.

'He must have escaped from his owner,' I suggested.

'Haven't you heard?' came the amazed response. 'It's been all over the local radio, appealing for the owner to come forward, telling people to contact us. The phone's never stopped ringing!'

'And I bet you've had some right nutters on,' I muttered to myself. 'Well,' I said, turning to the audience, 'the true owner will have to provide proof of ownership – you can't just hand him over to anyone, you know'.

'Er, we were hoping you might take care of that'. The duty vet now weighed in. 'I've examined it, you see, and can't find anything wrong other than a bruised wing. We don't have the facilities to look after it here'.

My heart sank. I could see what would happen: I'd end up accommodating another emotional cripple, just like Barney, who was too tame to fraternise with his own kind and add to my breeding stock, but also totally incapable of coping with freedom, as his recent mishap had amply demonstrated.

'I suppose I'd better have him for now,' I sighed. With as much enthusiasm as I could muster, I began to lower the owl back into his box.

'C'mon, Fred.' The name simply popped out. I could have used any words, but the owl responded instantly, turning its head and fixing me with a knowing stare. No doubt his response to a random name was just a coincidence, but I decided there and then that Fred he was, and Fred he would remain.

Having extracted a promise from the PDSA staff that they would not divulge my private telephone number to callers, I rushed Fred home and housed him, alone, in a spare aviary. Almost immediately, I set about the task of tracking down his owner by first of all telephoning the British Bird Council (BBC), who had originally issued the close ring that was secured around his leg. The woman I spoke to there was most unforthcoming, but eventually agreed to make a note of Fred's ring number and my contact details. It was then simply a matter of waiting to see if he would be claimed.

Fred was certainly no trouble. A gentle, undemanding soul, he was quite content to sit in an aviary and dine on two or three chicks a day. As I'd suspected, he showed no interest in any of my other barn owls and undertook very little activity of any kind. He seemed perfectly content with this thoroughly tedious existence. After a few months, despite his lethargy, which contrasted markedly with Barney's frequent attention-seeking displays, I began to grow quite fond of old Fred. I was convinced that he would become a permanent fixture. Then, one day, the telephone rang. On the line, to my surprise, was a rather assertive individual who claimed to be Fred's owner. Despite their promise, the PDSA had clearly given out my telephone number.

'I lost him last August,' he stated. As that was nearly a year before, I was more than a little suspicious.

'There's no way that this bird spent any time living in the wild before he was passed to me,' I retorted.

'It's definitely my bird'. He'd obviously been tipped off by the BBC. 'I lost it, along with another one. They either escaped or got stolen. When can I have it back?'

The caller was certainly persistent and none too pleased when I said that I'd have to check with the PDSA before I handed Fred over to anyone. Secretly, of course, I was hoping they'd say no. The caller, not to be so easily put off, began to provide more information, though in a slightly menacing tone of voice. He'd reported the presumed theft to the police, he said, and made a veiled threat to involve them again if I wasn't co-operative. He also reeled off the names of several of the birds' previous owners.

'Oh, I know him!' I recognised one of the individuals, a captive breeder and dealer, not a conservationist, but at least someone who, in my experience had always acted properly and followed the rules. At last I began to feel that I was probably not being told a cock-and-bull story. Having insisted that Fred was not mine to give away and that I was only minding him, I lost no time in contacting the PDSA. Reluctantly, I told them that I thought there was little option but to return the owl to the person claiming to be his owner.

It wasn't long after that I was on my way to return Fred to his last-known place of residence. On arrival, my forebodings seemed as if they might have been justified. Although I was sure that no deliberate cruelty would be involved, I could see instantly that Fred would be condemned, like thousands of other imprinted barn owls, to a dull existence in a cramped aviary set in a small suburban back garden. Just like a glorified budgie, I thought. Unlike parrots or canaries, however, barn owls do not learn to speak or sing mellifluous songs, nor do their feeding habits, as Barney's original owner had found out, make them suitable for indoor living. Anyone who has been lucky enough to see the bird in its natural habitat, fluttering over open ground like a huge white moth, would doubtless share my distaste at the thought of such a beautiful creature sitting, instead, hunched up and inactive within the four walls of an aviary. Feeling like a warder returning a convict to jail after a failed escape attempt, I began to wonder whether Fred's owner might be prepared to sell him to me. On the point of making him an offer, I began to think seriously about the situation that prevailed at home. Constantly struggling for aviary space, I already had some permanent residents: Barney, of course, who did at least act as a prop during my talks on conservation; and my tame magpie, Pica, who had lived with me for many years. Through my activities as a Licensed Rehabilitation Keeper, I also looked after a variety of other bird species, which had all to be accommodated, depending on their state of health, in cages and aviaries of many shapes and sizes. This in turn put immense pressure on the space and facilities available for breeding barn owls. Looked at from this point of view, I had to concede that returning Fred to his owner was the only rational thing to do. I couldn't afford another passenger. So, bidding him a fond farewell, I left Fred to continue his bland suburban existence.

Just as cash flow is said to be the lifeblood of any business, so a throughput of owls was the essence of my project. Occasionally, the required stock would come from a totally unexpected source. On the north bank of the river Mersey, sandwiched between Liverpool, Runcorn and Warrington, lies the chemical town of Widnes – an unlovely place associated with hard men in flat caps, dedicated to their whippets, meat pies and rugby league (not necessarily in that order). You could certainly be forgiven for thinking that this was no place

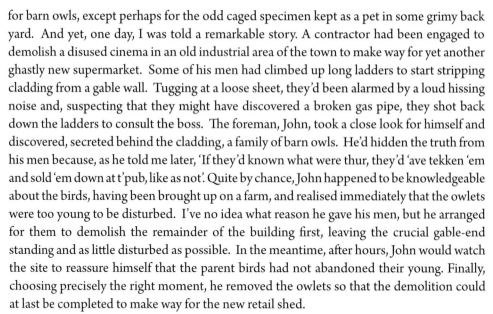

for barn owls, except perhaps for the odd caged specimen kept as a pet in some grimy back yard. And yet, one day, I was told a remarkable story. A contractor had been engaged to demolish a disused cinema in an old industrial area of the town to make way for yet another ghastly new supermarket. Some of his men had climbed up long ladders to start stripping cladding from a gable wall. Tugging at a loose sheet, they'd been alarmed by a loud hissing noise and, suspecting that they might have discovered a broken gas pipe, they shot back down the ladders to consult the boss. The foreman, John, took a close look for himself and discovered, secreted behind the cladding, a family of barn owls. He'd hidden the truth from his men because, as he told me later, 'If they'd known what were thur, they'd 'ave tekken 'em and sold 'em down at t'pub, like as not'. Quite by chance, John happened to be knowledgeable about the birds, having been brought up on a farm, and realised immediately that the owlets were too young to be disturbed. I've no idea what reason he gave his men, but he arranged for them to demolish the remainder of the building first, leaving the crucial gable-end standing and as little disturbed as possible. In the meantime, after hours, John would watch the site to reassure himself that the parent birds had not abandoned their young. Finally, choosing precisely the right moment, he removed the owlets so that the demolition could at last be completed to make way for the new retail shed.

It was a ranger from a local country park who passed the rescued owlets on to me and told me their fascinating story. When I later spoke to John, I felt I had to compliment him on his superb timing – the three plump, healthy owlets that the ranger produced were between five and six weeks old, the ideal age for relocation.

'It's a pity they 'ad to be disturbed,' he mused, 'but ah s'ppose that's progress. Parents buggered off, o' course!'

The big challenge now was what should be done with this windfall brood. Fortunately, some naturalist friends of mine agreed to help out by preparing a site from which the birds could be released as if they had been captive-bred. Even better, my friends agreed to carry out the release so that I could concentrate on my own birds. After keeping the youngsters under observation for a couple of days, I was sure that they were as fit and healthy as they appeared, and arranged to meet the others at the release site. Once there, the birds were ringed and placed in the nest box in the usual way. When I'd first received the owlets, I'd saved one of the pellets they'd regurgitated. Curious to have some idea of the prey they'd been raised on – I strongly suspected it was predominantly mice and rats – I asked one of the site operators, Charles, if he'd like to analyse the pellet for me. He subsequently reported that he'd found only vole and shrew remains, which suggested, assuming that the pellet's contents were typical, that the parent birds had found somewhere more rural to hunt than the immediate built-up surroundings of the old cinema.

Perhaps encouraged by his pellet analysis, Charles suggested that, if possible, the relocated owlets should be provided with a varied diet.

'I'm sure I've got field mice coming into my conservatory at home,' he claimed. 'I'll try to borrow some Longworth traps to catch them in. We could release them here, so the owlets might also be able to practise hunting'. Provided he was prepared to make the necessary effort, I was all for Charles's suggestion, although, based on my experience, I doubted whether any self-respecting wild mouse introduced into the release building would stick around long enough to give the owlets free target practice.

A few days later, Charles asked me to meet him at the release site. He was clearly pleased with himself, announcing that he'd captured several 'field mice'. When I arrived, along with Nick, the young chap who'd helped with the release at George's farm, Charles opened his car boot with a flourish and gestured towards a large glass tank which he'd furnished with balls of hay and a covering of wood shavings. In silence, Nick and I both studied the captives as they ricocheted around the tank in a desperate search for some cover. We exchanged knowing glances, which clearly signalled, amongst other things, that it was up to me to communicate our thoughts to Charles. My dilemma, in a nutshell, was how best to tell a keen naturalist that he'd confused the comparatively benign wood mouse with the indisputably pestilential house mouse. The former, as its alternative name of long-tailed field mouse suggests, has a very long, smooth tail, a sandy-brown coat and a white chest and belly. Although both species certainly have large eyes and ears and pointed noses, the common house mouse is much less attractive with a grey-brown greasy coat and a distinctly scaly tail. There's no getting away from it: they're easily distinguishable from one another.

When I pointed out the error, as tactfully as I could, Charles was aghast. This had more to do, I think, with the fact that there was an infestation of house mice in his home than his embarrassment at making such an obvious mistake. He shrank back from the open car boot as if the contents had suddenly become contagious, leaving Nick and me to work out the best way of transporting the mice to the release building, a short distance away. In an unexpected show of bravado, prompted no doubt by Charles's hesitation, Nick plunged his hand into the tank.

'I'll show you how to handle a mouse!' he declared, plucking one forth.

His captive, though, was having none of it. In a clear demonstration of the survival instinct that has ensured the worldwide success of the species, the tiny creature promptly bit Nick hard on the thumb and, as he momentarily loosened his grip, wriggled free and made for the nearest escape route. A tempting, dark tunnel presented itself, so the mouse darted up the sleeve of my young friend's baggy sweater. Nick now began to twitch and jerk, like someone suffering from St Vitus's dance, as the mouse scurried, unseen, up one sleeve, across his shoulders, down the other sleeve, and, emerging at the wrist, leapt the remaining three feet to the ground, before disappearing in a trice into the undergrowth.

'Er, I think we'll try something else,' Nick muttered, as the rest of us dissolved into hysterical laughter.

Abandoning the Laurel and Hardy approach, we concluded that the sensible action would be to carry the tank, with the remaining mice, to the release site. We then gently tipped it on one side, allowing the occupants to escape with the same speed and efficiency as their erstwhile companion.

From that point on, the whole relocation exercise proceeded smoothly, the youngsters receiving a back-up food supply of dead day-old chicks whilst they fledged and eventually dispersed. As for the relocated mice, Charles heard from the landowner 18 months later that an adult barn owl was hanging around the site. He collected some pellets for analysis, he told me, and I'd never guess what he found in them. As well as the remains of rats, common and pygmy shrews, and birds, he was absolutely confident that the bird's prey had included house mouse. I was far too polite to say so, and I valued our friendship too much, but I very much doubted that someone who'd failed to distinguish a wood mouse from a house mouse in the flesh could be trusted to get it right by examining their minute remains. I knew from my own analysis of pellets that the differences between the skulls of the two species are subtle, to say the least: as the standard guide on pellets states, the only certain way is to examine their dentition, by removing the first cheek teeth from the upper jaws and counting the number of roots (or holes in the jaw bone) – the wood mouse has four, whereas the house mouse can muster only three.

34 *A fortunate rescue*

Barn owls, like many other species, do manage to crop up in some rather unusual places. Sadly, for all the positive incidences, such as the Trafford Park and Widnes stories, and despite assurances about their survival abilities, such as the claim by an RSPB warden at Symonds Yat, a famous cliff overlooking the River Wye in Herefordshire, that barn owls regularly nested there without mishap alongside peregrine falcons, most of my unexpected encounters involved corpses or casualties. I know that I am not the only naturalist who, whilst driving along in a car, has a distinct tendency to start (a little unnervingly for my passengers) at any small white object lying by the roadside. More often than not, the 'casualty' turns out to be an abandoned plastic bag or disposable nappy, but occasionally a dramatic slamming on of brakes, or performing of a U-turn, has confirmed my worst fears: yet another barn owl mown down by traffic. One live find, however, occurred in totally unexpected circumstances.

Answering the telephone to a call from Ted one day, I assumed that he must be making one of his periodic requests for a fresh supply of dead day-old chicks. At the time, he was feeding a number of captive birds, including a permanently disabled tawny owl which he had agreed to look after for me. To the delight of his young daughter, if not of his wife Angela, he accommodated the owl in an aviary he'd built against the side of the farmhouse. Even Ted had to admit that this may have been a mistake. As he put it: 'She can't half hoot; she sounds as if she's sitting on the bedpost right next to you when she gets going'. Fortunately, he didn't seem to bear a grudge against me for his family's sleepless nights, though I was never sure that the same could be said for Angela. I soon found that I was wrong about the reason for his phone call.

'You'll never believe what I've found!' He sounded very excited. 'A barn owl!' he continued, before I could hazard a guess.

My first thought was that one of his captive owls must have escaped, but Ted answered my question without my needing to ask it.

'It's an unringed adult – a hen, I think. I've got her here in a box'.

Without waiting for an invitation, I told Ted I'd be there as quickly as I could. When I arrived at his farm a short time later, he insisted on first recounting at length how he'd come by the bird before allowing me to view it, though I was itching to peer into the box. Apparently, whilst wandering around the place, he'd spotted a gang of crows down in the fields pecking at a fluttering object which he took to be discarded litter, such as an old newspaper or plastic carrier bag. Then he'd suddenly realised that, far from being a piece of man-made detritus, the object of the corvids' attention was a bird, and what was more, that

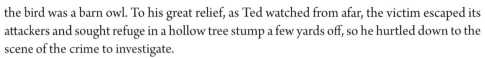

the bird was a barn owl. To his great relief, as Ted watched from afar, the victim escaped its attackers and sought refuge in a hollow tree stump a few yards off, so he hurtled down to the scene of the crime to investigate.

'I'd seen exactly where it went,' he explained, 'but could I find the bloomin' thing? I felt down every hole in that tree stump, but I found nothing. I was ready to give up'. I could picture him, cap in hand, leaning back and scratching his head in bewilderment. 'But on my last try, I stretched in up to my shoulder and just felt the bird's claws with the tips of my fingers'.

The fugitive had obviously retreated as deep into its hollow sanctuary as it possibly could, given the terrifying attack launched on it by the crows.

'It wasn't too happy when I hauled it out by one of its toes,' Ted concluded his tale. He was clearly proud of his piece of detective work, and I must say that I was impressed by it too.

At last, with the story complete, I had my chance to examine the rescued owl. Like the farmer, I was concerned that the bird's assailants may have inflicted some grievous bodily harm with their powerful bills. I knew from experience how devastating a weapon the corvid beak can be: not only had I witnessed my tame magpie, Pica, kill and then butcher with great efficiency several sparrows that had inadvertently strayed into his aviary, but I also remembered watching with mounting horror the systematic demolition, from within, of a wooden-walled aviary in which I'd temporarily placed a young rescued raven. In both cases, the beak was used alternately as a chisel and a jemmy.

To our great relief, what I found in the box appeared to be a perfectly healthy, if somewhat subdued, adult female barn owl, none the worse for the mugging she'd suffered.

'I think I'll hang on to her for a couple of days, just to check her flying ability, and so on', I suggested, before firmly closing the box and placing it in the boot of my car.

Sure enough, a brief spell in a quiet aviary proved that my first impression had been correct: the owl flew well, fed happily on the chicks I gave her, and showed no sign of any physical damage. I was sure that she'd had a very close shave indeed. Although that January's weather had been unseasonably mild, it wouldn't necessarily mean that owls could or would do all their hunting at night. Particularly in the winter months, they are prone to hunt during daylight hours – a boon to the ornithologist, but also a distinct opportunity for diurnal species to indulge in some mobbing, mugging, or something even worse. I was also relieved that the find hadn't been made in the summer months, as I would then have been faced with the dilemma of whether to keep the owl under observation for a couple of days, as I did, or to release her immediately in case she was caring for dependent young.

Fortunately for all, everything fell nicely into place. The weather stayed unusually fine and tolerably warm, so I arranged for the owl to be ringed by David, and Ted and I together released her close to the hollow tree in which she'd hidden from the crows. It was dusk, and the bird flew off strongly across the rough grassland surrounding a large sewage farm that bordered on Ted's land. Not only was this ideal foraging territory, but within a few hundred yards, there also lay a large, formal, but long-neglected, country estate which included areas of low-lying marshland bordering a meandering river. As I watched the owl disappear into the gloom of the night, I secretly wished her well.

When I next saw him, Ted told me that, about a fortnight after the release, some shooters of his acquaintance had reported seeing a barn owl sitting on a post by the sewage farm. I fervently hoped it was the bird we'd released and that she'd taken full advantage of her lucky second chance.

35   Hazards of the job

As well as priceless interactions with wildlife, my owl conservation activities have also brought me into contact with some fascinating human beings. I was flabbergasted one day when, on being asked how long his family had owned their estate, a young farmer replied nonchalantly 'Oh, since 1069'. That would take some beating, I thought; as I imagined the political nous that the whole clan must have possessed in order to hang on to the same land through many centuries of often turbulent change. Perhaps it was just down to eccentricity. The same individual proudly showed me a brace of nice fat trout he'd 'caught' by hurling a stick of dynamite into a local stream; and, once, creeping about in one of his barns at dead of night – with his prior permission – I spotted a trail of blood. Following it across the floor, I found, of all things, a poor moorhen that, for some inexplicable reason, had been shot and strung up on a hook.

I have also met highly practical people, including elderly ladies, totally unfazed at the prospect of climbing up and down ladders to access a release site; and, by contrast, others who have virtually fainted at the mention of feeding owls on dead day-old chicks. I wondered what they expected owls to eat: nice, convenient, dry pellets, perhaps as the PR woman at the zoo had imagined, or slices of prime fillet steak, gift-wrapped by the local butcher? With some would-be releasers, it rapidly became apparent that they saw the installation of owls on their properties as an extension of a homes-and-gardens design service: 'They won't make a mess will they?' Needless to say, such ill-informed folk unwittingly ruled themselves out of taking part in my project. Judging them unsuitable, I told them I had too few owls available to furnish their particular site, and that the best I could do was to 'put them on the list' (which, of course, did not exist). Occasionally, this would simply be construed as playing hard to get, prompting the unwelcome question: 'How much do I have to pay you then?' With a curt statement that I never bought or sold owls, I would promptly take my leave. Such landowners would not even make it on to my pretend list.

There were also some once-in-a lifetime experiences to be had by people who were not directly involved in releases, but who made the mistake of volunteering to help. Cleaning out aviaries and building nest boxes were two of the less noxious tasks available. Collecting and handling food supplies, though just as vital to the project, were distinctly less popular activities. In my project's early days, the wife of a work colleague, a committed vegetarian, happened to be working as a technician on a scientific study of eyesight. This apparently required large supplies of day-old chick retinas, meaning that all parts except the heads were surplus. Asked if I would like to have the decapitated corpses for my owls, I leapt at the offer, emphasising, however, that they must be fresh. For several years thereafter, my colleague would regularly trudge into the office bearing carrier bags full of grisly chick remains, which I would gratefully receive from him before rushing home to stick them in my freezer, rather than leave them lying around the office to go off or be discovered by my boss.

Despite the provision of freebies such as these, I also had to buy owl food in bulk, particularly in the breeding season. Although the charges made by the poultry industry were modest, the dealers always insisted on supplying their produce in multiples of five hundred or a thousand. I soon found out that I couldn't just bung a dustbin liner full of dead chicks into the freezer, as they then formed into a solid mass from which individual birds could be extracted only with the help of a hammer and chisel. So bagging chicks became a regular, and very tedious, part of the project. The aim of this eccentric activity was to end up with sandwich bags containing more manageable quantities, say, fifty chicks each. There seemed to be no alternative to laboriously counting out fifty at a time for as long as it took. Although I felt terribly guilty about it for years afterwards – this was a job I usually reserved for myself – I once accepted the offer of help from a couple of local university students I'd got to know. Both were Chinese nationals, one a medical student and the other a research scientist. If they'd volunteered only out of politeness, the same motive may perhaps have inhibited them from declining the task I proceeded to outline to them. Equipping them with gloves and face masks, I abandoned the pair on the front lawn of my house while I beetled off to attend to some other matter. They must have regarded the exercise as a kind of initiative test because, when I returned a couple of hours later, the volunteers proudly demonstrated to me how they'd devised a much more methodical system than counting out each individual corpse. Instead, the students had used a sheet of card to make a cone-shaped funnel large enough to hold precisely fifty chicks – no more, no less – and deployed it as a chute to fill the sandwich bags in a fraction of the time I would have taken to do it by hand. They beamed with pride as they gave me a demonstration, and I was only too happy to acknowledge the merits of taking a scientific approach.

Equally impressive was the readiness with which many of my contacts approached food storage. Despite dire warnings from me about the risks of salmonella contamination, very few releasers bothered to equip themselves with a dedicated freezer, as I had. Instead, they would happily stuff 'fifty-chick bags' in amongst the frozen peas and pizzas stored in their domestic appliances.

Sometimes, out of genuine concern, I would try a jokey, rather than my usual serious, approach:

'Watch out, you might get chick pie served up for tea!'

At other times, I would emphasise seriously the need for cleanliness:

'Make sure you always wash your hands after handling chicks.'

But my warnings fell on deaf ears. Even the professionals disregarded my advice, although, as a lawyer, I'm used to that. From my close acquaintance with the world of environmental health officers, I was well aware that any food establishment found with such items on their premises would instantly be on the receiving end of an emergency closure order. Yet this risk didn't seem to deter one of my friends who, in his freezers, merrily combined bagged-up chicks with home-cooked pies and cakes prepared for use in his Egon Ronay-recommended restaurant. Fortunately, as a regular customer, I don't remember chicken ever figuring prominently on his menu.

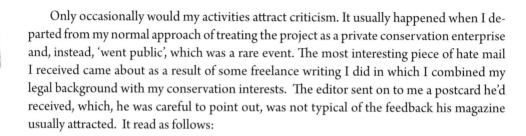

Only occasionally would my activities attract criticism. It usually happened when I departed from my normal approach of treating the project as a private conservation enterprise and, instead, 'went public', which was a rare event. The most interesting piece of hate mail I received came about as a result of some freelance writing I did in which I combined my legal background with my conservation interests. The editor sent on to me a postcard he'd received, which, he was careful to point out, was not typical of the feedback his magazine usually attracted. It read as follows:

'Dear Sir,

Recently His Royal Hypocrisy the Duke of Edinburgh killed two barn owls whilst out hunting.

 You claim to be a conservationist and solicitor trained, let's hear more about it from you then!*

Yours sincerely,

No Money for Private Action

A. PAUPER.

*The exclamation mark is because I doubt we will, in fact, I suspet [sic] you will be fawning all over him like all the rest of 'em.'

Needless to say, I didn't bother to reply, nor did I attempt to take the matter up with Buckingham Palace.

On occasion, it wasn't so much the people who alarmed me as the animals they kept. My years growing up in the Lake District, hearing my Dad's frequent dire warnings about the murderous bulls that might be lurking behind any hedge or wall, and having seen injuries such as the long, deep gash inflicted on a friend's hand when he'd attempted to feed his uncle's prize boar, had left me with a healthy regard for self-preservation, particularly around livestock. Predictably, however, it was other denizens of the farmyard who provided me with the most uncomfortably close encounters. The border collie, the breed most beloved of upland sheep farmers because of its tireless help with rounding up and herding the stock, can be dangerously unpredictable. On every visit, as children, to Bill and Pat's farm at Yewdale, my brothers and I would race instantly into the largest, coolest stone barn where we knew we would find their great shaggy border collie, Glenn. Without fail, he would be happy to see us, wagging his tail and stretching forward to let us stroke his neck and back. Not only was Glenn a good-natured dog, but we also felt doubly safe because of the stout collar and chain which kept him tethered in the barn. At the slightest hint of trouble, we knew we could simply move back beyond the chain's length to instant safety. Unfortunately, my adult experiences were not always so carefree.

After one or two unpleasant near-misses, I took to approaching closed barn doors with great care. Even if you'd gained the farmer's permission to look round his or her property, you simply never knew what might be lurking. An assumption that you would have been warned of any serious hazards was dangerously misplaced and, having opened the door, your eyes would need a few seconds to adjust to the black hole that confronted you. Whatever might be waiting within was under no such disadvantage, able to spring at the illuminated gap that had suddenly appeared, and at anything – or anyone – that stood in its way. Once or twice I only just managed to slam a door shut in time to prevent an escape, or an attack (from what, I was not always sure). Infinitely more unnerving, though, was the reverse situation, where I entered an empty building and an animal came in behind me. I once did this in an apparently empty barn only to spin round to find a pair of large dogs staring up at me.

'They'll be fine so long as you don't touch anything you shouldn't', said their cheery owner as he entered the barn, to my great relief, shortly afterwards. I later found out that they were Rhodesian ridgebacks, a muscular breed of dog developed to face up to cornered lions, thus allowing them to be more easily shot.

Only once, though, did I manage to get bitten. Visiting a release site where I knew the farmer was expecting me, I turned a corner of the farmhouse to be met by a large, excited border collie. I think my assailant was as surprised by the encounter as I was, but he was the one to make the first move, jumping up to sink his fangs in my upper arm. As I uttered various profanities, the farm children hurtled up and dragged the beast away by the remnant of a chain that was dangling from its neck.

'He must've escaped', they observed rather superfluously as I applied a handkerchief to my bruised and bleeding limb.

Though not personally attacked by any other farm animals, I have had my vehicle seriously mugged. When I first realised that I'd left my car window open on a visit one day, I thought it quite sweet that one of the farm cats had chosen to curl up and fall asleep on a blanket on the back seat. Only when I opened the door to evict the vagrant did I realise that he'd also personalised his new-found resting place with copious quantities of pungent cat wee. The same vehicle – it was a red Vauxhall Cavalier - suffered even greater indignities on another occasion, when I foolishly parked it in the corner of a field. Because it was such a warm evening, I left all the windows wide open, a move which evidently did not go unnoticed by the small herd of heifers whose field I was in. After fixing up a nest box in a nearby barn, I returned to find the car surrounded by the cattle, who'd clearly been indulging in an orgy of scratching, rubbing and licking. The bodywork was scratched and smeared all over with mud and cowshit, both wing mirrors were hanging off, and the whole interior was dripping in gelatinous saliva, as if someone had set about it with a wallpaper brush and a bucket of paste. The poor car certainly prompted some quizzical looks from the staff of my local valeting service.

Although often at risk, I've fortunately never had a serious incident whilst up a ladder. Others, however, have not been quite so fortunate. The most spectacular ladder incident took place in a friend's stables which, as he owned no horses, he was happy for me to use as an overspill breeding facility for barn owls. Gerry was a rather impetuous chap and, before I'd even fully realised what was going on, he'd seized a ladder and climbed up it to seek out any gaps in the brickwork that would need plugging to prevent barn owl escapes. My attention was also distracted by the presence of my two young sons. Unfortunately, in his haste to get on with the job, Gerry had erected the ladder at a rather shallow angle to the wall. As he reached the top, its feet suddenly slipped on the stable's concrete floor and down came my friend in a sort of controlled fall. Somehow landing on his feet, he let out a cry of pain as the hard metal ladder proceeded to bang him painfully on both shins. Worse was to follow: in a scene strongly reminiscent of a slapstick comedy, a half-brick then tumbled from the top of the wall and struck Gerry squarely on his glistening bald pate. Even the sound effect (a hollow clunk) could have come from a Hal Roach film. Rushing to Gerry's aid, I glared meaningfully at the boys who were at least struggling hard to keep their faces straight. Fortunately, my friend's injuries were not serious, although his shins were bruised and skinned, and his head wound was oozing blood. In the event, it was only his dignity that suffered any lasting damage.

Always up for a good party, I was very pleased one day to be unexpectedly invited to a book launch. And this, it seemed, was to be no ordinary bash. Organised by The Hawk and Owl Trust, of which I was a longstanding member, the event would mark the publication of the seminal work *The Barn Owl in The British Isles: Its Past, Present and Future*. Following extensive research funded by the Trust, the book had been written by Colin Shawyer, whom I knew and liked as a down-to-earth scientist. I felt reasonably confident, therefore, in accepting the invitation, that the event, at a posh London address, would not be dominated by the belted earls, retired major-generals and scions of the landed gentry whom, somewhat unfairly, I associated with the Trust. Besides, the guests of honour were to be Gerald Durrell and his wife, Lee. I'd been a fan of Durrell's work ever since my first encounter, at school, with his classic, *My Family and Other Animals*. Spectacularly missing the point, I'd openly sneered at the book's title, arrogantly assuming that the author had made an elementary grammatical mistake by equating his mother, brothers and sister with non-human life forms. The thought of my adolescent stupidity makes me cringe with embarrassment to this day. My criticism of his literary skills didn't put me off, however, and I soon began to read as many of Durrell's books as I could lay my hands on. So the opportunity to be at the same party as the great man, by then a world-renowned conservationist, was irresistibly attractive.

On the day of the launch, I duly hauled up outside an impressive Georgian mansion in a most desirable part of London. Just as 10 Downing Street is reputed to be (I've never managed to set foot inside), the building was much larger on the inside than it appeared to be from the outside. My heart sank therefore, when I was confronted by a mass of well-dressed, unfamiliar people all making polite small talk whilst helping themselves to wine and canapés. Wasn't that the Right Hon. so-and-so, the Minister of Agriculture, who'd just breezed past? What was he doing here? More used to rowdy gatherings of fellow naturalists, downing pints in a local pub and swapping biological banter in earthy language, I several times sought Dutch courage by quickly downing two or three large glasses of, doubtless high quality, wine offered by the smart, attentive waitresses. Just then, I spotted Gerald Durrell on the far side of the room, his beard and mane of thick silver hair making him instantly recognisable. Beyond him, through some open French windows, I could see a barn owl being prepped for its encounter with the great man. Photographers jostled for the best position, whilst PR people fussed over every detail. I was wondering whether I ought not to just to cut and run from this posh jamboree, when a friendly voice broke in on my thoughts.

'Is there anyone here you'd like to meet?'

I turned round, rather too rapidly as I was now feeling somewhat woozy, to see a face I vaguely recognised.

'Ooh yes, please!' I blurted out, adding 'Gerald Durrell!' and gesticulating across the room in the general direction of the guest of honour.

Totally unfazed by my outburst, or the apparent difficulty of the task, my affable host took me gently by the elbow and steered me with effortless ease through the crowded, noisy room. Before I had realised quite what was happening, I found myself face to face with none other than Mr Durrell himself. Standing there, slightly bemused, his wife at his side, this giant of the conservation world was evidently waiting for me to speak. Here was the moment I'd been waiting for. But what could I say? Hesitating at first, I eventually lurched forward. All I could think to do in my befuddled state was to take his outstretched hands and mumble:

'Mr Durrell, I just wanted to say what great pleasure I've had from reading your books.'

There was certainly no hesitation on the part of Mrs Durrell, who was clearly acting as her husband's minder for the occasion. Politely, and expertly, she moved her husband away, muttering something about the forthcoming barn owl photos. I cursed inwardly. Of course that's not what I'd bloody well wanted to say! He must have heard bland compliments like that a thousand times before. I'd wanted to talk barn owls, zoos, conservation with the doyen of British naturalists. But I knew that, thanks to several glasses of wine and my social awkwardness, I'd blown my chance.

Full of despondency, I watched the rest of the proceedings from a quiet corner, applauding at the right moments and consoling myself with several more glasses of wine, before staggering off to the railway station to catch the train home. The following day, along with millions of others, I read about the launch party in the newspaper and admired the striking photograph of Gerald Durrell with a beautiful barn owl on his gloved arm: the grand old man of conservation and an angel, its wings outstretched against a bright blue sky.

36   *Last release*

After a decade and a half of breeding barn owls and releasing them into the wild, I was beginning to feel that the time had come to reassess my project. Looking back over this relatively short period, I could see how attitudes had shifted away from the intensive use of farmland towards regimes that were becoming more benevolent towards wildlife. Increasing amounts of land were being set aside from agricultural use (and the farmers, of course, compensated for their losses) whilst planning restrictions were being eased to allow green belt and other open space to be put to a wider range of uses, some of them considerably more conservation-friendly than others. Whilst I hadn't exactly saturated my home territory with barn owls, I had branched out to more distant sites in Cheshire and Shropshire to carry out releases.

Alongside my work introducing birds into the wild, I'd had much help from voluntary organisations such as The Prince's Trust, who had constructed and erected nest boxes, encouraged landowners to adopt wildlife-friendly practices and generally raised awareness of the importance of wildlife conservation. So the time had now come, I thought, to consider whether releasing birds was still necessary or appropriate: in other words, I would study the evidence. ·

Not long before, poor old Barney had died. I had found her dead on the floor of her aviary one morning. 'Oh no!' I had exclaimed, gently stroking her cold body, which bore no external injuries and revealed no clues as to the cause of her sudden death. For more than fifteen years, this gentle friend had been my inspiration, helping me to demonstrate graphically to the public what a beautiful creature we were in danger of losing from our countryside, as well as being a constant reminder that tameness and captivity could never be adequate substitutes for the opportunity to fly free and breed in the wild. With my muse gone, and the hard evidence telling me that I'd probably done enough to give the local barn owl population a fighting chance of coming back from the brink, I took the decision to bring my project to an end.

But it wasn't quite as simple as that – nothing ever is. I had breeding stock to cater for, and there were also birds from previous releases that I was continuing to monitor. I therefore devised a programme of identifying breeding pairs that could be released by the adult release method, and sites from which to release them. There were, of course, surveys to be done, nest boxes to be made and installed, landowners to be briefed and, not to be overlooked – or underestimated in terms of the time and effort involved – licences to be applied for. Even with only a handful of pairs to be released, it proved to be a mammoth task. Desperate to prevent the birds from producing offspring in my aviaries, which would then have to be released before they fledged, I had to separate males from females and simply hope that they would still form a compatible pair when I brought them together again for the release process to begin. They would have to suffer enforced separation followed by a shotgun marriage.

Unfortunately, try as I might, I couldn't persuade the ineffably charming and ever-polite men from the Ministry (the Department of the Environment, Transport and the Regions) to support me in my tricky endeavour by allowing me some latitude – the odd harmless shortcut – in complying with their rules and procedures. I tried everything I could think of, a typical exchange going something like this:

> Me: 'Couldn't I house the birds on the proposed release site *before* I get a licence? It's only the same as keeping them in an aviary.'
> Civil Servant: 'I'm afraid the rules don't allow for that, sir.'
> Me: 'Can't you get an inspector out to have a look at my sites sooner?'
> Civil Servant: 'We have only a limited budget and our inspectors are on contract, so their time is already allocated.'
> Me: 'Will you accept applications now for future years as well as the current one? That would make my programme much easier to arrange.'
> Civil Servant: 'We're reviewing the licensing scheme at the moment but for the time being we can only license sites in the current year, I'm afraid.'

My every suggestion politely blocked, I eventually abandoned exploring ways through the bureaucratic maze and decided to concentrate instead on finding and surveying release sites, whilst continuing to deploy the ultimate contraceptive technique as far as my birds were concerned: enforced abstinence.

For the next couple of years, I worked hard on my programme of releases. Once a licence was granted, a pair of birds could be confined on the chosen site until they bred the next spring, when their offspring could be ringed and the parents allowed to fly free. By autumn, I would be completing ringing returns for the BTO and End of Year Reports for the Department, whilst surveying sites and completing application forms for new release sites. I was also doing a full-time job and bringing up my own family, of course. At times, I couldn't help feeling that I'd been hoist with my own petard – after all, I'd publicly advocated the setting-up of a licensing scheme, so I could hardly complain about it now.

It was in the midst of all this frenetic activity that the Department (by now transformed into the Department for Environment, Food and Rural Affairs, or Defra) decided to drop its bombshell. I found out what they'd meant by 'reviewing the licensing scheme'.

'The Future of the Barn Owl Release Scheme' was the ominous heading of a letter I received unexpectedly from the Species Conservation Policy Office (Species Conservation and Marine Team).

After a couple of short sentences on the background, the communication announced the end of the scheme in customarily impersonal government-speak:

> 'Having considered the responses and views of all those concerned it has been decided that the scheme should be discontinued. The majority of responses were in favour of this move. Over the past five years the number of licences issued has diminished and an insignificant number of birds have been released. The ending of the scheme will have no effect on the conservation of the species.'

As usual, the real sting came in the tail. After a few words about continuing to 'promote barn owl-friendly practices', the letter confirmed that licences could still be obtained, but that …

> '…the policy remit will be against issuing a licence unless English Nature advise otherwise. It will remain illegal to release a barn owl into the wild without a licence issued by Defra, the penalty for this offence is a maximum of £5,000 fine per specimen and/or six months custodial sentence.'

Having recovered from the shock of this dire news, I began to congratulate myself on having had the foresight – or good luck – to wind down my captive breeding and release project at just the right time. I had, by this stage, only one more pair of birds to be dealt with: a fit, young couple that had successfully reared a brood in captivity and therefore qualified as proven breeders. The male was a wild-bred bird which had been nursed back to health by Tony Warburton's World Owl Trust after being injured in a road accident; his mate was home grown from my own breeding stock. I had also found the ideal site, situated close, but not too close, to several others that I had used in previous years. All continued to go swimmingly as my application for a licence was granted, just before the government guillotine came down on the scheme, following a site inspection by one of their most senior and knowledgeable inspectors. The hugely enthusiastic farmer, Thomas, had created first class owl accommodation in one of his barns, I had placed the birds and all was ready to go. So this is it, I thought with more than a little regret: my swan song.

You should never, of course, count your chickens – or your owlets – until they are hatched. Just after I'd placed the owls on site, a national disaster struck in the form of an outbreak of foot-and-mouth disease. As a child in the Lake District, I'd lived through the last great epidemic, which resulted in all visits to Yewdale Farm and our beloved Bannisdale being prohibited for many months. It felt like suffering a bereavement. Certainly, this time round, there was graphic evidence of the effects of the disease. The north in particular was hit very hard and I remember on a trip to Scotland driving through northern Cumbria and being terribly shocked by the sight of huge funeral pyres of slaughtered livestock, belching out flames and thick black smoke across the beautiful Borders countryside.

The dreaded disease had not reached my area of the country, and I certainly didn't want to be the person responsible for bringing it there. I determined that all practical barn owl activity must therefore be suspended forthwith. At the earliest opportunity, I phoned the release site owner.

'Thomas, whatever you do, don't let them breed!'

'Why ever not – I thought that was the whole point?' He was understandably perplexed.

I quickly explained my reasoning, ending, I hoped, on an optimistic note.

'As soon as the crisis is over, we can go back to plan A. If necessary, we can just have the release licence renewed.' It was due to expire at the end of October.

Reluctantly, Thomas agreed to do as I asked, although I got the impression that he thought I was being over-cautious. He suggested that the best way to prevent the birds from breeding would be to deprive them of their nest box for the duration of the emergency. There were plenty of perching and roosting spots in the barn, but no obvious nesting sites.

My voluntary moratorium was backed up by guidance from bodies such as the BTO and, of course, Defra, the department actually responsible for battling with the outbreak. Even on the occasional visit to deliver fresh food supplies, I would have to dunk my footwear in a bowl of disinfectant stationed at the farm gate, and I kept strictly away from the barn itself, preferring to leave the feeding and monitoring to Thomas, who was present on the site in any event. Nevertheless, it was a hugely anxious time, as every news bulletin on the television or in the newspapers seemed to report another foot-and-mouth outbreak, or describe the heartache of a farmer whose precious livestock had to be culled. The only consolation, I told myself, was that this year the countryside would be a lot less busy and the owls I'd released would therefore suffer much less disturbance than usual during the all-important breeding season.

After a seemingly interminable wait, and many more reports of death and destruction from affected parts of the country, the all-clear was at last sounded by Defra. By the simple stratagem of removing their nest box, we'd succeeded in preventing the owls at Thomas' farm from producing eggs. I certainly hadn't relished the prospect of having to remove or prick perfectly viable barn owl eggs. At least, we hoped that the absence of eggs was down to the lack of somewhere to lay and not to another, unknown factor, such as a bird's infertility or the site's unsuitability. We would soon find out, because our plan now was to do a complete volte-face and use all the tried and tested methods of encouraging the owls to breed. At least, that was *my* plan. Thomas, I found, had a rather different approach. Instead of attaching the adapted tea chest which I had given him to a roof beam in the conventional way, he had, as he proudly showed me, sawn the top off a garish blue plastic barrel and fastened it on its side only a few feet off the floor of the barn. My box, I noticed, had been quietly discarded in a dark corner.

'You did wash the barrel out thoroughly, didn't you?' I asked. I'd seen the lethal effects of toxic fumes on captive owls at a previous release site. Privately, I very much doubted that the owls would use the barrel, but Thomas was so proud of his handiwork that I couldn't persuade him to alter his arrangements. I also struggled to convince him that he shouldn't be going up into the barn to look at his owls more than once a day, when they needed to be fed, as they would need privacy to stand a good chance of breeding.

A successful outcome was critical, not just because this was to be my last release, but also because I needed to persuade Defra to issue me with a fresh licence. The unused one had expired – by effluxion of time, as we lawyers would say – at the end of October. I dispatched the appropriate form, with an explanation of the reason why I had not used the previous licence, a reason which I felt sure the department would sympathise with, because of its own experience of handling the foot-and-mouth epidemic. I could not have been more wrong. Within a few days, back came the peremptory response:

'As advised in the department's letter of (such-and-such a date), the Barn Owl Release Scheme has been discontinued. No new licences will therefore be issued.'

'But I don't want a new licence, just a renewal of one!' I screamed at no-one in particular. Despite working in one myself, I had of course forgotten the immutable principles of any bureaucracy: rules are rules, there are no such things as exceptional circumstances and standard procedures will be blindly followed at all times.

What on earth was I to do now? On the one hand, Thomas and I were doing all we could to encourage the owls to breed, but on the other hand Defra was making it perfectly clear that we would face hefty criminal penalties if we were to act outside the rules. They had, of course, remembered to put that bit in their refusal letter. Should we go into reverse again, depriving the owls of their nest box (assuming, of course, that I could persuade Thomas to remove his precious half-barrel) or would it be better to gamble on eventually getting a licence and leave things as they were? Several polite but non-committal telephone conversations with civil servants later, I was no further forward and feeling increasingly desperate. At which point, Thomas telephoned.

'Hullo. Just thought you'd like to know – the hen's sittin' on eggs'.

I should have felt pleased, delighted even, but all I could do was groan.

'What's up – it's what we wanted ter happen, isn't it?'

I'd been shielding Thomas somewhat from the truth about the licence, simply saying there were some delays caused by inefficiency in the system – blaming the Government always plays well with farmers, I find. But now I felt I had to come clean – after all, he might end up standing next to me in the dock one day, if we weren't extremely careful. I knew, from professional experience, that claiming the birds just happened to escape, when we had in reality deliberately set them free, was not likely to go down too well with the average magistrate, or even worse, crown court judge.

'I'll keep trying,' I said. 'Just make sure they don't get out!'

I now had a definite period within which I must persuade Defra to license the release. From the date of laying, which I knew precisely, thanks to Thomas' obsessive observation of the owls, it would take 30 – 31 days for the eggs to hatch and a further four weeks for the owlets to reach the stage at which their parents should be allowed to fly free. If the barn were not opened up during the two-week period when their young were 4 – 6 weeks old, it would be too late: adults and young would be condemned to a life of captivity, the very antithesis of everything that my project had been about from the start. To fail at this final stage of my last release was simply unthinkable.

Several increasingly frantic telephone conversations with civil servants finally produced a sliver of hope: if I submitted a fresh licence application with a detailed account of the circumstances, they would see what they could do. It seemed, from gentle interrogation, that it was English Nature (now known as Natural England) who were putting the mockers on the issue of a licence, but they may simply have been used as a scapegoat. Restraining myself with the greatest difficulty from pointing out that Defra already held all the relevant information and that they were fully aware from my letters and telephone calls of the special circumstances – the previous application, site inspection, licence, placing of the barn owl pair on site, foot-and-mouth outbreak, intervention to prevent breeding, reapplication for a licence and so on – I knuckled down to setting out the entire argument again. It reminded me of occasional court cases I had to deal with where I had to plead my case three or four separate times because, for some reason or another, the previous hearing had ended without reaching any useful conclusions. The more often I repeated my argument, the more convinced I became that I was right. However, I thought, I must guard against complacency.

Once again, I set out in detail the full story of my would-be release. I emphasised that the clock was ticking and could not be stopped or turned back without drastic measures: destroying the newly-laid eggs and keeping the adults celibate and in captivity for the rest of their lives (although one of the civil servants did point out to me that the male bird could be released separately as it was wild-bred). Hoping that my carefully-crafted letter contained a compelling mix of emotional appeal and cold, compelling logic, I posted it off and waited anxiously for the response.

Within a few days, I received the phone call I'd been expecting – and dreading. A gleeful Thomas announced that the eggs were hatching, or so he thought: could I come and check? He must have wondered why I was so disconsolate as I confirmed that the faint chittering noises that we could hear as we stood a few feet from the barrel were the sounds made by newly-hatched owlets. Not wishing to seem impolite – I desperately wanted to avoid being asked a direct question about the licensing position – I left the farm and rushed home, where I instantly picked up the phone to Defra.

Perhaps it was my approach, or my undoubted state of agitation, that let me down. Whatever the cause, I was met with the frosty indifference of officialdom when I yet again explained my plight.

'According to our file, your application has been referred to English Nature, sir, and no, this department has no influence over the time the consultation will take'. I detected just a touch of irritation at my suggestion that Defra might try hurrying its consultee along. A greater degree of annoyance became apparent when I went on to propose that I speak to English Nature myself: that would not be possible. Feeling I had made no progress at all, and concerned that further pushing might actually be counter-productive, I simply urged the unhelpful civil servant to expedite matters. I couldn't resist one last dig, though:

'I just can't see how a site that was inspected and licensed last year can be unsuitable now!'

Putting down the phone, I feared that I might have overplayed my hand.

Over the next few anxious weeks, I received regular, excited bulletins from Thomas – his owlets were developing perfectly normally – but no communication at all from 'The Department'. I cursed the circumstances that had produced this impasse, and as each day went by I rehearsed in my mind what I would say to Thomas if the licence failed to arrive in time, or even worse, was refused: 'Thanks for all your help. I'm afraid I haven't got a licence, so I'll have to remove the owls now and take them into captivity'. Even played over in my mind, the words were unconvincing. When I imagined saying them to him as I sat in his comfortable farmhouse kitchen, watching the enthusiasm promptly drain from his big farmer's face, I couldn't help but shudder. What a way to end nearly twenty years of barn owl conservation, I thought: an uncooperative government department, a failed release, a disgruntled landowner and a garden full of perfectly fit captive birds that belonged in the wild.

As the eldest of the owlets approached its fourth week of life, I became increasingly twitchy. Should I try once more to chivvy the bureaucrats at Defra, or should I just keep my fingers firmly crossed? Perhaps I should warn Thomas that there was now a serious risk that we wouldn't be able to let the owls go after all. He'd begun to send me photographs that he'd taken of his beloved birds inside their half-barrel nest, obviously in anticipation of their imminent release. I felt I'd made a mess of everything.

Just as I was despairing that the window of opportunity for releasing the birds would soon be slammed shut (at six weeks, owlets can fly and are likely to leave the barn prematurely and be unable to find their way back), an envelope marked 'OHMS' plopped onto the door mat. Like receiving exam results, I knew that the contents contained my fate: either a licence or a letter of refusal. With trembling hands, I tore the envelope open and pulled out the contents: an anonymous-looking two page document. There was no covering letter, no explanatory note, not even a compliments slip, but I couldn't have cared less because in my hand I held, at last, the all-important licence to release barn owls. The licence was in the standard form, setting out all the nine conditions that I was familiar with from the tens of licences I'd had previously. It was signed by someone I'd never heard of who was, the document solemnly recorded, 'authorised by the Secretary of State to sign in that behalf'. Alternately congratulating and cursing Defra, I decided to waste no time in telling Thomas the good news.

From that point on, the release proceeded as smoothly as so many had before. It was perhaps as well: I wasn't sure that my seriously-frayed nervous system could have withstood any more setbacks. With a mixture of triumph and relief, I completed my last ever End of Year Report Form, confirming that the owls were still being seen around the farm, and dispatched it to the Department. Wandering out into the garden, I surveyed my line of aviaries, now standing redundant for the first time in many years.

'Well, I suppose that's that,' I murmured as I turned and walked slowly back indoors.

37   Reflections on barn owl conservation

The 64 thousand dollar question must be: has it all been worth it? Or, to put it another way: have barn owl numbers increased, thanks to my efforts, when they otherwise would not have? Has the cause of wildlife conservation been advanced? Does it matter anyway, in view of the serious threats facing the planet? Has the whole exercise been just one huge ego trip for yours truly? It's probably time to examine my conscience.

> ## HILL TOP FARM
>
> 2005. We do know that a neighbour a mile away has barn owls living in his barn (for the last few years). They breed successfully. We hope that they may have some connection with our released ones that you brought here.

If I were setting out the case for the defence, I'd be making all sorts of pious statements about the beauty of nature, the glories of British wildlife and the urgent rescue mission needed to save the barn owl. A brief spot of navel gazing, however, relieves me of any need to defend my activities. From an early age, I've been fascinated by wildlife and all things natural. Remember the nature table, the trips into the countryside and the attempts to introduce more exotic pets into the household than boring old dogs and goldfish.

As soon as I gained an income and a house of my own, I began to care for a whole variety of wild creatures, most of which needed help of some kind. I looked after orphaned foxes and injured kestrels, homeless lizards and poorly hedgehogs, stray ducks and fledgling blue tits with a view to returning them, wherever possible, to the wild. Not content with being a Licensed Rehabilitation Keeper (and, almost incidentally, a practising lawyer), I kept unusual pets too, such as a pair of stick insects, a magpie and a (literally) semi-house-trained polecat. But I decided that the care and rehabilitation of individual animals and birds, though personally rewarding and sometimes successful, would have, at best, only a minimal effect on Britain's fauna – something along the lines of one swallow not making a summer. I contrasted my efforts unfavourably with the likes of John Love's project to return the sea eagle to Scotland, or an old friend's surreptitious and totally unregulated programme of breeding polecats and reintroducing them, in considerable numbers, to some of their former haunts in northern England. It was meeting Jane and Teddy Ratcliffe, and hearing about their barn owl releases, that inspired me finally to take the plunge from being a licensed rehabilitation keeper to breeding and releasing an endangered species. In short, I now had the means, thanks to my day job, motive and opportunity to undertake species conservation work on a larger scale.

In these days of target-setting, performance monitoring and outputs, I suppose that the best indicator of the success of a project like mine would be the number of barn owls successfully introduced into the wild environment. In turn, their success would be judged by how many of them went on to reproduce, and by the effect their efforts had on the total number of barn owls in the wild. Taking this clinical, scientific approach leads inexorably to a consideration of hard, cold, factual data, such as the survival rates of released owls, perhaps comparing them with those of wild-bred birds. So far, the longevity record has been provided by an unfledged male barn owl that I ringed, together with its three siblings, at one of my release sites. It was found dead, the victim of a collision with road traffic, nearly eleven years later, only 11 km. from the site.

Survival of wild and captive-bred barn owls was exactly the subject of a study carried out by a one-time helper, Ian, for his masters degree. In fact, the conclusion of his erudite dissertation was that there is little difference between the two groups' respective survival rates. My own theory is that the released birds benefit from a reliable food source and the protective care of their human foster parents, whilst wild-bred owlets are more susceptible to natural food fluctuations – crashes in vole populations, particularly – but do have their parents around during their early flying careers to warn them of danger and to demonstrate relevant life skills, such as hunting and finding good places to roost. The only incontrovertible proof that a bird has survived for a given length of time is provided by any ringing returns that are made. It is certainly not scientifically valid to assume that any birds for which there are no ringing returns are still alive (along the lines that 'no news is good news'), not least because only a small percentage of ringed birds are subsequently recovered. It is very difficult, for instance, to recover a bird that has been eaten, although one farmer whose site I used did find the BTO ring amongst a few feathers from one of his released birds, which, reasonably enough, he assumed a predatory fox had found hard to swallow.

Nothing demonstrated to me more clearly the tension between science and conservation than the rising irritation of my friend, Robert, the zoo curator, when I presented him with regular updates on ringing recoveries of our captive-bred birds. Eventually, he brought himself to say it.

'I don't want to know about the failures. I'm looking for success stories'.

At first, his attitude upset me. What did he expect? It was one thing for the zoo to broadcast the birth of its latest baby elephant, or the acquisition of a cuddly new species, but didn't he realise that releasing birds into the dangers and uncertainties of the wild was a completely different challenge from operating within the controlled confines of the zoo? Eventually, though, I began to calm down. His underlying concerns were exactly the same as those put to me by the TV presenter during the conservation programme, and voiced rather less eloquently by many of the people – landowners, helpers and so on – who had worked with me over the years: how do you know whether it's working?

There has certainly been plenty of anecdotal evidence. In the years following my releases, there is often a distinct increase in the reported sightings of barn owls in the relevant localities. This is far from conclusive, though. Just as the incidence of particular types of crime sometimes seems to rise following publicity about a high-profile case, so the number of reported barn owl sightings might grow simply because of increased awareness and interest. The same could be said of the establishment of breeding pairs, which has also often coincided with releases carried out in the area. This was particularly the case where I released several sets of unrelated young from different sites within a mile or two of each other, usually spanning a period of two or three years. Although they didn't always choose one of my release sites to establish themselves in, the pairs did remain in the general release area. I could therefore put forward strong circumstantial evidence that my activities were having a positive effect, particularly when this was combined with the fact that all the sites I used were in locations from which barn owls had been absent for a number of years.

As far as possible, I have tried to verify the anecdotal evidence with more substantial data. Visiting a site to see things with your own eyes is one technique, but I have also sent out questionnaires to owners of sites, sometimes many years after carrying out a release. They would at least recognise a barn owl if they saw one, I thought. Although my assumption was, in the main, correct, I did have some surprises. Assured by one owner, whose two sites I'd used several times, that the nest box in her huge Dutch barn was definitely in use, I scaled the long ladder leading up to the box to check out her story for myself. Rashly sticking my head into the entrance hole, I was horrified to find a large and very displeased tawny owl glowering back at me. I moved aside as it leapt towards me, only too aware that the well-known natural history photographer, Eric Hoskins, had lost an eye to a breeding tawny. Fortunately, the angry bird swept past me and landed in some nearby trees. Behind her she left a solitary, round white egg. Shinning back down the ladder as quickly as I could, I briefly explained the situation to the onlookers, emphasising that this was an exercise that they shouldn't try to repeat and suggesting that we all retreat from the barn to allow the brooding owl to return. I knew that I'd got off lightly. I remember being told by a friend who worked at a wildlife park that one of his colleagues had done a similar thing to a nesting macaw. Instead of simply fleeing, like the owl, this bird, nesting deep inside an old stone building, had grabbed the intruder's nose with its powerful bill (developed to crack nuts – fortunately the bird didn't seize that part of his anatomy) and held on until the poor park warden was able to back off down his ladder with an extremely sore conk.

Unfortunately, surveys and inspections do not provide conclusive evidence that the birds present on a site are ones that I have released. Incontrovertible proof is only available from a bird's leg ring. Although the rings may seem relatively large and cumbersome when being fitted, they have an unfortunate ability to become almost invisible on a free-flying bird. Many is the time that I have strained through my binoculars, trying to detect the presence of a silver band on a barn owl's slender white leg, without being able to reach any definite conclusion. The job is made all the harder by the owls' nocturnal habits, but even in broad daylight, it is a virtually impossible task. Even more impossible, of course, is reading from a distance any of the information on the ring. The only sensible approach is to have the bird in the hand, but that is also problematic. Unless you were lucky enough to corner one in a confined space, such as a small loft, the most likely place to catch healthy, fledged birds would be at their roosting spot, such as a hollow in a tree, or in a nest box. Although techniques for catching owls at the nest are referred to in the BTO Ringers' Manual, I have always shied away from using them, mainly because of the dangers of disturbance that might result in damaged or deserted eggs or young. Except during my early releases, I have also avoided marking birds in some other way, for example by fitting a brightly-coloured plastic ring to the non-BTO-ringed leg, because of my wish to minimise interference with their natural state. Radio tracking is a possibility, but can last only for a limited time, and involves even greater interference with the birds than colour-ringing them, because of the need to attach a transmitting device to their plumage. So, on balance, I have opted to remain in a state of relative ignorance, convinced on the basis of circumstantial evidence that the project has worked, able to prove my case on the balance of probabilities, if not beyond reasonable doubt.

There are, though, other justifications for a project aimed at conserving a flagship species. Once you accept that the barn owl is at the top of a food chain and that its presence, or absence, is an indicator of the health of the countryside, you become much more focused on the wider conservation issues. That is why I have thought of myself as a conserver of voles, shrews and mice as much as the releaser of a rare and beautiful raptor. In turn, there can be no thriving populations of prey species without the conservation and recreation of their habitats and their food supplies. As any small child soon learns, worms, grubs and all the other tiny creatures that inhabit the soil are essential to the basic functioning of rural ecosystems. Reducing or eliminating the use of pesticides, setting land aside from cultivation or intensive grazing, and preserving habitats such as old barns, hedgerows and watercourses are essential to securing the wellbeing of the countryside, from the top to the bottom of the food chain. But you also have to bear in mind that, to the landowners, the countryside represents an asset, the source of their livelihood and their daily place of work. It might take considerable persuasion to wean them off their approach of maximising production and minimising inconvenience. This is where the good old barn owl comes in. Not to put too fine a point on it, the bird is just plain sexy. Whether floating ethereally above a lush meadow on a balmy summer's night, or staring out at you with a pair of sparkling black eyes, the barn owl is bound to provoke a strong emotional response. John Major characterised rural Britain's charms as 'the country of long shadows on cricket grounds [and] warm beer'. Whilst he was thinking of village life, for me the warm inner glow that comes with the feeling that all is well with the world is epitomised by the sight of a barn owl in its element, gliding amongst the farms and fields of Britain.

So, armed with a set of photographs or even the real thing, when Barney was up for it, I've encountered few problems persuading landowners to let me carry out releases on their properties. I'm convinced, however, that had I been proposing the conservation of something less glamorous, such as rodents or bugs, the reaction I got would have been much less enthusiastic. Not only were my activities tolerated and supported, but I was often greeted at the site with news of the latest conservation initiative:

'Ah've decided to cut down on them chemicals' or 'I don't plough right up to't field edges ne more'.

The beneficial effects would spread like ripples across a pond. Hearing on the grapevine about a neighbour's barn owl releases, some landowners would be keen to take measures aimed at tempting the birds to move into their territory. Nest boxes would suddenly be put up, set-aside land identified and renewed interest shown in environmentally-friendly farming methods. Counter-measures might then be unleashed by the neighbour, causing an escalation in a sort of good-natured green war. I was happy, of course, to play the part of mercenary, offering my services to any of the warring parties. As far as I was concerned, all these activities could only be beneficial to the barn owl and to the countryside in general. The gains were sometimes counter-balanced by losses, however. The fad for barn conversions, providing homes for people who fancy living in the country without getting covered in shit, continues to thrive. Many of the barns and other farm buildings that I've used over the last few years have suffered just such a fate, turned from little-used, neglected agricultural assets into neat and tidy, aseptic residential units occupied by folk with no connection with the land. Government policy has simply encouraged this approach to so-called redundant farm buildings. Although The Hawk and Owl Trust and other bodies have sought to mitigate the effects of such conversions by suggesting the designing-in of suitable facilities, I shouldn't think that many of the residents would welcome breeding barn owls in their attics, just as the presence of bats in their houses is seen by many as a curse rather than a blessing.

IVY HOUSE

2005. My parents (Mr & Mrs S.) no longer live at the above address. The new owners are about to move in – they intend to convert the barn that we raised many broods of barn owl chicks in.

When all is said and done, the honest answer to the question of whether all my efforts have been worthwhile is that I *think* they have. I certainly hope so, for a straightforward reason: that those who appreciate the natural world, and those who might come to appreciate it, should have the opportunity to experience all its glories. In Britain, judging by its frequent appearance on countless calendars, leaflets, cards and TV films, the barn owl is one of the country's greatest natural glories. I want everyone to be able to witness the scene that I and my elder son were privileged to see on a recent trip to one of the Hebridean islands. As we pulled up in our car one evening at a derelict farm house, we were met by the sight of four recently-fledged barn owls sitting shoulder to shoulder on a fence, as if posing for a photograph, whilst their attentive parents flew silently in the sky above. For once, these were not birds I'd released, but a wild-bred family flourishing in the British countryside. Long may such sights continue; and if in some small way I have helped to make it more likely, then I, for one, think that my efforts have all been worthwhile. For me, it's been the next best thing to farming, which was my very earliest career aspiration, and, as a bonus, it's been bloody good fun too!

APPENDIX: BARN OWL FACTS

The owls are divided into two families, the *Tytonidae,* which includes the barn owl, and the *Strigidae,* which includes perhaps the best-known British species, the tawny owl. There are thought to be 35 subspecies, or races, of barn owl (*Tyto alba*) throughout the world, which means that it is one of the most widespread species of bird. It has been around for a long time too: fossil records of barn owls and their diet have been found from the Miocene period (about 20 million years ago); and evidence of their presence in Britain 10,000 years ago, in the late Devensian, was reported in 1984.

When seen in flight, or perched outside the nest, barn owls look pure white. A closer look, however, reveals a subtle colouration of the back, tail and upper wings, consisting of a buff or pale-golden background, barred and flecked with grey, black and white. Some of this colouring may extend to a limited extent across the white surface of the breast, facial disc and underwings, particularly in females. Nevertheless, British birds are noticeably lighter on their fronts than the barn owls from further north and east and belong to the subspecies *Tyto alba alba*: the white-breasted barn owl.

The classic image of the barn owl is of a bird resembling a large moth fluttering silently, but somewhat randomly, over a large area of open ground. In fact, the bird is a consummate hunter, using its highly-developed form and skills to locate and capture its prey. First, the silence: this is achieved primarily by the softness of the bird's feathers, particularly the velvet-like pile on the upper surfaces of the flight feathers, and serration of the leading edge of the tenth primary feather on each wing. Silence is vital both to avoid being detected by potential prey and to enable the owl to locate that prey by sound. The second major feature complements the first: in common with other owls, the barn owl's relatively large head consists mainly of specialised feathers arranged into a facial disc. The disc is divided into two parabolic sound collectors which funnel the rustles and squeaks of prey items to the ear openings that are asymmetrically positioned in the head (the ears are hidden at the side of the head, and the barn owl has no ear tufts – which aren't true ears anyway – as long-eared and short-eared owls do). Such acute hearing combines with the bird's sharp eyesight to produce a highly successful predator, although experiments have shown that a barn owl's hunting success rate is likely to reduce in conditions of complete darkness. The final weapons in the barn owl's armoury are its legs and feet. Long, feathered legs dangle beneath the bird as it quarters its hunting ground at heights of 1.5 – 4.5 metres. Once prey is located, the owl drops suddenly, sometimes performing elaborate twists and turns before seizing its target in the needle-like talons of its feet.

In common with many other birds, barn owls produce pellets containing the indigestible remains of their prey. There is a physical barrier in the birds' stomachs which prevents anything except digested food from getting by, so this has to be regurgitated through the mouth in sausage-shaped parcels known as pellets or castings, consisting of skeletal and other remains tightly packed in animal fur. By collecting and analysing these, the barn owl's diet can be accurately established. Many years of study have shown that barn owls specialise in hunting small mammals, mainly the short-tailed vole, the wood mouse, juvenile brown rats and various species of shrew. The most significant of prey items is the short-tailed, or field, vole (*Microtus agrestis*) whose populations fluctuate, with peak densities occurring every three or four years. The barn owl's breeding success rate varies accordingly. As well as small mammals, the remains of many other prey items, including fish, frogs and birds, have been found in barn owl pellets, but these are relatively unusual.

The barn owl is not a nest builder. Whether using a cliff ledge, a hollow tree or a man-made structure such as a barn, the most that the hen bird will do is to form a shallow scrape in a collection of pellet debris. Onto this mat, usually during April, May or June, she will lay between two and nine smallish white eggs, each being laid two or three days after the previous one. It follows that when the eggs hatch, after an incubation lasting about a month, the young are similarly staggered in age. In a large brood, the oldest chick can therefore easily be several weeks older than the youngest and its chances of survival, particularly in periods of food shortages, will be much greater. There is also evidence of cannibalism, with the older owlets in a brood sometimes killing and eating their younger siblings.

The period of chick rearing is an intensely busy time for the male barn owl. His off-spring develop rapidly and, by their third or fourth week of life, he will need to provide each of them with three good-sized prey items per night. Not only might variations in vole numbers affect his ability to do this, but poor weather – particularly heavy rain, which quickly soaks the barn owl's soft feathering – may restrict the number and length of his foraging excursions. Nevertheless, he will feel impelled to do his best as hungry owlets make persistent calls for food, mainly loud snores and hisses, which only end when prey is finally provided.

Once fledged, young barn owls cautiously explore their surroundings, still relying on their parents to provide them with food. Gradually, the bonds loosen as the owlets gain in confidence and succeed in catching prey for themselves. Moving further and further afield, and at times being actively driven away by their parents, the owlets are effectively dispersed by the end of October. This is the period of greatest danger for them, being inexperienced birds without their own territories. If they make it safely through the coming winter – two out of every three will not – and find suitable mates and territories the following spring, these birds may help to create the next generation of barn owls.

Sadly, this iconic bird of the British countryside has long been suffering a decline in numbers and for that reason has been accorded special status, including protection under the Wildlife and Countryside Act 1981 (Schedules 1 and 9). It is illegal to kill, injure or take a wild barn owl or to take or destroy its eggs. It is also illegal to check nest sites or even to disturb a barn owl while it is at or near a breeding site, unless you hold a special (Schedule 1) licence. As described in this book, captive-bred barn owls cannot be released into the wild without the appropriate licence from the Department for Environment, Food and Rural Affairs (Defra), which has indicated in recent years that such licences will be issued only in exceptional circumstances.

Although clear evidence of the decline has been documented, the reasons for it are less certain. In some areas of the country, there has been a marked reduction in available nest sites, with many derelict or unused farms and outbuildings converted to residential use. Farming methods have also changed, with increased mechanisation and a preference for large-scale crop production. Changes to the climate have also been harmful: prolonged snow cover and lengthy periods of heavy rain can prevent the barn owl from finding enough food to sustain itself. In terms of mortality, it seems clear that increasing numbers of busy roads carrying fast-moving vehicles are a major cause of the species' decline. It is fair to say, however, that no single cause has been identified and that the steady reduction in barn owl numbers is most likely to be due to a combination of these factors, and a number of others, such as the use of rodenticides that are harmful to the birds.

More than 20 years ago, a national study, *The Barn Owl in the British Isles – Its Past, Present and Future* (see p151 under Further Reading), charted the reduction in the numbers of barn owls in England and Wales from an estimated 12,000 breeding pairs in 1932 to around 3,750 in 1982 – 1985, a decrease of 69%, and asked how the downward spiral could be reversed, or at least stemmed. Since then, there have been many conservation initiatives undertaken, ranging from habitat creation and the provision of artificial nest boxes through to captive breeding and release as described in this book. The latest information strongly suggests that the barn owl has managed to stage a recovery in this country, with the number of breeding pairs thought to have stabilised at around 8,000 – 9,000 in 2008. However, there is no room for complacency, and the organisations listed below have key roles to play in ensuring that the recovery in numbers of this truly beautiful bird is maintained and improved.

SOME USEFUL CONTACTS

The Barn Owl Trust
Waterleat, Ashburton, Devon TQ13 7HU
The Barn Owl Trust is a national registered charity based in Devon, dedicated to conserving barn owls and their environment.
(www.barnowltrust.org.uk)

Hawk and Owl Trust
PO Box 400, Bishops Lydeard, Taunton, TA4 3WH
The Hawk and Owl Trust is a registered charity working for owls and other birds of prey in the wild.
(www.hawkandowl.org)

Barn Owl Conservation Network
c/o Wildlife Conservation Partnership, 2 Mill Walk, Wheathampstead,
AL4 8DT
The BOCN is a project of The Hawk and Owl Trust and consists of a network of specialist voluntary advisers (including the author of this book), working to help the barn owl by promoting a nationwide habitat creation scheme along with the installation of nest boxes.
(www.bocn.org)

World Owl Trust
The Owl Centre, Muncaster Castle, Ravenglass, Cumbria, CA18 1RQ
The World Owl Trust is a registered charity which exists to advance wildlife conservation primarily by focusing on all owl species and their ecology.
(www.owls.org)

The British Trust for Ornithology
The Nunnery, Thetford, Norfolk, IP24 2PU
The British Trust for Ornithology (BTO) has existed since 1933 as an independent, scientific research trust, investigating the populations, movements and ecology of wild birds in the British Isles. It runs the bird ringing scheme referred to in this book.
(www.bto.org)

Department for Environment, Food and Rural Affairs

Nobel House, 17 Smith Square, London SW1P 3JR

The Department for Environment, Food and Rural Affairs (Defra) is the UK government department responsible for policy and regulations on the environment, food and rural affairs.

(www.defra.gov.uk)

Natural England

Head Office: 1 East Parade, Sheffield S1 2ET

Natural England's general purpose is to ensure that the natural environment is conserved, enhanced and managed for the benefit of present and future generations, thereby contributing to sustainable development. It is the government's adviser on the natural environment.

(www.naturalengland.org.uk)

FURTHER READING

Bunn, D.S., Warburton, A.B. and Wilson, R.D.S. *The Barn Owl*. T. and D. Poyser Ltd., 1982.

Ratcliffe, Jane. *Fly High, Run Free*. Chatto and Windus, London, 1979.

Shawyer, Colin. *The Barn Owl*. Arlequin Press, 1998.

Shawyer, Colin R. *The Barn Owl in the British Isles: Its Past, Present and Future*. The Hawk Trust, London, 1987.

Taylor, Iain. *Barn Owls: Predator-Prey Relations and Conservation*. Cambridge University Press, 1994.